Ancient Secrets Restored
The Books of ENOCH

A Complete Collection of 1, 2, and 3 Enoch
with Illustrated Commentary, Apocryphal Texts, and Exclusive
Digital Resources

LARGE PRINT

Introduction by Rush Nilson

Enoch 1
Author Enoch,
Translated by R.H.Charles

Enoch 2
Author Enoch,
Translated by W.R. Morfill

Enoch 3
Author Rabbi Ishmael,
Translated by Hugo Odeberg

★★★★★　★★★★★　★★★★★

PLEASE NOTE
THE FOLLOWING CAREFULLY

The **audiobook** and the **additional contents** can only be accessed by scanning the **QR code** on the page after the Table of Contents and visiting the **website address** indicated on that same page.

If you encounter any difficulties, feel free to write to us at:

info@manuscryptha.com   or   **rushnilson@manuscryptha.com**

Thank you for your understanding.

TABLE OF CONTENTS

The Timeline – Tracing the Legacy of Hidden Texts

INTRODUCTION	i
Unlocking the Wisdom of the Forgotten Texts	i
The Lost Voices of Sacred Tradition	i
The Enochian Legacy	ii
Beyond Enoch	iv
A Journey into the Depths of Esoteric Wisdom	v
1 ENOCH	**1**
Historical Context	1
Key Themes	2
Theological and Symbolic	4
Modern Applications	5
Editorial Note on Structure and Introductions	6
Structure of the Book	7
ETHIOPIAN BOOK OF ENOCH	**8**
Section I (Chapters I–XXXVI) The Watchers' Rebellion and Divine Judgment	8
Section II (Chapters XXXVII – LXXI) Parables of the Elect and the Coming Judgment	22
Section III (Chapters LXXII—LXXXII) Mysteries of Creation and the Heavenly Order	42
Section IV (Chapters LXXXIII—XC) Prophetic Dreams and the Future of Humanity	52
Section V (Chapters XCI—CIV) The Path of Righteousness and Divine Warnings	63
FRAGMENT OF THE BOOK OF NOAH	74

2 ENOCH — 81

- Historical Context — 81
- Key Themes — 83
- Theological and Symbolic Insights — 84
- Modern Applications — 86
- Editorial Note on Structure and Introductions — 87
- Structure of the Book — 88

SLAVONIC BOOK OF SECRETS — 90

- Section I - The Heavenly Journey — 90
- Section II - Divine Creation and Wisdom — 97
- Section III - Ethics and Righteous Living — 104
- Section IV - Enoch's Legacy and Prophecies — 113
- Conclusion to the Second Book of Enoch — 116

3 ENOCH — 119

- Historical Context — 119
- Key Themes — 121
- Theological and Symbolic Insights — 122
- Modern Applications — 124
- Editorial Note on Structure and Introductions — 125
- Structure of the Book — 126

HEBREW BOOK OF PALACES — 128

- Section I - The Revelation of Metatron — 128
- Section II - Trasformation Into an Angelic Being — 132
- Section III - Visions of The Divine Throne — 135
- Section IV - Mystical Hierarchies and Heavenly Realms — 149
- Conclusion to the Third Book of Enoch — 162

APPENDIX 1
THE ASCENSION OF ISAIAH   164

  Historical and Literary Context   164
  Theological Significance   165
  Relationship to Other Ancient Texts   166
  Reception and Influence   168
  Author's Note on the Introductions   170
  Structure of the Text   172

THE ASCENSION OF ISAIAH   174

  The Martyrdom Of Isaiah (I-V)   174
  The Testament Of Hezekiah (II:13 - IV:18)   177
  The Visione of Isaiah (VI-XI)   181

APPENDIX 2
A STUDY OF ANGELS AND CELESTIAL HIERARCHIES   192

  Angels in Mysticism and Scripture   192
  The Nine Orders of Angels: Celestial HierarchieS   194
  The Watchers (Grigori): Fallen Angels and the Nephilim   195
  Metatron: The Prince of the Presence   196
  Sacred Names, Words, and Mystical Language   196
  Functions and Roles of Specific Angels   197
  Heavenly Realms and Angelic Structures   202
  Divine Judgment and the Role of Angels   203
  Symbolism and Modern Reflections   204
  Applying Ancient Wisdom Today   205
  Conclusion: Unveiling the Mysteries of the Divine   207

ADDITIONAL DIGITAL CONTENT

Scan the QR CODE to access all digital content!!!

or visit this website address:

manuscryptha.com/enochdigital

+ EBOOK VERSION
+ THE ENTIRE DIGITAL LIBRARY OF MANUSCRYPTHA.

AUDIOBOOK (100+ HOURS)

Listen to the complete Trilogy of Enoch, together with the Ethiopian Bible and the Gnostic Gospels.

VIDEO LESSONS (200+ HOURS)

Discover powerful insights from leading scholars and teachers.

BONUS EXTENDED TEXTS
UNIQUE APOCRYPHAL TEXTS
AND LOST WRITINGS

1. **The Book of Noah** – English & Latin texts with commentary on the pre-Flood age.

2. **The Book of Giants** – Fragments revealing the fate of the Nephilim and Watchers.

3. **The Assumption of Moses** – Paraphrased Edition – Moses' final testament, newly rendered for today's reader.

★★★★★   ★★★★★   ★★★★★

PLEASE NOTE
THE FOLLOWING CAREFULLY

The **audiobook** and the **additional contents** can only be accessed by scanning the **QR code** on the previous page and visiting the **website address** indicated on that same page.

If you encounter any difficulties, feel free to write to us at:

info@manuscryptha.com   or   *rushnilson@manuscryptha.com*

Thank you again,
RUSH NILSON

THE TIMELINE
TRACING THE LEGACY OF HIDDEN TEXTS

The apocryphal and mystical texts gathered in this volume span across centuries, each emerging from distinct historical and theological contexts. To aid readers in situating these writings within their broader historical framework, a timeline has been included to provide a chronological perspective on their origins, development, and influence.

Unlike canonical scriptures, which were consolidated into formal religious traditions, these texts followed a different path of transmission, preserved through sectarian communities, mystical traditions, and esoteric circles. Some were revered in certain religious traditions, while others were lost, rediscovered, and reassessed in later centuries. This timeline serves as a guide to understanding the historical placement of the Books of Enoch, the Ascension of Isaiah, and the study of angelic hierarchies, allowing readers to grasp how these writings evolved alongside or outside mainstream religious thought.

By placing these works in their historical and theological continuum, this timeline offers a valuable tool for both scholars and spiritual seekers, providing insight into the development of Jewish apocalypticism, early Christian mysticism, and angelological traditions. It is not merely a record of dates and events, but a window into the unfolding of esoteric wisdom across the ages.

ANTEDILUVIAN
PRE-FLOOD ERA
From Enoch to the Great Flood

3000 BC
Enoch

"The Watchers descend to Earth and beget the giants."
(Seventh descendant of Adam, great grandfather of Noah. Mentioned in Genesis 5:21-24. Enoch is known for his righteousness and prophetic visions. According to tradition, he was taken to heaven without experiencing death. The Book of Enoch, attributed to him, describes his visions of heaven, the fall of the Watchers (fallen angels), and hidden cosmic secrets.)

"The Nephilim spread violence and ask Enoch to intercede."
(An ancient apocryphal text found among the Dead Sea Scrolls. It expands on the story of the Watchers and their giant offspring, the Nephilim, who bring chaos and violence to the Earth. The giants, fearing divine punishment, plead with Enoch to intercede on their behalf, but judgment is inevitable.)

2700 BC
The Book of Giants

2500-2000 BC
Noah and the Great Flood

"God sends the Flood to cleanse the Earth and destroy the giants."
(A righteous man and direct descendant of Enoch, Noah is chosen by God to survive the Flood, which serves as divine retribution against the corruption of mankind and the Nephilim. He builds an ark to preserve life, as described in Genesis 6-9. The flood marks the end of the Pre-Flood world and the beginning of a new era.)

POSTDILUVIAN
POST-FLOOD ERA
From Abraham to the Birth of Christianity

"After the Flood, humans repopulate the Earth."
(A direct descendant of Noah through Shem, Abraham is considered the patriarch of the Israelites, Ishmaelites, and many other nations. According to Genesis 12-23, God establishes a covenant with him, promising that his descendants will be as numerous as the stars. His story marks the beginning of the monotheistic tradition, and he is central to Judaism, Christianity, and Islam.)

2000-1800 BC — Abraham

1400-1200 BC — Moses

"Giants are still mentioned (such as Og of Bashan and the Rephaim)."
(The great prophet and leader of the Israelites, Moses is chosen by God to deliver the Hebrews from Egyptian slavery and receive the Ten Commandments on Mount Sinai (Exodus 3-20). The biblical narrative also references the survival of some giants after the Flood, such as Og, king of Bashan (Deuteronomy 3:11), and the Rephaim, a race of ancient giants dwelling in Canaan.)

"Giants become symbols of the fall of the wicked."
(One of the major prophets of the Old Testament, Isaiah warns of divine judgment upon the corrupt nations. In Isaiah 14:9-20, fallen rulers are metaphorically compared to the giants (Rephaim) in Sheol, symbolizing their inevitable downfall. His prophecies also foretell the coming of the Messiah and the redemption of humanity.)

700 BC — Isaiah

1st Century AD — Mary

"Mother of Jesus, marking the transition to Christianity."
(A descendant of King David, Mary is chosen to bear Jesus Christ, fulfilling the Messianic prophecies. According to Christian tradition, she is visited by the Archangel Gabriel and conceives Jesus through divine intervention (Luke 1:26-38). Revered as the Mother of God (Theotokos), her role bridges the Old and New Covenants, heralding a new era of faith.)

INTRODUCTION

UNLOCKING THE WISDOM OF THE FORGOTTEN TEXTS

Throughout history, certain texts have remained on the fringes of mainstream religious traditions, whispered about in esoteric circles, studied in secret, and revered by those who sought to uncover the hidden dimensions of faith. The Books of Enoch, along with other mystical writings, belong to this vast and intricate web of apocryphal traditions—works that, despite their exclusion from biblical canons, have profoundly shaped religious thought, influenced theological discourse, and ignited the imaginations of seekers and scholars alike.

The significance of these texts lies not only in their antiquity but in their continued relevance, offering unique perspectives on divine revelation, cosmic order, angelic hierarchies, and the role of humanity in the grand design of creation. From the earliest Jewish apocalyptic traditions to later mystical interpretations, these writings have endured across centuries, carrying with them echoes of an ancient wisdom that refuses to be forgotten. This collection brings together three books attributed to Enoch, a central figure in both biblical and extrabiblical traditions, as well as additional writings that expand upon themes of divine ascent, prophecy, and celestial mysteries.

The decision to include The Ascension of Isaiah and The Study of Angels and Celestial Hierarchies alongside the Enochian texts is not incidental; rather, it serves to enrich the reader's journey through themes of heavenly ascension, esoteric wisdom, and spiritual transformation. These works, though distinct in origin, share a common thread—each provides a glimpse beyond the veil, revealing aspects of divine reality and cosmic order that were once accessible only to visionaries and mystics. Together, they invite the reader into a realm of hidden knowledge, where the boundaries between heaven and earth dissolve, and where the mysteries of divine justice, angelic mediation, and spiritual enlightenment unfold.

THE LOST VOICES OF SACRED TRADITION

Across cultures and religious traditions, certain texts have been preserved, revered, and canonized, while others have been set aside, lost, or intentionally suppressed. The apocryphal writings, often existing on the periphery of mainstream religious acceptance, carry within them a different kind of authority—not one enforced by ecclesiastical decree, but one born from their ability to speak to the deepest spiritual yearnings of humanity. These are the texts that challenge, illuminate, and reveal, offering an alternative yet complementary lens through which to view divine revelation and cosmic truth.

The Books of Enoch exemplify this phenomenon. While 1 Enoch was widely influential in Second Temple Judaism and is even quoted in the New Testament, it was later excluded from the biblical canon in most traditions. Yet, it persisted in Ethiopian Christianity, where it remains a part of sacred scripture to this day. 2 Enoch, though not preserved in the same way, survived through Slavonic Christian traditions, reflecting its continued relevance beyond Jewish circles. 3 Enoch, meanwhile, marks a transition into the world of early Jewish mysticism, providing a vision of the celestial order that would later influence Merkabah traditions and Kabbalistic thought.

These texts, though left outside of the mainstream biblical tradition, never truly vanished. Their survival—through scattered manuscripts, hidden archives, and oral tradition—demonstrates that their wisdom was too powerful to be erased. Their reemergence in modern scholarship has reignited interest in their theological, esoteric, and historical significance, proving that what was once forgotten or disregarded still has a voice that speaks across time.

Beyond the Enochian corpus, other apocryphal writings share this fascinating trajectory of preservation, loss, and rediscovery. The Ascension of Isaiah, for example, offers a vision of heavenly realms and divine revelation, mirroring themes found in Enoch's ascent. Similarly, the Study of Angels and Celestial Hierarchies explores the intricate structure of the divine order, reinforcing concepts central to Enochian thought. Their inclusion in this volume is intended to broaden the scope of exploration, allowing the reader to experience a fuller panorama of mystical and apocalyptic literature.

To engage with these texts is to step into a world where history, theology, and mysticism converge. They invite us to ask questions that go beyond the limitations of traditional religious discourse, urging us to seek the hidden wisdom that lies beneath the surface of ancient traditions. Whether studied for their historical importance, theological implications, or spiritual insights, these works hold a power that remains as compelling today as it was in the ancient world.

THE ENOCHIAN LEGACY—MYSTICISM, PROPHECY, AND COSMIC ORDER

The Books of Enoch stand at the crossroads of apocalyptic prophecy, mystical ascent, and celestial revelation, offering a grand vision of divine justice and cosmic structure. Unlike many other apocryphal texts, which often supplement or expand biblical narratives, the Enochian tradition presents a wholly unique cosmology, one that redefines the relationship between heaven and earth, angels and humanity, time and eternity. The Enochian legacy is not merely that of a prophet, but of a scribe, visionary, and mediator, a figure whose journey into the divine realm unveils hidden truths about creation, judgment, and redemption.

INTRODUCTION

At the heart of these texts is the pursuit of wisdom beyond human comprehension, a quest that is embodied in Enoch's ascent through the heavens. 1 Enoch, the earliest and most widely studied of these books, describes angelic rebellion, cosmic order, and the impending judgment of both celestial and earthly beings. Its themes of divine justice and eschatological prophecy directly influenced later apocalyptic literature, including the Book of Daniel, the Book of Revelation, and various Second Temple Jewish writings. The narrative of the Watchers—fallen angels who descend to corrupt humanity—remains one of the most striking depictions of celestial transgression, symbolizing the eternal struggle between knowledge, power, and divine obedience.

2 Enoch, also known as *Slavonic Enoch*, shifts the focus toward mystical cosmology, celestial hierarchies, and ethical instruction. Unlike its predecessor, which details the moral corruption of angels and their catastrophic impact on the world, *2 Enoch* provides a structured vision of the heavens, where divine wisdom is revealed in layers of light, justice, and cosmic balance. This text introduces a deeper theological meditation on the nature of creation, portraying the celestial realm as a living embodiment of divine order, where stars, angels, and cosmic forces operate in harmony with God's will.

3 Enoch represents yet another transformation of the Enochian tradition, shifting from prophetic eschatology to Jewish mysticism, particularly the Merkabah (Chariot) tradition that later influenced Kabbalistic thought. Here, Enoch is no longer simply a prophet or visionary, but an elevated being—Metatron, the Prince of the Presence—who stands closest to the divine throne. This portrayal encapsulates the mystical aspiration to transcend human limitations, reinforcing the belief that spiritual ascension and divine communion are attainable through purity, wisdom, and devotion. The text also expands on angelology, presenting a hierarchical and highly structured cosmos, where angelic forces govern every aspect of creation and execute divine will with absolute precision.

Taken together, the Books of Enoch form a continuous thread of divine revelation, each adding new layers of complexity to humanity's understanding of the cosmos, the nature of divine justice, and the role of celestial beings. Their endurance throughout centuries, despite exclusion from most biblical canons, speaks to their lasting spiritual and theological significance. These texts have not only shaped ancient Jewish eschatology, but also influenced early Christian thought, Islamic mysticism, and later esoteric traditions, proving that their wisdom extends beyond the historical context of their composition.

To engage with the Enochian texts is to enter a world where history, prophecy, and mysticism merge, offering a glimpse into a universe where celestial beings govern the cosmos, divine justice is absolute, and human destiny is shaped by forces beyond visible reality. The Enochian legacy continues to challenge, inspire, and illuminate, serving as both a theological cornerstone and a mystical guide for those who seek to understand the deeper truths hidden within sacred tradition.

BEYOND ENOCH—THE HIDDEN DIMENSIONS OF FAITH AND DIVINE ASCENT

While the Books of Enoch serve as the foundation of this collection, their inclusion is not an isolated choice, but part of a broader vision that seeks to explore the hidden dimensions of divine ascent, angelology, and apocalyptic prophecy. This is why, alongside the Enochian texts, this volume also presents two additional writings that complement and expand upon the themes of celestial revelation and mystical ascent: *The Ascension of Isaiah* and *The Study of Angels and Celestial Hierarchies*. These works, though distinct in origin and tradition, share a profound thematic resonance with the Enochian material, further deepening the reader's exploration of the unseen realms of divine order and judgment.

The Ascension of Isaiah is a visionary text that, much like *3 Enoch*, describes the soul's passage through the heavenly realms, revealing the hidden structures of the divine world and the ultimate fate of the righteous and the wicked. Isaiah's celestial journey is a counterpart to Enoch's ascent, reflecting similar preoccupations with angelic hierarchies, divine judgment, and cosmic revelation. In both cases, a prophet is granted extraordinary access to the heavenly realms, encountering celestial beings, divine mysteries, and the realities of the spiritual cosmos. This parallel between the figures of Enoch and Isaiah suggests that heavenly ascension was not an isolated literary motif, but a recurring mystical tradition that permeated both Jewish apocalypticism and early Christian thought.

The inclusion of *The Study of Angels and Celestial Hierarchies* further enriches this exploration, offering a systematic theological reflection on the nature, function, and hierarchy of angelic beings. If the Enochian texts and the Ascension of Isaiah provide the mystical and prophetic experiences of heavenly ascent, this appendix serves as a structured framework that contextualizes these celestial realities. Understanding how the divine order is maintained, how angels function within cosmic governance, and how spiritual ascent is achieved is crucial for grasping the full impact of Enoch's and Isaiah's revelations.

Together, these texts present a multifaceted vision of divine ascent, celestial mediation, and esoteric knowledge, each contributing a unique perspective on the hidden dimensions of faith. The prophets and mystics who experienced these visions were not merely passive recipients of revelation, but active participants in a larger cosmic drama, bearing witness to the realms beyond human perception. Through their experiences, they provide a glimpse into the ultimate spiritual journey—the soul's return to its divine source.

By reading these works in tandem, one begins to perceive a cohesive spiritual framework—one that suggests that hidden wisdom is accessible to those who seek it, and that divine ascent is not merely a visionary experience, but a reflection of a deeper cosmic reality. These texts, taken together, form a bridge between prophecy and mysticism, history and revelation, theology and esoteric tradition, offering modern readers a path into the mysteries of the divine.

INTRODUCTION

A JOURNEY INTO THE DEPTHS OF ESOTERIC WISDOM

The texts gathered in this volume are more than just ancient writings—they are gateways into a world where prophecy, mysticism, and divine revelation converge. From the Books of Enoch, with their intricate visions of angelic hierarchies and cosmic justice, to the Ascension of Isaiah, which reveals the path of the soul through celestial realms, and the Study of Angels and Celestial Hierarchies, which systematizes the role of divine beings, each work presents a unique piece of the larger puzzle of esoteric tradition.

Engaging with these texts is not a passive exercise. They challenge the reader to contemplate the nature of divine authority, the structure of the cosmos, and humanity's place within it. They present a reality in which angels govern the universe, in which hidden knowledge is revealed to the righteous, and in which the forces of justice, mercy, and cosmic balance are constantly at play. These are not simply theological concepts; they are visions of a spiritual reality that transcends time and tradition, inviting those who seek understanding to step beyond conventional religious thought and into the realm of mystical insight.

For centuries, these texts have inspired scholars, theologians, mystics, and seekers of hidden wisdom, offering glimpses into a world that exists beyond the veil of ordinary perception. They have shaped apocalyptic literature, mystical traditions, and esoteric teachings across different faiths, serving as threads that connect the ancient past to the present search for spiritual truth. Their endurance speaks to their power and significance, proving that despite their exclusion from canonical traditions, their influence has never faded.

To read these works is to embark on a journey—one that is both historical and deeply personal. They encourage reflection, challenge assumptions, and offer new ways of understanding divinity, judgment, and the spiritual ascent of the soul. Whether approached as historical artifacts, theological explorations, or sources of personal enlightenment, they remain as relevant today as they were in the ancient world, continuing to illuminate the timeless quest for hidden wisdom and divine knowledge.

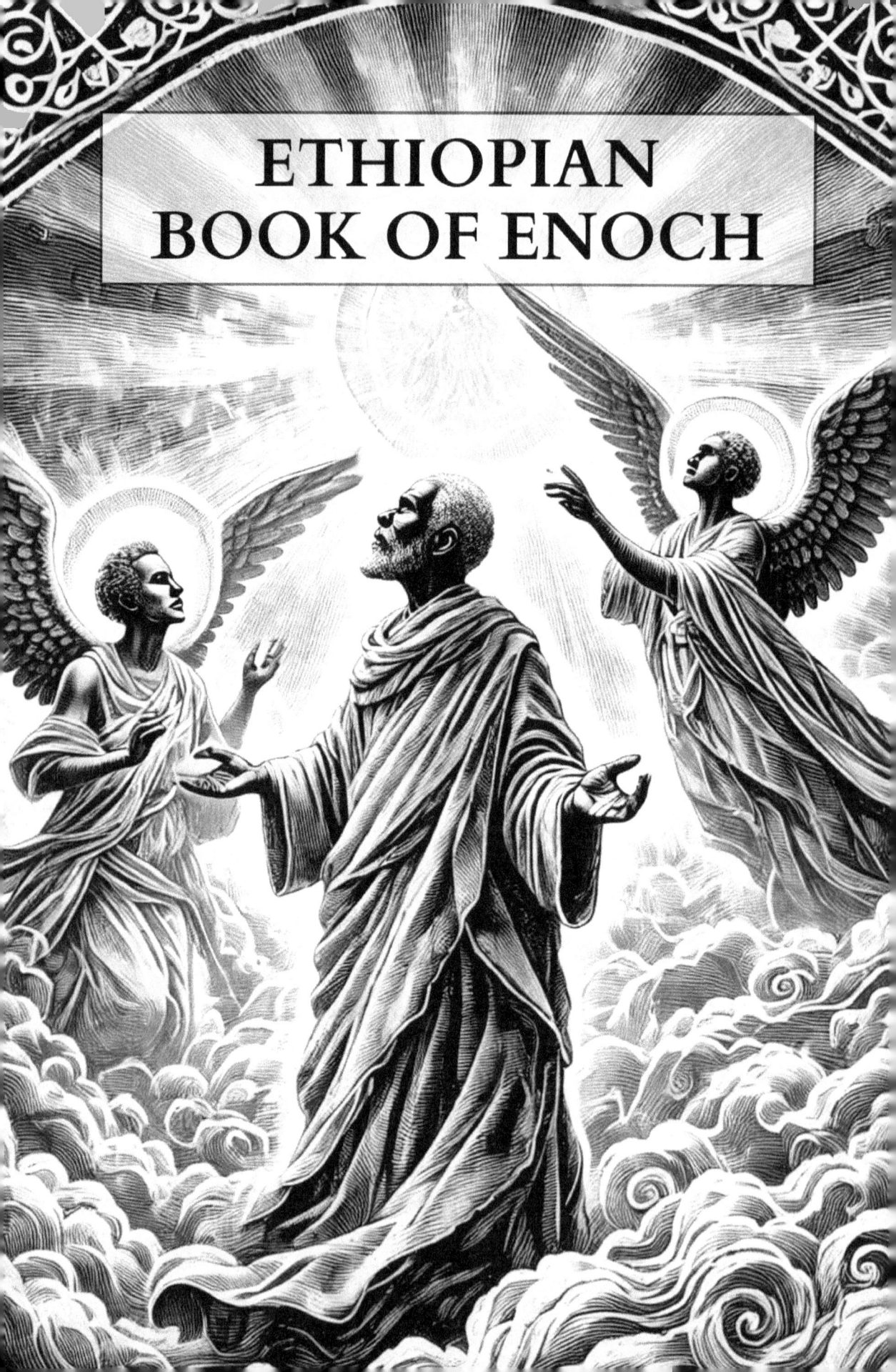

1 ENOCH

INTRODUCTION

HISTORICAL CONTEXT

The First Book of Enoch (also known as 1 Enoch or The Ethiopian Book of Enoch) stands as one of the most significant and early apocryphal writings in Jewish tradition. Composed between the 3rd century BCE and the 1st century CE, it emerged during a period of profound religious, political, and social upheaval within the Second Temple era (515 BCE–70 CE). This was a time when Jewish identity was being shaped by both external influences and internal divisions, making apocalyptic literature like 1 Enoch particularly relevant as a response to uncertainty and oppression.

The Hellenistic period, following the conquests of Alexander the Great (4th century BCE), introduced Greek philosophical and cultural ideals into Jewish thought. Some Jewish sects, particularly the Sadducees, embraced certain aspects of Hellenism, while others, such as the Pharisees and Essenes, resisted it, seeking to preserve traditional interpretations of Jewish law. This environment of theological tension contributed to the rise of apocalyptic literature, a genre deeply concerned with divine judgment, cosmic battles, and eschatological prophecies—themes that dominate 1 Enoch. The text reflects the yearning for divine intervention during periods of foreign rule and religious strife, portraying a hidden cosmic order in which the righteous would ultimately be vindicated and the wicked punished.

Originally written in Aramaic, the common language of the Jewish people at the time, 1 Enoch was later translated into Greek as its influence spread beyond Jewish communities. However, the most complete surviving version exists in Ge'ez, the classical liturgical language of Ethiopia. While only fragmentary Aramaic manuscripts have been discovered among the Dead Sea Scrolls, the Ge'ez translation has preserved the book in its entirety, highlighting its importance within Ethiopian Christianity, where it remains canonical scripture. This text's remarkable preservation in Ethiopia underscores its lasting impact, having journeyed through Jewish diaspora communities and early Christian traditions before becoming deeply embedded in Ethiopian religious heritage.

Despite its profound theological and literary influence, 1 Enoch was excluded from the Jewish Tanakh and most Christian biblical canons. However, it continued to be highly regarded in certain religious circles. Evidence of its significance in Second Temple Judaism is found in the Dead Sea Scrolls, where fragments of the text were preserved by the Essenes, a sect known for their apocalyptic worldview. Additionally, 1 Enoch is explicitly quoted in the New Testament, particularly in the Epistle of Jude (Jude 14–15), demonstrating its impact on early Christian thought. This reference suggests that at least some early Christians viewed it as an authoritative work, even if it was later excluded from the biblical canon in most traditions.

The preservation of 1 Enoch within Ethiopian Christianity is a testament to its enduring legacy. When Ethiopia adopted Christianity in the 4th century CE under King Ezana, the text was safeguarded as part of the Ethiopian biblical tradition, where it has remained ever since. Unlike in Western Christianity, where the text became largely forgotten or relegated to the realm of extra-biblical literature, it has been actively studied, transmitted, and revered within Ethiopian religious scholarship. Its survival not only provides a unique glimpse into ancient Jewish apocalypticism but also serves as a bridge between Jewish, Christian, and Ethiopian traditions, demonstrating how texts once central to one tradition can take on new significance in another.

Through its themes of cosmic justice, divine revelation, and angelic hierarchies, 1 Enoch continues to captivate scholars, theologians, and seekers of hidden wisdom, offering an alternative yet complementary narrative to the canonical scriptures. Its complex history, from Jewish origins to Ethiopian preservation, reflects the diverse ways in which religious traditions evolve, adapt, and survive across centuries, ensuring that its mystical and prophetic messages remain relevant to this day.

KEY THEMES

The First Book of Enoch presents a sweeping vision of divine justice, cosmic order, and eschatological prophecy, reflecting the concerns and aspirations of ancient believers navigating a world of uncertainty. Far from being a mere collection of visions, the text weaves together apocalyptic revelations, moral exhortations, and celestial mysteries, offering readers a profound meditation on the nature of sin, righteousness, and the ultimate fate of humanity. Its themes resonate deeply across generations, speaking to those who seek hidden wisdom, divine governance, and the interplay between heaven and earth.

One of the most compelling narratives in 1 Enoch is the fall of the Watchers, a group of angels who abandon their divine station to descend to earth, where they take human wives and introduce forbidden knowledge to mankind. Their union with mortals results in the birth of the Nephilim, hybrid beings described as giants who become a symbol of unchecked power, corruption, and divine transgression. The Watchers, in their defiance, impart to humanity secret arts—alchemy, astrology, weaponry, and sorcery—which, though promising enlightenment, ultimately lead to destruction. This theme of forbidden knowledge and its consequences mirrors ancient concerns about the dangers of unrestrained ambition and moral decay, warning that the pursuit of power without divine guidance leads to chaos. The punishment of the Watchers serves as a stark reminder of divine retribution and the unyielding order of the cosmos, reinforcing the need for obedience to divine law.

The text is equally concerned with divine judgment and cosmic redemption. The Watchers and the Nephilim face annihilation, demonstrating that no being—whether celestial or mortal—is beyond the reach of divine justice. Yet, alongside this stark portrayal of judgment, 1 Enoch offers a vision of deliverance for the righteous, promising vindication, renewal, and eternal reward. This dual theme of judgment and redemption serves not only as a reassurance to the oppressed, affirming that divine justice will ultimately prevail, but also as a moral imperative, urging humanity toward repentance and vigilance. The judgment of the Watchers is not merely a historical event within the text but an ongoing cosmic reality, a template for the moral struggle between obedience and rebellion that transcends time.

The apocalyptic nature of 1 Enoch is further emphasized through its rich visionary language, portraying heaven, hell, and celestial realms in striking detail. Enoch's ascent into the heavens, where he is granted revelations of angelic hierarchies, divine thrones, and the mechanisms of judgment, aligns with broader apocalyptic traditions that seek to unveil the hidden structure of reality. His visions of fire, stars, and divine luminaries not only reflect ancient cosmological views but also foreshadow elements found in later Christian and Islamic eschatology, making 1 Enoch a foundational text for understanding the development of apocalyptic thought. These celestial journeys function as both prophecy and warning, revealing the majesty of divine governance while reinforcing the inevitability of judgment for both angels and humans alike.

Closely linked to these themes is 1 Enoch's exploration of cosmology and heavenly mysteries, particularly through its intricate descriptions of astronomical cycles, celestial bodies, and divine order. The text portrays the movement of the stars and the luminaries as expressions of divine obedience, contrasting their perfect alignment with the disorder brought by human and angelic rebellion. The cycles of the heavens serve as a moral and spiritual lesson, reminding readers that divine law governs all of creation, and those who act in defiance of this order are destined to fall. Through these revelations, 1 Enoch not only presents a sacred science of the cosmos but also underscores the interdependence between divine law, natural order, and human morality.

Beyond its apocalyptic and cosmological dimensions, 1 Enoch serves as a moral treatise, offering a clear ethical framework for its readers. The text condemns greed, corruption, violence, and oppression, calling instead for a life of humility, justice, and faithfulness. These exhortations to the righteous remnant emphasize the enduring struggle of the faithful against the forces of corruption, portraying the righteous as those who stand firm despite adversity. Unlike many apocalyptic texts that focus solely on divine intervention, 1 Enoch places significant responsibility on individuals, urging them to actively choose righteousness in preparation for the coming judgment. In this way, the text functions not only as prophecy but also as pastoral guidance, offering reassurance that steadfastness in faith leads to divine favor.

Through its cosmic visions, ethical warnings, and revelations of divine justice, 1 Enoch remains a powerful meditation on the fate of humanity and the unseen forces that shape existence. Its themes continue to captivate readers across generations, offering a lens through which to understand the ancient struggle between rebellion and obedience, corruption and purity, judgment and mercy. Whether approached as an apocalyptic prophecy, a moral exhortation, or a cosmic revelation, its message endures, calling its readers to recognize their place within the grand design of creation and to live in accordance with the divine will.

THEOLOGICAL AND SYMBOLIC

The First Book of Enoch holds profound theological and symbolic significance, serving as a bridge between divine justice, cosmic order, and the fate of humanity. Its intricate visions and apocalyptic themes reveal a structured universe governed by moral law, where righteousness leads to elevation and rebellion invites judgment. The text functions as both a revelation of celestial mysteries and a moral exhortation, guiding readers toward an understanding of their role in the divine order.

At its core, 1 Enoch presents Enoch as a mediator between heaven and earth, a figure chosen to receive divine secrets and bear witness to the hidden structure of the cosmos. His journey into the heavens symbolizes spiritual ascent and divine favor, embodying the ideal of absolute righteousness. His translation into immortality, bypassing death altogether, prefigures later theological concepts of resurrection, eternal life, and divine glorification—themes that resonate deeply within early Christian and mystical traditions. Through his unwavering obedience and faithfulness to God's will, Enoch becomes an archetype of spiritual perfection, reinforcing the idea that righteousness leads to union with the divine.

The symbolic imagery within 1 Enoch offers a compelling vision of the unseen forces governing creation. The celestial hierarchy, the Watchers' descent, and the structure of divine thrones all serve as metaphors for the interplay between obedience and defiance, order and chaos. The Watchers' rebellion embodies the eternal struggle between divine law and the corruption of power, demonstrating the consequences of transgression. Their punishment and binding serve as a stark reminder that divine justice is absolute, ensuring that no act of defiance goes unanswered. Meanwhile, Enoch's role as a scribe of judgment and wisdom reinforces the necessity of moral accountability, urging humanity to align with the cosmic order established by God.

Beyond its immediate theological impact, 1 Enoch profoundly influenced later religious traditions, particularly in early Christianity and Islamic eschatology. Its descriptions of angelic hierarchies, cosmic judgment, and divine retribution shaped the development of Christian and Gnostic beliefs about the afterlife, celestial beings, and the end of days. Many themes found in 1 Enoch—including the role of angels in human affairs, the punishment of the wicked, and the ultimate restoration of creation—echo throughout the New Testament, early Christian apocrypha, and later mystical writings. The text's apocalyptic language and visions of divine justice continue to inspire interpretations of God's mercy and judgment, offering both warnings to the unfaithful and hope for redemption to the righteous.

Through its complex theological framework and vivid symbolism, 1 Enoch remains a foundational text in apocalyptic literature, serving as both a guide to the mysteries of the divine realm and a moral beacon for those who seek alignment with God's will. Its teachings endure across centuries, reminding readers of the delicate balance between righteousness and corruption, justice and mercy, judgment and restoration.

MODERN APPLICATIONS

The First Book of Enoch remains profoundly relevant today, serving as a source of wisdom, reflection, and academic inquiry for both spiritual seekers and scholars. Its themes of divine justice, moral accountability, and cosmic order continue to resonate across cultures and traditions, offering insights into humanity's enduring quest for meaning. The text's ability to bridge ancient revelation with contemporary ethical and theological concerns ensures that it remains a valuable tool for those who seek to understand the nature of the divine, the structure of the cosmos, and the moral responsibilities of humankind.

For those engaged in spiritual growth, 1 Enoch provides a framework for meditation on divine mysteries and the human condition. Its vivid visions of heaven, judgment, and redemption serve as powerful contemplative guides, prompting reflection on the nature of good and evil, the consequences of sin, and the promise of salvation. The fall of the Watchers and the emergence of the Nephilim mirror modern struggles with temptation, corruption, and moral decay, making the text strikingly relevant for those grappling with ethical dilemmas and the role of divine intervention in human affairs. The apocalyptic imagery of 1 Enoch does not merely depict an end-time scenario but also serves as a call to self-examination and transformation, urging readers to consider their spiritual alignment with the divine order.

Beyond its spiritual insights, 1 Enoch provides ethical and moral guidance, offering a compelling vision of justice, humility, and righteousness. The text's denunciations of greed, violence, and oppression challenge both individuals and societies to reflect on their actions and strive for ethical living. In a world plagued by inequality, environmental crises, and social injustice, its calls for accountability and moral responsibility feel especially urgent. The idea that righteousness leads to divine favor while corruption invites cosmic judgment serves as both a cautionary message and a source of hope, reinforcing the notion that ethical living is not merely a personal choice but a cosmic imperative.

For scholars, 1 Enoch provides invaluable insights into the development of Jewish apocalyptic thought and its influence on early Christian and Islamic eschatology. Its detailed accounts of angelology, cosmology, and divine hierarchies illuminate ancient understandings of the supernatural world and its governance. The text's parallels with canonical scriptures, such as the Book of Daniel and the Book of Revelation, demonstrate its role in shaping later religious traditions. Comparative studies have further revealed how 1 Enoch influenced early Christian and Gnostic writings, as well as later mystical traditions, making it an essential resource for those studying Second Temple Judaism, biblical history, and religious syncretism.

The discovery of Aramaic fragments of 1 Enoch among the Dead Sea Scrolls has also provided critical evidence of the theological diversity of Second Temple Judaism. Its preservation in Ethiopian Christianity, where it is still considered canonical, highlights the text's adaptability and enduring spiritual authority. For researchers in biblical archaeology, comparative religion, and textual studies, 1 Enoch continues to be a cornerstone of scholarship, shedding light on the evolution of apocalyptic literature and eschatological thought across cultures.

In an age marked by spiritual alienation, existential uncertainty, and global crises, 1 Enoch offers timeless lessons on faith, redemption, and divine order. Its visions of cosmic upheaval and renewal resonate with contemporary discussions about moral reckoning, climate change, and the human search for spiritual renewal. The text's emphasis on judgment and restoration encourages reflection on both personal and collective transformation, reinforcing the belief that spiritual awakening and moral realignment are necessary steps toward cosmic harmony. By engaging with 1 Enoch, modern readers find not just an ancient apocalyptic vision, but a profound and enduring call to introspection, righteousness, and hope.

EDITORIAL NOTE ON STRUCTURE AND INTRODUCTIONS

To enhance the accessibility and comprehension of The First Book of Enoch, it has been decided to introduce thematic divisions within the text, each accompanied by an explanatory introduction. While the original manuscript of 1 Enoch does not contain these structural divisions, they have been incorporated into this edition to provide clarity and deeper insight into the book's theological, historical, and mystical dimensions.

The introductions to each section have been newly written for this edition, offering contextual analysis, thematic exploration, and interpretative guidance. These additions aim to bridge the gap between ancient apocalyptic thought and modern understanding, making the text more accessible to scholars, spiritual seekers, and those newly engaging with apocryphal literature. The content of 1 Enoch itself remains unaltered, ensuring the integrity of the original work while presenting it in a format that allows for structured reflection and study.

By providing these introductions, this edition seeks to illuminate the depth of 1 Enoch, guiding readers through its complex symbolism, cosmic visions, and moral teachings while preserving its historical authenticity and apocalyptic intensity.

STRUCTURE OF THE BOOK

The *First Book of Enoch* is organized into five distinct sections, each addressing specific theological and cosmological themes:

1. The Watchers' Rebellion and Divine Judgment (Chapters I–XXXVI):

This section introduces Enoch's visions and chronicles the fall of the Watchers, the rebellious angels who descend to Earth, mate with human women, and corrupt humanity. It provides detailed accounts of judgment upon the fallen angels, their punishment, and the restoration of divine order. Themes of sin, rebellion, and divine justice dominate this section, emphasizing God's sovereignty.

2. Parables of the Elect and the Coming Judgment (Chapters XXXVII–LXXI):

This section is composed of three parables that expand on divine mysteries, including visions of the Messiah, heavenly secrets, and the final judgment. It introduces concepts of resurrection and the Son of Man, which later influenced Christian theology.

3. Mysteries of Creation and the Heavenly Order (Chapters LXXII–LXXXII):

Also known as the Book of the Heavenly Luminaries, this section explores celestial cycles, astronomy, and calendars. It provides insight into the cosmic order and portrays the stars and heavenly bodies as obedient servants of God, contrasting them with human disobedience.

4. Prophetic Dreams and the Future of Humanity (Chapters LXXXIII–XC):

This section contains symbolic and prophetic dreams, presenting a history of humanity from creation to the final judgment. It uses allegory and vivid imagery to convey divine plans and warnings.

5. The Path of Righteousness and Divine Warnings (Chapters XCI–CVIII):

Concluding the book, this section combines ethical teachings and prophetic warnings. It emphasizes themes of repentance, justice, and redemption, offering encouragement to the righteous while condemning the wicked.

ETHIOPIAN BOOK OF ENOCH

Section I (Chapters I-XXXVI)

THE WATCHERS' REBELLION AND DIVINE JUDGMENT

This section, often referred to as the *Book of the Watchers*, focuses on the dramatic narrative of the fallen angels (Watchers) who descend to Earth, mate with human women, and corrupt humanity. It explores themes of sin, forbidden knowledge, and divine judgment. Enoch's visions of angelic punishment highlight the consequences of rebellion against divine order and emphasize the sovereignty of God.

Readers are introduced to the origins of evil and corruption, setting the stage for the cosmic struggle between light and darkness that resonates throughout the rest of the book. This section also underscores Enoch's role as an intercessor, mediating between heaven and earth.

I-V. Parable of Enoch on the Future Lot of the Wicked and the Taghteous

CHAPTER I.

The words of the blessing of Enoch, wherewith he blessed the elect "and" righteous, who will be living in the day (of tribulation, when all the wicked "and godless" are to be removed. 2. And he took up his parable and said—Enoch a righteous man, whose eyes were opened by God, saw the vision of the Holy One in the heavens, 'which' the angels showed me, and from them I heard everything, and from them I understood as I saw, but not for this generation, but for a remote one which is for to come. 3. Concerning the elect I said, and took up my parable concerning them: The Holy Great One will come forth from His dwelling, 4, And the eternal God will tread upon the earth, Ge on Mount Sinai, And appear in the strength of His might from the heaven of heavens 5. And all shall be smitten with fear, And the Watchers shall quake, And great fear and trembling shall seize them unto the ends of the earth. 6. And the high mountains shall be shaken, And the high hills shall be made low, And shall melt like wax before the flame. 7. And the earth shall be "wholly' rent in sunder, And all that is upon the earth shall perish, And there shall be a judgement upon all (men). 8. But with the righteous He will make peace, And will protect the elect, And mercy shall be upon them. And they shall all belong to God, And they shall be prospered, And they shall 'all' be blessed. And He will help them all', And light shall appear unto them, And

He will make peace with them'. 9, And behold! He cometh with ten thousands of 'His' holy ones To execute judgement upon all, And to destroy 'all' the ungodly: And to convict all flesh Of all the works 'of their ungodliness? which they have ungodly committed, And of all the hard things which ungodly sinners have spoken against Him.

CHAPTER II.

Observe ye every thing that takes place in the heaven, how they do not change their orbits, "and! the luminaries which are in the heaven, how they all rise and set in order each in its season, and transgress not against their appointed order. 2. Behold ye the earth, and give heed to the things which take place upon it from first to last, "how steadfast they are', how 'none of the things upon earth' change, "but! all the works of God appear 'to you'. 3. Behold the summer and the winter, "how the whole earth is filled with water, and clouds and dew and rain lie upon it".

CHAPTER III.

Observe and see how (in the winter) all the trees "scem as though they had withered and shed all their leaves, except fourteen trees, which do not lose their foliage but retain the old foliage from two to three years till the new comes.

CHAPTER IV.

And again, observe ye the days of summer how the sun is above the earth over against it. And you seek shade and shelter by reason of the heat of the sun, and the earth also burns with glowing heat, and so you cannot tread on the earth, or on a rock by reason of its heat.

CHAPTER V.

Observe ye" how the trees cover themselves with green leaves and bear fruit: wherefore give ye heed 'and know! with regard to all "His works', and recognize how He that liveth for ever hath made them so. 2. And 'all' His works go on 'thus! from year to year 'for ever', and all the tasks 'which! they accomplish for Him, and 'their tasks' change not, but according as "God" hath ordained so is 1t done. 3. And behold how the sea and the rivers in like manner accomplish 'and change not! their tasks "from His commandments'. 4. But ye— ye have not been steadfast, nor done the commandments of the Lord, But ye have turned away and spoken proud and hard words With your impure mouths against His greatness. Oh, ye hard-hearted, ye shall find no peace. 5. Therefore shall ye execrate your days, And the years of your life shall perish, And 'the years of your destruction' shall be multiplied in eternal execration, And ye shall find no mercy. a. In those days ye shall make your names an eternal execration unto all the righteous, b. And by you shall 'all' who curse, curse c. 'And all' the sinners and godless' shall imprecate by you, 7 c. And for you the godless there shall be a curse. 6d. And all the... shall rejoice, e. And there shall be forgiveness of sins, fJ. And every mercy and peace and forbearance: g. There shall be salvation unto them, a goodly light. i. And for all of you sinners there shall be no salvation, j. But on you all shall abide a curse'. 7a. But for the elect there shall be light and grace and peace, b. And they shall inherit the earth. 8. And then there shall be bestowed upon the elect wisdom, And they shall all live and never again sin, Either through ungodliness or through pride: But they who are wise shall be humble. 9. And they shall not again transgress, Nor shall they sin all the days of their life, Nor shall they die of (the divine) anger or wrath, But they shall complete the number of the days of their life. And their lives shall be increased in peace, And the years of their joy shall be multiplied, In eternal gladness and peace, All the days of their life.

VI-XI. The Fall of the Angels: the Demoralisation of Mankind

The Intercession of the Angels on behalf of Mankind. The Dooms pronounced by God on the Angels: the Messianie Kingdom (a Noah fragment)

CHAPTER VI.

And it came to pass when the children of men had multiplied that in those days were born unto them beautiful and comely daughters. 2, And the angels, the children of the heaven, saw and lusted after them, and said to one another: 'Come, let us choose us wives from among the children of men and beget us children,' 3, And Semjiza, who was their leader, said unto them: 'I fear ye will not indeed agree to do this deed, and I alone shall have to pay the penalty of a great sin.' 4, And they all answered him and said: 'Let us all swear an oath, and all bind ourselves by mutual imprecations not to abandon this plan but to do this thing' 5. Then sware they all together and bound themselves by mutual imprecations upon it, 6. And they were in all two hundred; who descended "in the days! of Jared on the summit of Mount Hermon, and they called it Mount Hermon, beeause they had sworn and bound themselves by mutual imprecations upon it. 7. And these are the names of their leaders: Sémiaz4z, their leader, Arakiba, Riméél, Kokabiél, Tamiél, Ramiél, Danél, Ezéqéél, Bardqijal, Asiél, Armarés, Bataré]l, Ananél, Zaqiél, Sams4péél, Satarél, Taré), Jomjiél, Sariél 8. These are their chiefs of tens.

CHAPTER VII.

And all the others together with them took unto themselves wives, and each chose for himself one, and they began to go in unto them and to defile themselves with them, and they taught them charms and enchantments, and the cutting of roots, and made them acquainted with plants. 2. And they became pregnant, and they bare great giants, whose height was three thousand ells: 3. Who consumed all the acquisitions of men, 4, The giants 5. And they began to sin against birds, and beasts, and reptiles, and fish, and when men could no longer sustain them, turned against them and devoured mankind. to devour one another's flesh, and drink the blood. 6. Then the earth laid accusation against the lawless ones,

CHAPTER VIII.

And Azazél taught men to make swords, and knives, and shields, and breastplates, and made known to them the metals (of the earth).and the art of working them, and bracelets, and ornaments, and the use of antimony, and the beautifying of the eyelids, and all kinds of costly stones, and all colouring tinctures, 2. And there arose much godlessness, and they committed fornication, and they were Jed astray, and became corrupt in all their ways. 3. Semjaza taught enchantments, and root-cuttings, Armirds the resolving of enchantments, Bardqijal (taught) astrolozy, Kékabél the constellations, Ezéq86l the knowledge of the clouds, (Araqiél the signs of the earth, Shamsiél the signs of the sun), and Sarié] the course of the moon. 4, And as men perished, they cried, and their cry went up to heaven....

CHAPTER IX.

And then Michael, Uriel, Raphael, and Gabriel looked down from heaven and saw much blood being shed upon the earth, and all lawlessness being wrought upon the earth. 2. And they said one to another: 'The earth made } without inhabitant cries the voice of their crying} up to the gates of heaven, 8. "And now to you, the holy ones of heaven", the souls of men make their suit, saying, " Bring our cause before the Most High",'? 4. And they said to the Lord of the ages: 'Lord of lords, God of gods, King of kings (and God of the ages), the throne of Thy glory (standeth) unto all the generations of the ages, and Thy name holy and glorious and blessed unto all the ages! 5. Thou hast made all things, and power over all things hast Thou: and all things are naked and open in Thy sight, and all things Thou seest, and nothing can hide itself from Thee. 6. Thou seest what Azizél hath done, who hath taught all unrighteousness on earth and revealed _the_eternal secrets which were (preserved) in heaven, which men were striving to learn: 7. And Semjazi, to whom Thou hast given authority to bear rule over his associates. 8, And they have gone to the daughters of men upon the earth, and have slept with the women, and have defiled themselves, and revealed to them all kinds of sins. 9. And the women have borne giants, and the whole earth has thereby been filled with blood and unrighteousness. 10. And now, behold, the souls of those who have died are crying and making their suit to the gates of heaven, and their lamentations have ascended: and cannot cease because of the lawless deeds which are wronght on the earth. 11, And Thou knowest all things before they come to pass, and Thou seest these things and Thou dost suffer them, and Thou dost not say to us what we are to do to them in regard to these.'

CHAPTER X.

Then said the Most High, the Holy and Great One spake, and sent Uriel to the son of Lamech, and said to him: 2. (Go to Noah and) tell him in my name " Hide thyself! ", and reveal to him the end that is approaching: that the whole earth will be destroyed, and a deluge is about to come upon the whole earth, and will destroy all that is on it. 3. And now instruet him that he may escape and his seed may be preserved for all the generations of the world.' 4, And again the Lord said to Raphael: ' Bind Azizél hand and foot, and cast him into the darkness: and make an we in the desert, which is in Didaél, and cast him therein. 5. And place upon him rough and jagged rocks, and cover him with darkness, and let him abide there for ever, and cover his face that he may not see light. 6. And on the day of the great judgement he shall be cast into the fire. 7. And heal the earth which the angels have _ corrupted, and proclaim the healing of the earth, that they may heal the plague, and that all the children of men may not perish through all the secret things that the Watchers have disclosed and have taught their sons. 8. And the whole earth has been corrupted through the works that were taught by Azazél: to him ascribe all sin.' 9. And to Gabriel said the Lord: 'Proceed against the bastards and the reprobates, and against the children of fornication: and destroy [the children of fornication and] the children of the Watchers from amongst men: [and cause them to go forth]: send them one against the other that they may destroy each other in battle: for length of days shall they not have. 10. And no request that they (i.e. their fathers) make of thee shall be granted unto their fathers on their behalf; for they hope to live an eternal life, and that each one of them will live five hundred years.' 11. And the Lord said unto Michael: 'Go, bind Semjizi and his associates who have united themselves with women so as to have defiled themselves with them in all their uncleanness. 12. And, when their sons have slain one another, and they have seen the destruction of their beloved ones, bind them fast for seventy generations in the valleys of the earth, till the day of their judgement and of their consummation, till the judgement that is for ever and ever is consummated. 13. In those days they shall be led off to the abyss of fire: (and) to the torment and the prison in which they shall be confined for ever. 14, And whosoever shall be condemned and destroyed will from thenceforth be bound together with them to the end of all generations. 15. And destroy all the spinits of the reprobate and the children of the Watchers, because they have wronged mankind. 16. Destroy all wrong from the face of the earth and let every evil work come to an end: and let the plant of righteousness and truth appear: 'and it shall prove a blessing: the works of righteousness and truth' shall be planted in truth and joy for evermore. 17. And then shall all the righteous escape, And shall live till they beget thousands of children, And all the days of their youth and their old age shall they complete in peace. 18. And then shall the whole earth be tilled in righteousness, and shall all be planted with trees and be full of blessing. 19, And all desirable trees shall be planted on it, and they shall plant vines on it: and the vine which they plant thereon shall yield wine in abundance, and as for all the seed which is sown thereon each measure (of it) shall bear a thousand, and each measure of olives shall yield ten presses of oil, 20. And cleanse thou the earth from all oppression, and from all unrighteousness, and from all sin, and from all godlessness: and all the uncleanness that is wrought upon the earth destroy from off the earth. 21. 'And all the children of men shall become righteous', and all nations shall offer adoration and shall praise Me, and all shall worship Me. 22. And the earth shall be cleansed from all defilement, and from all sin, and from all punishment, and from all torment, and I will never again send (them) upon it from generation to generation and for ever.

CHAPTER XI

And in those days I will open the store chambers of blessing which are in the heaven, so as to send them down 'upon the earth' over the work and labour of the children of men. 2. And truth and peace shall be associated together throughout all the days of the world and throughout all the generations of men.'

XII-XVI. Dream Vision of Enoch

His intercession for Azdzél and the fallen Angels: and his announcement to them of their first and final doom.

CHAPTER XII.

Before these things Enoch was hidden, and no one of the children of men knew where he was hidden, and where he abode, and what had become of him. 2, And his activities had to do with the Watchers, and his days were with the holy ones. 3. And I Enoch was blessing the Lord of majesty and the King of the ages, and lo! the Watchers called me—Enoch the scribe—and said to me: 4, 'Enoch, thou scribe of righteous-ness, 20, fdeclare} to the Watchers of the heaven who have left the high heaven, the holy eternal place, and have defiled themselves with women, and have done as the children of earth do, and have taken unto themselves wives: "Ye have wrough great destruction on the earth: 5. And ye shall have no peace nor forgiveness of sin: and inasmuch as tthey7 delight themselves in } their} children, 6. The murder of } their tT beloved ones shall ;they} sec, and over the destruction of } their} children shall + they} lament, and shall make supplication unto eternity, but mercy and peace shall ye not attain."

CHAPTER XIII.

And Enoch went and said: ' Azazél, thou shalt have no peace: a severe sentence has gone forth against thee to put thee in bonds ; 2. And thou shalt not have toleration nor + request} granted to thee, because of the unrighteousness which thou hast taught, and because of all the works of godlessness and unrighteousness and sin which thou hast shown to men.' 3. Then I went and spoke to them all together, and they were all afraid, and fear and trembling seized them. 4. And they besought me to draw up a petition for them that they might find forgiveness, and to read their petition in the presence of the Lord of heaven. 5. For from thenceforward they could not speak (with Him) nor lift up their eyes to heaven for shame of their sins for which they had been 'condemned. 6. Then I wrote out their petition, and the prayer fin regard to their spirits 'and their deeds individually and in regard to their request s that they should have forgiveness and lengthy. 7 eon I went off and sat down at the waters of Dan, in the land of Dan, to the south of the west of Hermon: I read their petition till I fell asleep. § 8. And behold a dream came to me, and visions fell down upon me, and I saw visions of chastisement, 'and a voice came bidding (me)! to tell it to the sons of heaven, and reprimand them. 9. And when I awaked, I came unto them, _and they were all sitting gathered together, weeping: in 'Abelsjail, which is between Lebanon and Sénésér, with their faces covered. 10. And I recounted before them all the visions which I had seen in sleep, and I began to speak the words of righteousness,.and to reprimand the heavenly Watehers.

CHAPTER XIV.

The book of the words of righteousness, and of the reprimand of the eternal Watchers in' accordance with the command of the Holy Great One in that vision. 2. I saw in my sleep what I will now say with a tongue of flesh and with the breath of my mouth: which the Great One has given to men to converse therewith and understand with the heart. 3. As He has created and given "to man the power of understanding the word of wisdom, so hath He created me also and given™ me the power of reprimanding the Watchers, the children of heaven. 4, I wrote out your petition, and in my vision it appeared thus, that your petition will not be granted unto you "throughout all the days of eternity, and that judgement has been finally passed upon you: yea (your petition) will not be granted unto you", 5. And from henceforth you shall not ascend into heaven unto all eternity, and "in bonds! of the earth the decree has gone forth to bind you for all the days of the world, 6. And (that) previously you shall have seen the destruction of your beloved sons and ye shall have no pleasure in them, but they shall fall before you by the sword. 7. And your petition on their behalf shall not be granted, nor yet on your own: even though you weep and pray and speak all the words contained in the writing which I have written, 8. And the vision was shown to me thus: Behold, in the vision clouds invited me and a mist summoned me, and the course of the stars and the lightnings sped and hastened me, and the winds in the vision caused me to fly and lifted me upward, and bore me into heaven, 9, And I went in till I drew nigh to a wall which is built of crystals and surrounded by tongues of fire: and it began to affright me, 10. And I went into the tongues of fire and drew nigh to a large house which was built of crystals: and the walls of the house were like a tesselated floor (made) of crystals, and its groundwork was of crystal. 11. Its ceiling was like the path of the stars and the lightnings, and between them were fiery cherubim, and their heaven was (clear as) water. 12. A flaming fire surrounded the walls, and its portals blazed with fire. 13, And I entered into that house, and it was hot as fire and cold as ice: there were no delights of life therein: fear covered me, and trembling gat hold upon me. 14. And as I quaked and trembled, I fell upon my face, And I beheld a vision, 15. And lo! there was a second house, greater than the former, and the entire portal stood open before me, and it was built of flames of fire. 16. And in every respect it so excelled in splendour and magnificence and extent that I cannot describe to you its splendour and its extent. 17. And its floor was of fire, and above it were lightnings and the path of the stars, and 18. And I looked and saw therein" a lofty throne: its appearance was as crystal, and the its ceiling also was flaming fire. wheels thereof as the shining sun, and there was the vision of cherubim. 19. And from underneath the throne came streams of flaming fire so that I could not look thereon. 20. And the Great Glory sat thereon, and His raiment shone more brightly 21. None of the angels could enter and could behold His face by reason of the magnificence and glory, and no flesh could behold Him. 22, The flaming fire was round about Him, and a great fire than the sun and was whiter than any snow. stood before Him, and none around could draw nigh Him: ten thousand times ten thousand (stood) before Him, yet He needed no counsellor. 23, And the most holy ones who were nigh to Him did not leave by night nor depart from Him. 24, And until then I had been prostrate on my face, trembling: and the Lord called me with His own mouth, and said to me: 'Come hither, Enoch, and hear my word.' 25. 'And one of the holy ones came to me and waked me', and He made me rise up and approach the door: and I bowed my face downwards.

CHAPTER XV.

And He answered and said to me, and I heard His voice: 'Fear not, Enoch, thou righteous man and scribe of righteousness: approach hither and hear my voice. 2. And go, say to "the Watchers of heaven", who have sent thee to intercede for them : "' Youshould intercede" for men, and not men for you: 3. Wherefore have ye left the high, holy, and_eternal heaven, and lain with women, and defiled yourselves with the daughters of men and taken to yourselves wives, and done like the children of earth, and begotten giants (as your) sons. 4, And though ye were holy, spiritual, living the eternal life, you have defiled yourselves with the blood of women, and have begotten (children) with the blood of flesh, and, as the children of men, have lusted after flesh and blood as those 'also' do who die and perish. 5. Therefore have I given them wives also that they might impregnate them, and beget children by them, that thus nothing might be wanting to them on oe 6. But you were 'formerly! spiritual, living the eternal life, and immortal for all generations of the world. 7, And therefore I have not appointed wives for you; for as for the spiritual ones of the heaven, in heaven is their dwelling. 8. And now, the giants, who are produced from the spirits and flesh, shall be called evil spirits upon the earth, and on the earth shall be their dwelling. 9 Evil spirits have proceeded from their bodies; because they are born from men, "and™ from the holy watchers is their beginning and primal origin; 'they shall be evil spirits on earth, and! evil spirits shall they be called. [10. As for the spirits of heaven, in heaven shall be their dwelling, but as for the spirits of the earth which were born upon the earth, on the earth shall be their dwelling.] 11. And the spirits of the giants afflict, oppress destroy, attack, do battle, and work destruction on the earth, and cause trouble: they take no food, "but nevertheless hunger" and thirst, and cause offences. 12. And these spirits shall rise up against the children of men and against the women, because they have proceeded 'from them'.

CHAPTER XVI.

From the days of the slaughter and destruction and death 'of the giants', from the souls of whose flesh the spirits, having gore forth, shall destroy without incurring judgement —thus shall they destroy until the day of the consummation, the great "judgement! in which the age shall be consummated, over the Watchers and the godless, yea, shall be wholly consummated." 2. And now as to the Watchers who have sent thee to intercede for them, who had been "aforetime® in heaven, (say to them) : 3. "You have been in heaven, but 'all' the mysteries had not yet been revealed to you, and you knew worthless ones, and these in the hardness of your hearts you have made known to the women, and through these mysteries women and men work mueh evil on earth." 4. Say to them therefore: "You have no peace."

XVII-XXXVI. Hnoch's Journeys through the Earth and Sheol.

XVII-XIX. The First Journey

CHAPTER XVII.

And they took 'and brought' me to a place in which those who were there were like flaming fire, and when they wished, they appeared as men. 2. And they brought me to the place of darkness, and to a mountain the point of whose summit reached to heaven. 8. And I saw the places of the luminaries 'and the treasuries of the stars' and of the thunder, 'and! in the uttermost depths, where were a fiery bow and arrows and their quiver, "and a fiery sword" and all the lightnings. 4. And they took me to the living waters, and to the fire of the west, which receives every setting of the sun. 5. And I came to a river of fire in which the fire flows like water and discharges itself into the great sea towards the west. 6. I saw the great rivers and came to the great 'river and to the great! darkness, and went to the place where no flesh walks. 7. I saw the mountains of the darkness of winter and the place whence all the waters of the deep flow. 8. I saw the mouths of all the rivers of the earth and the mouth of the deep.

CHAPTER XVIII.

I saw the treasuries of all the winds; I saw how He had furnished with them the whole creation and the firm foundations of the earth. 2. And I saw the corner-stone of the earth: I saw the four winds which bear [the earth and] the firmament of the heaven. 3. "And I saw how the winds stretch out the vaults of heaven", and have their station between heaven and earth: "these are the pillars of the heaven". 4, I saw the winds of heaven which turn and bring the circumference of the sun and all the stars to their setting. 5. I saw the winds on the earth carrying the clouds: I saw "the paths of the angels: I saw" at the end of the earth the firmament of the heaven above. 6. And I proceeded and saw a place which burns day and night, where there are seven mountains of magnificent stones, three towards the east, and three towards the south. 7, And as for those towards the east (one) was of great earth: there the heavens were completed. 1]. And I saw a deep abyss, with columns "of heavenly fire, and among them I saw columns" of fire fall, which were beyond measure alike towards the height and towards the depth. 12. And beyond that abyss I saw a place which had no firmament of the heaven above, and no firmly founded earth beneath it: there was no water upon it, and no birds, but it was a waste and horrible place. 13. I saw there seven stars like great burning mountains, and to me, when I inquired regarding them, 14, The angel said : 'This place is the end of heaven and earth: this has become a prison for the stars and the host of heaven. 15. And the stars which roll over the fire are they which have transcressed the commandment of the Lord in the beginning of their rising, because they did not come forth at their appointed times. 16. And He was wroth with them, and bound them till the time when their guilt should be consummated (even) 'for ten thousand years'.'

CHAPTER XIX.

And Uriel said to me: ' Here shall stand the angels who have connected themselves with women, and their spirits assuming many different forms are defiling mankind and shall lead them astray into sacrificing to demons "as gods", (here shall they stand), till "the day of" the great judgement in which they shal] be judged till they are made an end of. 2. And the women also of the angels who went astray shall become sirens.' 3. And I, Enoch, alone saw the vision, the ends of all things: and no man shall see as J have seen.

Names and Functions of the Seven Archangels.

CHAPTER XX.

And these are the names of the holy angels who watch. 2. Uriel, one of the holy angels, who is over the world and over Tartarus. 3. Raphael, one of the holy angels, who is over the spirits of men. 4, Raguel, one of the holy angels who }takes vengeance ont the world of the luminaries. 5. Michael, one of the holy angels, to wit, he that is set over the best part of mankind "and" over chaos. __ 6. Sara- qaél, one of the holy angels, who is set over the spirits, who sin in the spirit. 7. Gabriel, one of the holy angels, who is over Paradise and the serpents and the Cherubim. 8, Remiel, one of the holy angels, whom God set over those who rise.

XXI-XXXVI. The Second Journey of Enoch.

Preliminary and final place of punishment of the fallen angels (stars).

CHAPTER XXI.

And I proceeded to where things were chaotic. 2. And I saw there something horrible: I saw neither a heaven above nor a firmly founded earth, but a place chaotic and horrible. 3. And there I saw seven stars of the heaven bound together in it, like great mountains and burning with fire. 4, Then I said: 'For what sin are they bound, and on what account have they been cast in hither?' 5. Then said Uriel, one of the holy angels, who was with me, and was chief over them, and said: ' Enoch, why dost thou ask, and why art thou eager for the truth ? 6. These are of the number of the stars "of heaven"^ which have transgressed the commandment of the Lord, and are bound here till ten thousand years^ the time entailed by their sins, are consummated/ 7. And from thence I went to another place, which was still more horrible than the former, and I saw a horrible thing : a great fire there which burnt and blazed, and the place was cleft as far as the abyss, being full of great descending columns of fire : neither its extent or magnitude could I see, nor could I conjecture. 8. Then I said : * How fearful is the place and how terrible to look upon ! 9. Then Uriel answered me, one of the holy angels who was with me, and said unto me ; ' Enoch, why hast thou such fear and affright?" And I answered: 'Because of this fearful place, and because of the spectacle of the pain.' 10. And he said unto me: This place is the prison of the angels, and here they will be imprisoned for ever'

Sheol or the Underworld.

CHAPTER XXII.

And thence I went to another place, and he showed me in the west ""another""^ great and high mountain [and] of hard rock. 2. And there was in it four hollow places^ deep and wide and very smooth. How smooth are the hollow places and deep and dark to look at. 3. Then Raphael answered, one of the holy angels who was with me, and said unto me: ' These hollow places have been created for this very purpose, that the spirits of the souls of the dead should assemble therein, yea that all the souls of the children of men should assemble here. 4. And these places have been made to receive them till the day of their judgement and till their appointed period [till the period appointed], till the great judgement (comes) upon them.' 5, I saw the spirits of the children of men who were dead, and their voice went forth to heaven and made suit. 6. Then I asked Raphael the angel who was with me, and I said unto him: ' This spirit—whose is it whose voice goeth forth and maketh suit? 7, And he answered me saying: ' This is the spirit which went forth from Abel whom his brother Cain slew, and he makes his suit against him till his seed is destroyed from the face of the earth, and his seed is annihilated from amongst the seed of men . Then 1 asked regarding it, and regarding all the hollow places: ' Why is one separated from the other? 9. And he answered me and said unto me:' These three have been made that the spirits of the dead might be separated. And such a division has been made (for) the spirits of the righteous, in which there is the bright spring of water. 10. And such has been made for sinners when they die and are buried in the earth and judgement has not been executed on them in their lifetime. 11. Here their spirits shall be set apart in this great pain till the great day of judgement and punishment and torment of those who curse for ever, and retribution for their spirits. There He shall Und them for ever. 12. And such a division has been made for the spirits of those who make their suit, who make disclosures concerning their destruction, when they were slain in the days of the sinners. 13. Such has been made for the spirits of men who were not righteous sinners, who were complete in transgression, and of the transgressors they shall be companions: but their spirits shall not be slain in the day of judgement nor shall they be raised from thence.' 14.

Then I blessed the Lord of glory and said: ' Blessed be my Lord, the Lord of righteousness^ who ruleth for ever.

The Fire that deals with the Luminaries of Heaven.

CHAPTER XXIII.

From thence I went to another place to the west of the ends of the earth. 2. And I saw a "burning" ire which ran without resting^ and paused not from its course day or night but (ran) regularly. 3. And I asked saying: ' What is this which rests not? ' 4. Then Raguel one of the holy angels who was with me, answered me "^and said unto me: This course '^of fire which thou hast seen is the fire in the west which persecutes all the luminaries of heaven.'

XXIV—XXV. The Seven Mountains in the North-West and the Tree of Life.

CHAPTER XXIV.

And from thence I went to another place of the earth, and he showed me a mountain range of fire which burnt ""day and^ night. 2. And I went beyond it and saw seven magnificent mountains all differing each from the other, and the stones (thereof) were magnificent and beautiful, magnificent as a whole, of glorious appearance and fair exterior : three towards the east, one founded on the other, and three towards the south, one upon the other, and deep rough ravines, no one of which joined with any other. 3. And the seventh mountain was in the midst of these, and it excelled them in eight, resembling the seat of a throne: and fragrant trees encircled the throne. 4. And amongst them was a tree such as I had never yet smelt, neither was any amongst them nor were others like it: it had a fragrance beyond all fragrance, and its leaves and blooms and wood wither not for ever: and its fruit ^is beautiful, and its fruit resembles the dates of a palm. 5. Then I said: 'How" beautiful is this tree, and fragrant, and its leaves are fair, and its blooms very delightful in appearance.' 6. Then answered Michael, one of the holy and honoured angels who was with me, and was their leader.

CHAPTER XXV.

And he said unto me: Enoch, why dost thou ask me regarding the fragrance of the tree, and 'why dost thou wish to learn the truth? ' 2. Then I answered him "saying": I wish to know about everything, but especially about this tree 3. And he answered saying: ' This high mountain which thou hast seen, whose summit is like the throne of God, is His throne, where the Holy Great One, the Lord of Glory, the Eternal King, will sit, when He shall come down to visit the earth with goodness. 4. And as for this fragrant tree no mortal is permitted to touch it till the great judgement, when He shall take vengeance on all and bring (everything) to its consummation for ever. It shall then be given to the righteous and holy. 5. Its fruit shall be for food to the elect: it shall be transplanted to the holy place, to the temple of the Lord, the Eternal King. 6. Then shall they rejoice with joy and be glad. And into the holy place shall they enter; And its fragrance shall be in their bones, And they shall live a long life on earth, Such as thy fathers lived: And in their days shall no "sorrow or" plague Or torment or calamity touch them 7. Then blessed I the God of Glory, the Eternal King, who hath prepared such things for the righteous, and hath created them and promised to give to them.

Jerusalem and the Mountaim, Ravines, and Streams.

CHAPTER XXVI.

And I went from thence to the middle of the earth, and I saw a blessed place 'in which there were trees with branches abiding and blooming [of a dismembered tree]. 2. And there I saw a holy mountain, "and" underneath the mountain to the east there was a stream and it flowed towards the south. 3. And I saw towards the east another mountain higher than this, and between them a deep and narrow ravine: in it also ran a stream 'underneath the mountain. 4. And to the west thereof there was another mountain, lower than the former and of small elevation, and a ravine deep and dry between them: and another deep and dry ravine was at the extremities of the three ^mountains". 5. And all the ravines were deep "and narrow", (being formed) of hard rock, and trees were not planted upon them. 6. And I marvelled "at the rocks, and I marvelled" at the ravine, yea, I marvelled very much.

The Purpose of the Accursed Valley.

CHAPTER XXVII.

Then said I: For what object is this blessed land, which is entirely filled with trees, and this accursed valley between? 2. "Then Uriel, one of the holy angels who was with me, answered and said: This accursed valley is for those who are accursed for ever: here shall all "the accursed" be gathered together who utter with their lips against the Lord unseemly words and of His glory speak hard things. Here shall they be gathered together, and here shall be their place of judgement. 3. In the last days there shall be upon them the spectacle of righteous judgement in the presence of the righteous for ever: here shall the merciful bless the Lord of Glory, the Eternal King. 4. In the days of judgement over the former, they shall bless Him for the mercy in accordance with which He has assigned them (their lot) 5. Then I blessed the Lord of Glory and set forth His "glory" and landed Him gloriously.

XXVIII–XXXIII. Farther Journey to the East.

CHAPTER XXVIII.

And thence I went "towards the east", into the midst "of the mountain range" of the desert, and I saw a wilderness and it was solitary, full of trees and plants. 2. "And" water gushed forth from above. 3. Rushing like a copious watercourse [which flowed] towards the north-west it caused clouds and dew to ascend on every side.

CHAPTER XXIX.

And thence I went to another place in the desert, and approached to the east of this mountain range. 2. And "there" I saw aromatic trees exhaling the fragrance of frankincense and myrrh, and the trees also were similar to the almond tree.

CHAPTER XXX.

And beyond these, I went afar to the east, and I saw another place, a valley (full) of water. 2. And "therein there was'" a tree, the colour(?) of fragrant trees such as the mastic. 3. And on the sides of those valleys I saw fragrant cinnamon. And beyond these I proceeded to the east.

CHAPTER XXXI.

And I saw other mountains, and amongst them were "groves of trees, and there flowed forth from them nectar, which is named sarara and galbanum. 2. And beyond these mountains I saw another mountain "to the east of the ends of the earth, "whereon were aloe trees", and all the trees were full of stacte, being like almond trees. 3. And when one burnt it, it smelt sweeter than any fragrant odour.

CHAPTER XXXII.

And after these fragrant odours, as I looked towards the north over the mountains I saw seven mountains full of choice nard and fragrant trees and cinnamon and pepper. 2. And thence I went over the summits of all these mountains, far towards the east ^of the earth^, and passed above the Erythraean sea, and went far from it, and passed over "the angel Zotiel. 3. And I came to the Garden of Righteousness, and saw beyond those trees many large trees growing there and of goodly fragrance, large, very beautiful and glorious, and the tree of wisdom whereof they eat and know great wisdom. 4. "That tree is in height like the fir, and its leaves are like (those of) the Carob tree: and its fruit is like the clusters of the vine, very beautiful: and the fragrance of the tree penetrates afar. 5. Then I said: 'How' beautiful is the tree, and how attractive is its look! 6. Then Raphael, the holy angel who was with me, answered me "and said" : 'This is the tree of wisdom, of which thy father old (in years) and thy aged mother, who were before thee, have eaten, and they learnt wisdom and their eyes were opened, and they knew that they were naked and they were driven out of the garden.'

SECTION I - THE WATCHERS' REBELLION AND DIVINE JUDGMENT

CHAPTER XXXIII.

And from thence I went to the ends of the earth and saw there great beasts, and each differed from the other; and (I saw) birds also differing in appearance and beauty and voice, the one differing from the other. 2. And to the east of those beasts I saw the ends of the earth whereon the heaven rests, and the portals of the heaven open. 3. And I saw how the stars of heaven come forth, and I counted the portals out of which they proceed, and wrote down all their outlets, of each individual star by itself, according to their number and their names, their courses and their positions, and their times and their months, as Uriel the holy angel who was with me showed me. 4. He showed all things to me and wrote them down for me: also their names he wrote for me, and their laws and their companies.

Enoch's Journey to the North.

CHAPTER XXXIV.

And from thence I went towards the north to the ends of the earth, and there I saw a great and glorious device at the ends of the whole earth. 2. And here I saw three portals of heaven open in the heaven: through each of them proceed north winds: when they blow there is cold, hail, frost, snow, dew, and rain. 3. And out of one portal they blow for good: but when they blow through the other two portals, fit is with violence and affliction on the earth, and they blow with violence!

CHAPTER XXXV.

And from thence I went towards the west to the ends of the earth, and saw there three portals of the heaven open such as I had seen in the feastf, the same number of portals, and the same number of outlets.

The Journey to the South.

CHAPTER XXXVI.

And from thence I went to the south to the ends of the earth, and saw there three open portals of the heaven: and thence there come dew, rain, fand wind. 2. And from thence I went to the east to the ends of the heaven, and saw here the three eastern portals of heaven open and small portals above them, 3. Through each of these small portals pass the stars of heaven and run their course to the west on the path which is shown to them. 4. And as often as I saw I blessed always the Lord of Glory, and I continued to bless the Lord of Glory who has wrought great and glorious wonders, to show the greatness of His work to the angels and to spirits and to men, that they might praise His work and all His creation: that they might see the work of His might and praise the great work of His hands and bless Him for ever.

Section II (Chapters XXXVII – LXXI)

PARABLES OF THE ELECT AND THE COMING JUDGMENT

This section, often referred to as the *Book of the Watchers*, focuses on the dramatic narrative of the fallen angels (Watchers) who descend to Earth, mate with human women, and corrupt humanity. It explores themes of sin, forbidden knowledge, and divine judgment. Enoch's visions of angelic punishment highlight the consequences of rebellion against divine order and emphasize the sovereignty of God.

Readers are introduced to the origins of evil and corruption, setting the stage for the cosmic struggle between light and darkness that resonates throughout the rest of the book. This section also underscores Enoch's role as an intercessor, mediating between heaven and earth.

The Parables.

CHAPTER XXXVII.

The second vision which he saw, the vision of wisdom—which Enoch the son of Jared^ the son of Mahalalel, the son of Cainan, the son of Enos, the son of Seth, the son of Adam, saw. 2. And this is the beginning of the words of wisdom which I lifted up my voice to speak and say to those which dwell on earth: Hear, ye men of old time, and see, ye that come after, the words of the Holy One which I will speak before the Lord of Spirits. 3. It were better to declare (them only) to the men of old time, but even from those that come after we will not withhold the beginning of wisdom. 4. Till the present day such wisdom has never been given by the Lord of Spirits as I have received according to my insight, according to the good pleasure of the Lord of Spirits by whom the lot of eternal life has been given to me. 5. Now three parables were imparted to me, and I lifted up my voice and recounted them to those that dwell on the earth.

THE FIRST PARABLE.

XXXVIII. The Coming Judgement of the Wicked.

CHAPTER XXXVIII.

When the congregation of the righteous shall appear, And sinners shall be judged for their sins, And shall be driven from the face of the earth: 2. And when the Righteous One shall appear before the eyes of the righteous. Whose elect works hang upon the Lord of Spirits, And light shall appear to the righteous and the elect who dwell on the earth, Where then will be the dwelling of the sinners, And where the resting-place of those who have denied the Lord of Spirits? It had been good for them if they had not been born. 3. When the secrets of the righteous shall be revealed and the sinners judged, And the godless driven from the presence of the righteous

SECTION II - PARABLES OF THE ELECT AND THE COMING JUDGMENT

and elect, 4. From that time those that possess the earth shall no longer be powerful and exalted: And they shall not be able to behold the face of the holy, For the Lord of Spirits has caused His light to appear On the face of the holy, righteous, and elect. 5. Then shall the kings and the mighty perish And be given into the hands of the righteous and holy 6. And thenceforward none shall seek for themselves mercy from the Lord of Spirits: For their life is at an end.

The Ahocle of the Righteous and of the Elect One: the Praises of the Blessed.

CHAPTER XXXIX.

And it shall come to pass in those days that elect and holy children will descend from the high heaven and their seed f will become one with the children of men. 2. And in those days Enoch received books of zeal and wrath, and books of disquiet and expulsion.] And mercy shall not be accorded to them; saith the Lord of Spirits, 3. And in those days a whirlwind carried me off from the earth, And set me down at the end of the heavens. 4. And there I saw another vision, the dwelling-places of the holy, And the resting-places of the righteous. 5. Here mine eyes saw their dwellings with His righteous angels, And their resting-places with the holy. And they petitioned and interceded and prayed for the children of men, And righteousness flowed before them as water, And mercy like dew upon the earth: Thus it is amongst them for ever and ever. 6 a. And in that place mine eyes saw the Elect One of righteousness and of faith, 7 a. And I saw his dwelling-place under the wings of the Lord of Spirits. 6 b. And righteousness shall prevail in his days. And the righteous and elect shall be without number before Him for ever and ever. 7 b. And all the righteous and elect before Him shall be strong f as fiery lights, And their mouth shall be full of blessing, And their lips extol the name of the Lord of Spirits, And rig-hteousness before Him shall never fail, [And uprightness shall never fail before Him]. 8. There I wished to dwell, And my spirit longed for that dwelling-place: And there heretofore hath been my portion, For so has it been established concerning me before the Lord of Spirits. 9. In those days I praised and extolled the name of the Lord of Spirits with blessings and praises, because He hath destined me for blessing and glory according to the good pleasure of the Lord of Spirits. 10. For a long time my eyes regarded that place, and I blessed Him and praised Him, saying: 'Blessed is He, and may He be blessed from the beginning and for evermore. 11. And before Him there is no ceasing. He knows before the world was created what is for ever and what will be from generation unto generation. 13. Those who sleep not bless Thee: they stand before Thy glory and bless, praise, and extol, saying: " Holy, holy, holy, is the Lord of Spirits: He filleth the earth Avith spirits. 13. And here my eyes saw all those who sleep no : they stand before Him and bless and say: ' Blessed be Thou, and blessed be the name of the Lord for ever and ever, 14. And my face was changed ; for I could no longer behold.

The Four Archangels
CHAPTER XL.

And after that I saw thousands of thousands and ten thousand times ten thousand I saw a multitude beyond number and reckoning, who stood before the Lord of Spirits. 2. And on the four sides of the Lord of Spirits I saw four presences, different from those that sleep not, and I learnt their names: for the angel who went with me made known to me their names, and showed me all the hidden things. 3. And I heard the voices of those four presences as they uttered praises before the Lord of glory. 4. The first voice blesses the Loi-d of Spirits for ever and ever. 5. And the second voice I heard blessing the Elect One and the elect ones who hang upon the Lord of Spirits. 6. And the third voice I heard pray and intercede for those who dwell on the earth and supplicate in the name of the Lord of Spirits. 7. And I heard the fourth voice fending off the Satans and forbidding them to come before the Lord of Spirits to accuse them who dwell on the earth. 8. After that I asked the angel of peace who went with me, who showed me everything that is hidden: 'Who are these four presences which I have seen and whose words I have heard and written down? 9. And he said to me: ' This first is Michael, the merciful and long-suffering: and the second, who is set over all the diseases and all the wounds of the children of men, is Raphael : and the third, who is set over all the powers, is Gabriel: and the fourth, who is set over the repentance unto hope of those who inherit eternal life, is named Phanuel/ 10. And these are the four angels of the Lord of Spirits and the four voices I heard in those days.

CHAPTER XLI.

And after that I saw all the secrets of the heavens, and how the kingdom is divided, and how the actions of men are weighed in the balance. 2. And there I saw the mansions of the elect and the mansions of the holy, and mine eyes saw there all the sinners being driven from thence which deny the name of the Lord of Spirits, and being dragged off: and they could not abide because of the punishment which proceeds from the Lord of Spirits. 3. And there mine eyes saw the secrets of the lightning and of the thunder, and the secrets of the winds, how they are divided to blow over the earth, and the secrets of the clouds and dew, and there I saw from whence they proceed in that place and from whence they saturate the dusty earth. 4. And there I saw closed chambers out of which the winds are divided, the chamber of the hail and winds, the chamber of the mist, and of the clouds, and the cloud thereof hovers over the earth from the beginning of the world. 5. And I saw the chambers of the sun and moon, whence they proceed and whither they come again, and their glorious return, and how one is superior to the other, and their stately orbit, and how they do not leave their orbit, and they add nothing to their orbit and they take nothing from it, and they keep faith with each other, in accordance with the oath by which they are bound together. 6. And first the sun goes forth and traverses his path according to the commandment of the Lord of Spirits, and mighty is His name for ever and ever. 7. And after that I saw the hidden and the visible path of the moon, and she accomplishes the course of her path in that place by day and by night—the one holding a position opposite to the other before the Lord of Spirits. And they give thanks and praise and rest not; For unto them is their thanksgiving rest. 8, For the sun changes oft for a blessing or a curse, And the course of the path of the moon is light to the righteous, And darkness to the sinners in the name of the Lord, Who made a separation between the light and the darkness. And divided the spirits of men. And strengthened the spirits of the righteous. In the name of His righteousness. 9. For no angel hinders and no power is able to hinder; for He appoints a judge for them all and he judges them all before Him.

The Dwelling-places of Wisdom and of Unrighkonmess.

CHAPTER XLII.

Wisdom found no place where she might dwell; Then a dwelling-place was assigned her in the heavens. 2. Wisdom went forth to make her dwelling among the children of men, And found no dwelling-place: Wisdom returned to her place. And took her seat among the angels. 3. And unrighteousness went forth from her chambers: Whom she sought not she found. And dwelt with them, As rain in a desert And dew on a thirsty land.

XLIII—XLIV. Adronomical Secrets.

CHAPTER XLIII.

And I saw other lightnings and the stars of heaven, and I saw how He called them all by their names and they hearkened unto Him. 2. And I saw how they are weighed in a righteous balance according to their proportions of light: (I saw] the width of their spaces and the day of their appearing, and how their revolution produces lightning: and (I saw) their revolution according to the number of the angels, and (how) they keep faith with each other. 3. And I asked the angel who went with me who showed me what was hidden: ' What are these? ' 4. And he said to me: 'The Lord of Spirits hath showed thee their parabolic meaning (lit. ' their parable '): these are the names of the holy who dwell on the earth and believe in the name of the Lord of Spirits for ever and ever.

CHAPTER XLIV.

Also another phenomenon I saw in regard to the lightnings: how some of the stars arise and become lightnings and cannot part with their new form.

THE SECOND PARABLE

The Lot of the Apostates: the New Heaven and the New Earth.

CHAPTER XLV.

And this is the Second Pai*able concerning those who deny the name of the dwelling of the holy ones and the Lord of Spirits. 2. And into the heaven they shall not ascend, And on the earth they shall not come: Such shall be the lot of the sinners Who have denied the name of the Lord of Spiritp Who are thus preserved for the day of suffering and tribulation. 3. On that day Mine Elect One shall sit on the throne of glory And shall try their works, And their places of rest shall be innumerable. And their souls shall grow strong within them when they see Mine elect ones, And those who have called upon My glorious name: 4. Then will I cause Mine Elect One to dwell among them. And I will transform the heaven and make it an eternal blessing and light, 5. And I will transform the earth and make it a blessing: And I will cause Mine elect ones to dwell upon it: But the sinners and evil-doers shall not set foot thereon, 6. For I have provided and satisfied with peace My righteous ones And have caused them to dwell before Me: But for the sinners there is judgement impending with Me, So that I shall destroy them from the face of the earth.

The Head of Days and the Son of Man.

CHAPTER XLVI.

And there I saw One who had a head of days, And His head was white like wool, And with Him was another being whose countenance had the appearance of a man, And his face was full of graciousness, like one of the holy angels. 2. And I asked the angel who went with me and showed me all the hidden things, concerning that Son of Man, who he was, and whence he was, (and) why he went with the Head of Days? 3. And he answered and said unto me: This is the Son of Man who hath righteousness, With whom dwelleth righteousness. And who revealeth all the treasures of that which is hidden, Because the Lord of Spirits hath chosen him, And whose lot hath the pre-eminence before the Lord of Spirits in uprightness for ever. 4. And this Son of Man whom thou hast seen Shall f raise up f the kings and the mighty from their seats, [And the strong from their thrones] And shall loosen the reins of the strong. And break the teeth of the sinners; 5. [And he shall put down the kings from their thrones and kingdoms] Because they do not extol and praise Him, Nor humbly acknowledge whence the kingdom was bestowed upon them. 6. And he shall put down the countenance of the strong, And shall fill them with shame. And darkness shall be their dwelling, And worms shall be their bed, - And they shall have no hope of rising from their beds, Because they do not extol the name of the Lord of Spirits. 7. And these are they who judge the stars of heaven, [And raise their hands against' the Most High], And tread upon the earth and dwell upon it. And all their deeds manifest unrighteousness, And their power rests upon their riches, And their faith is in the gods which they have made with their hands, And they deny the name of the Lord of Spirits, 8. And they persecute the houses of His congregations, And the faithful who hang upon the name of the Lord of Spirits.

The Prayer of the Righteous for Vengeance and their Joy at its Coming.

CHAPTER XLVII.

And in those days shall have ascended the prayer of the righteous. And the blood of the righteous from the earth before the Lord of Spirits. 2. In those days the holy ones who dwell above in the heavens Shall unite with one voice And supplicate and pray [and praise. And give thanks and bless the name of the Lord of Spirits] On behalf of the blood of the righteous which has been shed. And that the prayer of the righteous may not be in vain before the Lord of Spirits, That judgement may be done unto them, And that they may not have to suffer for ever. 3. In those days I saw the Head of Days when He seated himself

SECTION II - PARABLES OF THE ELECT AND THE COMING JUDGMENT

upon the throne of His glory, And the books of the living were opened before Him And all His host which is in heaven above and His counsellors stood before Him, 4. And the hearts of the holy were filled with joy; Because the number of the righteous had been offered, And the prayer of the righteous had been heard, And the blood of the righteous been required before the Lord of Spirits.

The Fount of Righteousness: the Son of Man—the Stay of the Righteous: Judgement of the Kings and the Mighty.

CHAPTER XLVIII.

And in that place I saw the fountain of righteousness Which was inexhaustible:

And around it were many fountains of wisdom; And all the thirsty drank of them, And were filled with wisdom, And their dwellings were with the righteous and holy and elect. 3. And at that hour that Son of Man was named In the presence of the Lord of Spirits, And his name before the Head of Days. 3. Yea, before the sun and the signs were created, Before the stars of the heaven were made, His name was named before the Lord of Spirits. 4. He shall be a staff to the righteous whereon to stay themselves and not fall, And he shall be the light of the Gentiles, And the hope of those who are troubled of heart. 5. All who dwell on earth shall fall down and worship before him, And will praise and bless and celebrate with song the Lord of Spirits. 6. And for this reason hath he been chosen and hidden before Him, Before the creation of the world and for evermore. 7. And the wisdom of the Lord of Spirits hath revealed him to the holy and righteous; For he hath preserved the lot of the righteous; Because they have hated and despised this world of unrighteousness; And have hated all its works and ways in the name of the Lord of Spirits: For in his name they are saved, And according to his good pleasure hath it been in regard to their life, 8. In these days downcast in countenance shall the kings of the earth have become, And the strong who possess the land because of the works of their hands; For on the day of their anguish and affliction they shall not (be able to) save themselves, 9. And I will give them over into the hands of Mine elect As straw in the fire so shall they burn before the face of the holy: As lead in the water shall they sink before the face of the righteous, And no trace of them shall any more be found. 10. And on the day of their affliction there shall be rest on the earth, And before them they shall fall and not rise again: And there shall be no one to take them with his hands and raise them: For they have denied the Lord of Spirits and His Anointed. The name of the Lord of Spirits be blessed.

The Tower and Wisdom of The Elect One.

CHAPTER XLIX.

For wisdom is poured out like water, And glory faileth not before him for evermore. 2. For he is mighty in all the secrets of righteousness, And unrighteousness shall disappear as a shadow, And have no continuance; Because the Elect One standeth before the Lord of Spirits, And his glory is for ever and ever, And his might unto all generations. 3. And in him dwells the spirit of wisdom, And the spirit which gives insight, And the spirit of understanding and of might, And the spirit of those who have fallen asleep in righteousness. 4. And he shall judge the secret things. And none shall be able to utter a lying word before him; For he is the Elect One before the Lord of Spirits according to His good pleasure.

The Glorification and Victory of the Righteous: the Repentance of the Gentiles.

CHAPTER L.

And in those days a change shall take place for the holy and elect, And the light of days shall abide upon them, And glory and honour shall turn to the holy, 2. On the day of affliction on which evil shall have been treasured up against the sinners. And the righteous shall be victorious in the name of the Lord of Spirits: And He will cause the others to witness (this) That they may repent And forgo the works of their hands. 3. They shall have no honour through the name of the Lord of Spirits, Yet through His name shall they be saved, And the Lord of Spirits will have compassion on them, For His compassion is great. 4. And He is righteous also in His judgement, And in the presence of His glory unrighteousness also shall not maintain itself: At His judgement the unrepentant shall perish before Him. 5. And from henceforth I will have no mercy on them, saith the Lord of Spirits.

The Resurrection of the Dead, mid the Separation oy the Judge of the Righteous and the Wicked.

CHAPTER LI.

And in those days shall the earth also give back that which has been entrusted to it, And Sheo also shall give back that which it has received, And hell shall give back that which it owes. 5 a. For in those days the Elect One shall arise, 2. Arid he shall choose the righteous and holy from among them: Eor the day has drawn nigh that they should be saved. 3. And the Elect One shall in those days sit on My throne. And his mouth shall pour forth all the secrets of wisdom and counsel: For the Lord of Spirits hath given (them) to him and hath glorified him. 4. And in those days shallihe mountains leap like rams, And the hills also shall skip like lambs satisfied with milk, And the faces of [all] the angels in heaven shall be lighted up with joy. 5 b. And the earth shall rejoice, c. And the righteous shall dwell upon it, d. And the elect shall walk thereon.

The Seven Metal Mountains and the Elect One.

CHAPTER LII.

And after those days in that place where I had seen all the visions of that which is hidden—for I had been carried off in a whirlwind and they had borne me towards the west. 2. There mine eyes saw all the secret things of heaven that shall be^ a mountain of iron, and a mountain of copper, and a mountain of silver, and a mountain of gold, and a mountain of soft metal, and a mountain of lead. 3. And I asked the angel who went with me, saying, ' What things are these which I have seen in secret? 4. And he said unto me: All these things which thou hast seen shall serve the dominion of His Anointed that he may be potent and mighty on the earth. 5. And that angel of peace answered, saying unto me: Wait a little and there shall be

SECTION II - PARABLES OF THE ELECT AND THE COMING JUDGMENT

revealed unto thee all the secret things, which surround the Lord of Spirits. 6. And these mountains which thine eyes have seen, The mountain of iron, and the mountain of copper, and the mountain of silver, And the mountain of gold, and the mountain of soft metal, and the mountain of lead, All these shall be in the presence of the Elect One, As wax before the fire, And like the water which streams down from above [upon those mountains], And they shall become powerless before his feet. 7. And it shall come to pass in those days that none shall be saved. Either by gold or by silver. And none be able to escape. 8. And there shall be no iron for war. Nor shall one clothe oneself with a breastplate. Bronze shall be of no service. And tin [shall be of no service and] shall not be esteemed, And lead shall not be desired. 9. And all these things shall be [denied and] destroyed from the surface of the earth. When the Elect One shall appear before the face of the Lord of Spirits.'

<u>The Valley of Judgement: the Angels of Punishment: the Communities of the Elect One.</u>

CHAPTER LIII.

There mine eyes saw a deep valley with open mouths, and all who dwell on the earth and sea and islands shall bring to him gifts and presents and tokens of homage, but that deep valley shall not become full. 2. And their hands commit lawless deeds, And the sinners devour all whom they lawlessly oppress: Yet the sinners shall be destroyed before the face of the Lord of Spirits, And they shall be banished from off the face of His earth, And they shall perish for ever and ever.

3. For I saw all the angels of punishment abiding (there) and preparing all the instruments of Satan. 4. And I asked the angel of peace who went with me: For whom are they preparing thfese instruments? ' 5. And he said unto me: They prepare these for the kings and the mighty of this earth, that they may thereby be destroyed. 6. And after this the Righteous and Elect One shall cause the house of his congregation to appear: henceforth they shall be no more hindered in the name of the Lord of Spirits. 7. And these mountains shall not stand as the earth before his righteousness, But the hills shall be as a fountain of water And the righteous shall have rest from the oppression of sinners.'

CHAPTER LIV.

And I looked and turned to another part of the earth, and saw there a deep valley with burning fire. 2. And they brought the kings and the mighty, and began to cast them into this deep valley. 3. And there mine eyes saw how they made these their instruments, iron chains of immeasurable weight. 4. And I asked the angel of peace who went with me, saying ' For whom are these chains being prepared? ' 5. And he said unto me: ' These are being prepared for the hosts of Azazel, so that they may take them and cast them into the abyss of complete condemnation, and they shall cover their jaws with rough stones as the Lord of Spirits commanded. 6. And Michael, and Gabriel, and Raphael, and Phanuel shall take hold of them on that great day, and cast them on that day into the burning furnace, that the Lord of Spirits may take vengeance on them for their unrighteousness in becoming subject to Satan and leading astray those who dwell on the earth.

LIV. 7—LV. 2. Noachic Fragment on the first World Judgement.

And in those days shall punishment come from the Lord of Spirits, and He will open all the chambers of waters which are above the heavens, and of the fountains which are beneath the earth. 8. And all the waters shall be joined with the waters: that which is above the heavens is the masculine, and the water which is beneath the earth is the feminine. 9. And they shall destroy all who dwell on the earth and those who dwell under the ends of the heaven. 10. And when they have recognized their unrighteousness which they have wrought on the earth, then by these shall they perish.

CHAPTER LV.

And after that the Head of Days repented and said: 'In vain have I destroyed all who dwell on the earth'. 2. And He sware by His great name: 'Henceforth I will not do so to all who dwell on the earth, and I will set a sign in the heaven: and this shall be a pledge of good faith between Me and them for ever, so long as heaven is above the earth. And this is in accordance with My command.

LV. 3—LVI. 4. Final Judgement of Azazel, the Watchers and their children.

When I have desired to take hold of them by the hand of the angels on the day of tribulation and pain because of this, I will cause My chastisement and My wrath to abide upon them, saith God, the Lord of Spirits. 4. Ye mighty kings who dwell on the earth, ye shall have to behold Mine Elect One, how he sits on the throne of glory and judges Azazel, and all his associates, and all his hosts in the name of the Lord of Spirits.

CHAPTER LVI

1. And I saw there the hosts of the angels of punishment going, and they held scourges and chains of iron and bronze. 2. And I asked the angel of peace who went with me, saying: 'To whom are these who hold the scourges going?' 3. And he said unto me: 'To their elect and beloved ones that they may be cast into the chasm of the abyss of the valley. 4. And then that valley shall be filled with their elect and beloved, And the days of their lives shall be at an end, And the days of their leading astray shall not thenceforward be reckoned.

LVI. 5-8. Lasi struggle of heathen Powers against Israel.

And in those days the angels shall return

And hurl themselves to the east upon the Parthians and Medes: They shall stir up the kings, so that a spirit of unrest shall come upon them, And they shall rouse them from their thrones, That they may break forth as lions from their lairs, And as hungry wolves among their flocks. 6. And they shall go up and tread under foot the land of His elect ones, [And the land of His elect ones shall be before them a threshing-floor and a highway]: 7. But the city of my righteous shall be a hindrance to their horses. And they shall begin to fight among themselves, And their right hand shall be strong against themselves, And a man shall not know his brother, Nor a son his father or his mother. Till there be no number of the corpses through their slaughter, And their punishment be not in vain. 8. In those days Sheol shall open its jaws. And they shall be swallowed up therein. And their destruction shall be at an end ; Sheol shall devour the sinners in the presence of the elect.' The Return from the Dispersion.

CHAPTER LVII.

And it came to pass after this that I saw another host of wagons, and men riding thereon, and coming on the winds from the east, and from the west to the south. 2. And the noise of their wagons was heard, and when this turmoil took place the holy ones from heaven remarked it, and the pillars of the earth were moved from their place, and the sound thereof was heard from the one end of heaven to the other, in one day. 3. And they shall all fall down and worship the Lord of Spirits. And this is the end of the second Parable.

THE THIRD PARABLE

LVIII. The Blessedness of the Saints.

CHAPTER LVIII.

And I began to speak the third Parable concerning the righteous and elect. 2. Blessed are ye, ye righteous and elect. For glorious shall be your lot. 3. And the righteous shall be in the light of the sun. And the elect in the light of eternal life The days of their life shall be unending. And the days of the holy without number. 4. And they shall seek the light and find righteousness with the Lord of Spirits: There shall be peace to the righteous in the name of the Eternal Lord. 5. And after this it shall be said to the holy in heaven That they should seek out the secrets of righteousness, the heritage of faith; For it has become bright as the sun upon earth, And the darkness is past. 6. And there shall be a light that never endeth, And to a limit (lit. ' number ') of days they shall not come. For the darkness shall first have been destroyed, [And the light established before the Lord of Spirits] And the light of uprightness established for ever before the Lord of Spirits.

The Lights and the Thunder.

CHAPTER LIX.

In those days mine eyes saw the secrets of the lightnings, and of the lights, and the judgements they execute (lit. ' their judgement *) : and they lighten for a blessing or a curse as the Lord of Spirits willeth. 2. And there I saw the secrets of the thunder, and how when it resounds above in the heaven, the sound thereof is heard, and he caused me to see the judgements executed on the earth, whether they be for wellbeing and blessing, or for a curse according to the word of the Lord of Spirits. 3. And after that all the secrets of the lights and lightnings were shown to me, and they lighten for blessing and for satisfying.]

BOOK OF NOAH A FRAGMENT

Quaking of the Heaven: Behemoth and Leviathan: the Elements.

CHAPTER LX.

In the year five hundred, in the seventh month, on the fourteenth day of the month in the life of Enoch. In that Parable I saw how a mighty quaking made the heaven of heavens to quake, and the host of the Most High, and the angels, a thousand thousands and ten thousand times ten thousand, were disquieted with a great disquiet. 2. And the Head of Days sat on the throne of His glory, and the angels and the righteous stood around Him. 3. And a great trembling seized me, And fear took hold of me, And my loins gave way, And dissolved were my reins. And I fell upon my face. 4. And Michael sent another angel from among the holy ones and he raised me up, and when he had raised me up my spirit returned ; for I had not been able to endure the look of this host, and the commotion and the quaking of the heaven. 5. And Michael said unto me: 'Why art thou disquieted with such a vision? Until this day lasted the day of His mercy and He hath been merciful and long-suffering towards those who dwell on the earth. 6. And when the day, and the power, and the punishment, and the judgement come, which the Lord of Spirits hath prepared for those who worship not the righteous law, and for those who deny the righteous judgement, and for those who take His name in vain—that day is prepared for the elect a covenant, but for sinners an inquisition. When the punishment of the Lord of Spirits shall rest upon them, it shall rest in order that the punishment of the Lord of Spirits may not come in vain, and it shall slay the children with their mothers and the children with their fathers. Afterwards the judgement shall take place according to His mercy and His patience.' 7. And on that day were two monsters parted, a female monster named Leviathan, to dwell in the abysses of the ocean over the fountains of the waters. 8. But the male is named Behemoth, who occupied with his breast a waste wilderness named Duidain, on the east of the garden where the elect and righteous dwell, where my grandfather was taken up, the seventh from Adam, the first man whom the Lord of Spirits created. 9. And I besought the other angel that he should show me the might of those monsters, how they were parted on one day and cast, the one into the abysses of the sea, and the other unto the dry land of the wilderness. 10. And he said to me: ' Thou son of man, herein thou dost seek to know what is hidden.' 11. And the other angel who went with me and showed me what was hidden told me, what is first and last in the heaven in the height, and beneath the earth in the depth, and at the ends of the heaven, and on the foundation of the heaven. 13. And the chambers of the winds, and how the winds are divided, and how they are weighed, and (how) the portals of the winds are reckoned, each according to the power of the wind, and the power of the lights of the moon, and according to the power that is fitting : and the divisions of the stars according to their names, and how all the divisions are divided. 13. And the thunders according to the places where they fall, and all the divisions that are made among the lightnings that it may lighten, and their host that they may at once obey. 14. For the thunder has places of rest (which) are assigned (to it) while it is waiting for its peal; and the thunder and lightning are inseparable, and although not one and undivided, they both go together through the spirit and separate not. 15. For when the lightning lightens, the thunder utters its voice, and the spirit enforces a pause during the peal, and divides equally between them ; for the treasury of their peals is like the sand, and each one of them as it peals is held in with a bridle, and turned back by the power of the spirit, and pushed forward according to the many quarters of the earth. 16. And the spirit of the sea is masculine and strong, and according to the might of his strength he draws it back with a rein, and in like manner it is driven forward and disperses amid all the mountains of the earth. 17. And the spirit of the hoar-frost is his own angel, and the spirit of the hail is a good angel. 18. And the spirit of the snow has forsaken (his chamber) on account of his strength—there is a special spirit therein, and that which ascends from it is like smoke, and its name is frost. 19. And the spirit of the mist is not united with them in their chambers, but it has a special chamber; for its course is glorious both in light and in darkness, and in winter and in summer, and in its chamber is an angel. 20. And the spirit of the dew has its dwelling at the ends of the heaven, and is connected with the chambers of the rain, and its course is in winter and summer: and its clouds and the clouds of the mist are connected, and the one gives to the other. 21. And when the spirit of the rain goes forth from its chamber, the angels come and open the chamber and lead it out, and when it is diffused over the whole earth it unites with the water on the earth. And whensoever it unites with the water on the earth. ... 22. For the waters are for those who dwell on the earth; for they are nourishment for the earth from the Most High who is in heaven: therefore there is a measure for the rain, and the angels take it in charge. 23. And these things I saw towards the Garden of the Righteous. 24. And the angel of peace who was with me said to me: 'These two monsters, prepared conformably to the greatness of God, shall feed. . . .

Angels go off to measure Paradise: the Judgement of the Righteous by the Meet One: the Praise of the Meet One and of God.

CHAPTER LXI.

And I saw in those days how long- cords were given to those angels, and they took to themselves wings and flew, and they went towards the north. 2. And I asked the angel, saying unto him: ' Why have those (angels) taken these cords and gone off? ' And he said unto me: 'They have gone to measure." 3. And the angel who went with me said unto me:' These shall bring the measures of the righteous. And the ropes of the righteous to the righteous. That they may stay themselves on the name of the Lord of Spirits for ever and ever. 4. The elect shall begin to dwell with the elect, And those are the measures which shall be given to faith And which shall strengthen righteousness. 5. And these measures shall reveal all the secrets of the depths of the earth, And those who have been destroyed by the desert, And those who have been devoured by the beasts And those who have been devoured by the fish of the sea, That they may return and stay themselves On the day of the Elect One; For none shall be destroyed before the Lord of Spirits, And none can be destroyed. 6. And all who dwell above in the heaven received a command and power and one voice and one light like unto fire. 7. And that One (with) their first words they blessed. And extolled and lauded with wisdom. And they were wise in utterance and in the spirit of life. 8. And the Lord of Spirits placed the Elect One on the throne of glory. And he shall judge all the works of the holy above in the heaven. And in the balance shall their deeds be weighed. 9. And when he shall lift up his countenance To judge their secret ways according to the word of the name of the Lord of Spirits, And their path according to the way of the righteous judgement of the Lord of Spirits, Then shall they all with one voice speak and bless. And glorify and extol and sanctify the name of the Lord of Spirits. 10. And He will summon all the host of the heavens, and all the holy ones above, and the host of God, the Cherubin, Seraphin, and Ophannin, and all the angels of power, and all the angels of principalities, and the Elect One, and the other powers on the earth (and) over the water 11. On that day shall raise one voice, and bless and glorify and exalt in the spirit of faith, and in the spirit of wisdom, and in the spirit of patience. and in the spirit of mercy, and in the spirit of judgement and of peace, and in the spirit of goodness, and shall all say with one voice: ' Blessed is He, and may the name of the Lord of Spirits be blessed for ever and ever.' 12. All who sleep not above in heaven shall bless Him: All the holy ones who are in heaven shall bless him, And all the elect who dwell in the garden of life: And every spirit of light who is able to bless, and glorify, and extol, and hallow Thy blessed name. And all flesh shall beyond measure glorify and bless Thy name for ever and ever. 13. For great is the mercy of the Lord of Spirits, and He is long-suffering. And all His works and all that He has created He has revealed to the righteous and elect In the name of the Lord of Spirits.'

Judgement of the Kings and the Mighty: Blessedness of the Righteous.

CHAPTER LXII.

And thus the Lord commanded the kings and the mighty and the exalted, and those who dwell on the earth, and said: ' Open your eyes and lift up your horns if ye are able to recognize the Elect One. 2. And the Lord of Spirits seated him on the throne of His glory. And the spirit of righteousness was poured out upon him. And the word of his mouth slays all the sinners. And all the unrighteous are destroyed from before his face. 3. And there shall stand up in that day all the kings and the mighty, And the exalted and those who hold the earth. And they shall see and recognize How he sits on the throne of its glory. And righteousness is judged before him, And no lying word is spoken before him. 4. Then shall pain\ come upon them as on a woman in travail, [And she has pam in bringing forth] When her child enters the mouth of the womb, And she has pain m bringing forth. 5. And one portion of them shall look on the other. And they shall be terrified, And they shall be downcast of countenance. And pain shall seize them. When they see that Son of Man Sitting on the throne of his glory. 6. And the kings and the mighty and all who possess the earth shall bless and glorify and extol him who rules over all, who was hidden. 7. For from the beginning the Son of Man was hidden, And the Most High preserved him in the presence of His might, And revealed him to the elect. 8. And the congregation of the elect and holy shall be sown, And all the elect shall stand before him on that day. 9. And all the kings and the mighty and the exalted and those who rule the earth Shall fall down before him on their faces, And worship and set their hope upon that Son of Man, And petition him and supplicate for mercy at his hands. 10. Nevertheless that Lord of Spirits will so press them That they shall hastily go forth from His presence, And their faces shall be filled with shame, And the darkness shall grow deeper on their faces. 11. And He -will deliver them to the angels for punishment, To execute vengeance on them because they have oppressed His children and His elect. 12. And they shall be a spectacle for the righteous and for His elect: They shall rejoice over them, Because the wrath of the Lord of Spirits resteth upon them, And His sword is drunk with their blood. 13. And the righteous and elect shall be saved on that day, And they shall never thenceforward see the face of the sinners and unrighteous. 14. And the Lord of Spirits will abide over them, And with that Son of Man shall they eat And lie down and rise up for ever and ever. 15. And the righteous and elect shall have risen from the earth, And ceased to be of downcast countenance 16. And they shall have been clothed with garments of glory. And these shall be the garments of life from the Lord of Spirits: And your garments shall not grow old, Nor your glory pass away before the Lord of Spirits.

The unavailing Repentance of the Kings and the Mighty.

CHAPTER LXIII.

In those days shall the mighty and the kings who possess the earth implore (Him) to grant them a little respite from His angels of punishment to whom they were delivered, that they might fall down and worship before the Lord of Spirits, and confess their sins before Him. 2. And they shall bless and glorify the Lord of Spirits, and say:

' Blessed is the Lord of Spirits and the Lord of kings,

And the Lord of the mighty and the Lord of the rich,

And the Lord of glory and the Lord of wisdom,

3. And splendid in every secret thing is Thy power from generation to generation,

And Thy glory for ever and ever:

Deep are all Thy secrets and innumerable,

And Thy righteousness is beyond reckoning.

4. We have now learnt that we should glorify

And bless the Lord of kings and Him who is king over kings.'

5. And they shall say:

' Would that we had rest to glorify and give thanks

And confess our faith before His glory!

6. And now we long for a little rest but find it not:

We follow hard upon and obtain (it) not:

And light has vanished from before us,

And darkness is our dwelling-place for ever and ever:

7. For we have not believed before Him Nor glorified the name of the

Lord of Spirits, [nor glorified our Lord] But our hope was in the sceptre of our kingdom, And in our glory. 8. And in the day of our suffering and tribulation He saves us not. And we find no respite for confession That our Lord is true in all His works, and in His judgements and His justice, And His judgements have no respect of persons. 9. And we pass away from before His face on account of our works, And all our sins are reckoned up in righteousness. 10. Now they will say unto themselves: ' Our souls are full of unrighteous gain, but it does not prevent us from descending from the midst thereof into the burden of Sheol. 11. And after that their faces shall be filled with darkness And shame before that Son of Man, And they shall be driven from his presence. And the sword shall abide before his face in their midst. 12. Thus spake the Lord of Spirits: 'This is the ordinance and judgement with respect to the mighty and the kings and the exalted and those who possess the earth before the Lord of Spirits.'

Vision of the fallen Angels in the Place of Punishment.

CHAPTER LXIV.

And other forms I saw hidden in that place. 2. I heard the voice of the angel saying: ' These are the angels who descended to the earth, and revealed what was hidden to the children of men and seduced the children of men into committing sin.

Enoch foretells to Noah the Beliige and his own Preservation.

CHAPTER LXV.

And in those days Noah saw the earth that it had sunk down and its destruction was nigh. 2. And he arose from thence and went to the ends of the earth, and cried aloud to his grandfather Enoch: and Noah said three times with an embittered voice: ' Hear me, hear me, hear me/ 3. And I said unto him: ' Tell me what it is that is falling out on the earth that the earth is in such evil plight and shaken, lest perchance I shall perish with it/ 4. And thereupon there was a great commotion on the earth, and a voice was heard from heaven, and I fell on my face. 5. And Enoch my grandfather came and stood by me, and said unto me: 'Why hast thou cried unto me with a bitter cry and weeping? 6. And a command has gone forth from the presence of the Lord concerning those who dwell on the earth that their ruin is accomplished because they have learnt all the secrets of the angels, and all the violence of the Satans, and all their powers —the most secret ones—and all the power of those who practice sorcery, and the power of witchcraft, and the power of those who make molten images for the whole earth : 7. And how silver is produced from the dust of the earth, and how soft metal originates in the earth. 8. For lead and tin are not produced from the earth like the first: it is a fountain that produces them, and an angel stands therein, and that angel is pre-eminent. 9. And after that my grandfather Enoch took hold of me by my hand and raised me up, and said unto me: 'Go, for I have asked the Lord of Spirits as touching this commotion on the earth. 10. And He said unto me: " Because of their unrighteousness their judgement has been determined upon and shall not be withheld by Me for ever. Because of the sorceries which they have searched out and learnt, the earth and those who dwell upon it shall be destroyed/' 11. And these—they have no place of repentance for ever, because they have shown them what was hidden, and they are the damned : but as for thee, my son, the Lord of Spirits knows that thou art pure, and guiltless of this reproach concerning the secrets, 12. And He has destined thy name to be among the holy, And will preserve thee amongst those who dwell on the earth, And has destined thy righteous seed both for kingship and for great honours, And from thy seed shall proceed a fountain of the righteous and holy without number for ever/

The Angels of the Waters bidden to hold them in Check.

CHAPTER LXVI.

And after that he showed me the angels of punishment who are prepared to come and let loose all the powers of the waters which are beneath in the earth in order to bring judgement and destruction on all who [abide and] dwell on the earth. 2. And the Lord of Spirits gave commandment to the angels who were going forth, that they should not cause the waters to rise but should hold them in check; for those angels were over the powers of the waters. 3. And I went away from the presence of Enoch.

God's Promise to Noah: Places of Punishment of the Angels and of the Kings.

CHAPTER LXVII.

And in those days the word of God came unto me, and He said unto me: 'Noah, thy lot has come up before Me, a lot without blame, a lot of love and uprightness. 2. And now the angels are making a wooden (building), and when they have completed that task I will place My hand upon it and preserve it, and there shall come forth from it the seed of life, and a change shall set in so that the earth will not remain without inhabitant. 3. And I will make fast thy seed before me for ever and ever, and I will spread abroad those who dwell with thee: it shall not be unfruitful on the face of the earth, but it shall be blessed and multiply on the earth in the name of the Lord.' 4. And He will imprison those angels, who have shown unrighteousness, in that burning valley which my grandfather Enoch had formerly shown to me in the west among the mountains of gold and silver and iron and soft metal and tin. 5. And I saw that valley in which there was a great convulsion and a convulsion of the waters. 6. And when all this took place, from that fiery molten metal and from the convulsion thereof in that place, there was produced a smell of sulphur, and it was connected with those waters, and that valley of the angels who had led astray (mankind) burned beneath that land. 7. And through its valleys proceed streams of fire, where these angels are punished who had led astray those who dwell upon the earth. 8. But those waters shall in those days serve for the kings and the mighty and the exalted, and those who dwell on the earth, for the healing of the body, but for the punishment of the spirit; now their spirit is full of lust, that they may be punished in their body, for they have denied the Lord of Spirits and see their punishment daily, and yet believe not in His name. 9. And in proportion as the burning of their bodies becomes severe, a corresponding change shall take place in their spirit for ever and ever; for before the Lord of Spirits none shall utter an idle word. 10. For the judgement shall come upon them, because they believe in the lust of their body and deny the Spirit of the Lord. 11. And those same waters shall undergo a change in those days; for when those angels are punished in these waters, these water-springs shall change their temperature, and when the angels ascend, this water of the springs shall change and become cold. 12. And I heard Michael answering and saying: 'This judgement wherewith the angels are judged is a testimony for the kings and the mighty who possess the earth. 13. Because these waters of judgement minister to the healing of the body of the kings and the lust of their body; therefore they will not see and will not believe that those waters will change and become a fire which burns for ever.

Michael and Raphael astonied at the Severity of the Judgement.

CHAPTER LXVIII.

And after that my grandfather Enoch gave me the teaching of all the secrets in the book and in the Parables which had been given to him, and he put them together for me in the words of the book of the Parables. 2. And on that day Michael answered Raphael and said: 'the power of the spirit transports and makes me to tremble because of the severity of the judgement of the secrets, the judgement of the angels: who can endure the severe judgement which has been executed, and before which they melt away?' 3. And Michael answered again, and said to Raphael: 'Who is he whose heart is not softened concerning it, and whose reins are not troubled by this word of judgement (that) has gone forth upon them because of those who have thus led them out?' 4. And it came to pass when he stood before the Lord of Spirits, Michael said thus to Raphael: 'I will not take their part under the eye of the Lord; for the Lord of Spirits has been angry with them because they do as if they were the Lord. 5. Therefore all that is hidden shall come upon them for ever and ever ; for neither angel nor man shall have his portion (in it), but alone they have received their judgement for ever and ever.'

The Names and Functions of the (fallen Angels and) Satans: the secret Oath.

CHAPTER LXIX.

And after this judgement they shall terrify and make them to tremble because they have shown this to those who dwell on the earth. 2. And behold the names of those angels [and these are their names: the first of thrm is Samjaza, the second Artaqifa, and the third Armen, the fourth Kokabel, the fifth Turael, the sixth Rumjal, the seventh Danjal, the eighth Neqael, the ninth Baraqel, the tenth Azazel, the eleventh Armaros, the twelfth Batarjal, the thirteenth Busasejal, the fourteenth Hananel, the fifteenth Turel, and the sixteenth Simapesiel, the seventeenth Jetrel, the eighteenth Tumael, the nineteenth Turel, the twentieth Rumael, the twenty-first Azazel. 3. And these are the chiefs of their

SECTION II - PARABLES OF THE ELECT AND THE COMING JUDGMENT

angels and their names, and their chief ones over hundreds and over fifties and over tens.] The name of the first Jeqon: that is, the one who led astray [all] the sons of God, and brought them down to the earth, and led them astray through the daughters of men. 5. And the second was named Asbeel: he imparted to the holy sons of God evil counsel, and led them astray so that they defiled their bodies with the daughters of men. 6. And the third was named Gadreel : he it is who showed the children of men all the blows of death, and he led astray Eve, and showed [the weapons of death to the sons of men] the shield and the coat of mail, and the sword for battle, and all the weapons of death to the children of men. 7. And from his hand they have proceeded against those who dwell on the earth from that day and for evermore. 8. And the fourth was named Penemue: he taught the children of men the bitter and the sweety and he taught them all the secrets of their wisdom. 9, And he instructed mankind in writing with ink and paper, and thereby many sinned from eternity to eternity and until this day. 10. For men were not created for such a purpose, to give confirmation to their good faith with pen and ink. 11. For men were created exactly like the angels, to the intent that they should continue pure and righteous, and death, which destroys everything, could not have taken hold of them, but through this their knowledge they are perishing, and through this power it is consuming me. 12. And the fifth was named Kasdeja: this is he who showed the children of men all the wicked smitings of spirits and demons, and the smitings of the embryo in the womb, that it may pass away, and [the smitings of the soul] the bites of the serpent, and the smitings which befall through the noontide heat, the son of the serpent named Taba'et. 13. And this is the task of Kasbeel, the chief of the oath which he showed to the holy ones when he dwelt high above in glory, and its name is Biqa. 14. This (angel) requested Michael to show him the hidden name^ that he might enunciate it in the oath, so that those might quake before that name and oath who revealed all that was in secret to the children of men. 15. And this is the power of this oath, for it is powerful and strong, and he placed this oath Akae in the hand of Michael. 16. And these are the secrets of this oath ... And they are strong through his oath: And the heaven was suspended before the world was created, And for ever. 17. And through it the earth was founded upon tbe water, And from the secret recesses of the mountains come beautiful waters. From the creation of the world and unto eternity. 18. And through that oath the sea was created. And as its foundation He set for it the sand against the time of (its) anger, And it dare not pass beyond it from the creation of the world unto eternity. 19. And through that oath are the depths made fast, And abide and stir not from their place from eternity to eternity. 20. And through that oath the sun and moon complete their course, And deviate not from their ordinance from eternity to eternity.21. And through that oath the stars complete their course, And He calls them by their names. And they answer Him from eternity to eternity. [22. And in like manner the spirits of the water, and of the winds, and of all zephyrs, and (their) paths from all the quarters of the winds. 23. And there are preserved the voices of the thunder and the light of the lightnings: and there are preserved the chambers of the hail and the chambers of the hoar-frost, and the chambers of the mist, and the chambers of the rain and the dew. 24. And all these believe and give thanks before the Lord of Spirits, and glorify (Him) with all their power, and their food is. in every act of thanksgiving: they thank and glorify and extol the name of the Lord of Spirits for ever and ever.] 25. And this oath is mighty over them, And through it [they are preserved and] their paths are preserved, And their course is not destroyed.

Close of the Third Parable.

And there was great joy amongst them, And they blessed and glorified and extolled Because the name of that Son of Man had been revealed unto them. 27. And he sat on the throne of his glory. And the sum of judgement was given unto the Son of Man, And he caused the sinners to pass away and be destroyed from off the face of the earth, And those who have led the world astray. 28. With chains shall they be bound. And in their assemblage-place of destruction shall they be imprisoned, And all their works vanish from the face of the earth. 29. And from henceforth there shall be nothing corruptible. For that Son of Man has appeared. And has seated himself on the throne of his glory. And all evil shall pass away before his face, And the word of that Son of Man shall go forth And be strong before the Lord of Spirits. This is the third Parable of Enoch.

The final Translation of Enoch.

CHAPTER LXX.

And it came to pass after this that his name during his lifetime was raised aloft to that Son of Man and to the Lord of Spirits from amongst those who dwell on the earth. 2. And he was raised aloft on the chariots of the spirit and his name vanished among them. 3. And from that day I was no longer numbered amongst them; and he set me between the two winds, between the north and the west, where the angels took the cords to measure for me the place for the elect and righteous. 4. And there I saw the first fathers and the righteous who from the beginning dwell in that place.

Two earlier Visions of Enoch.

CHAPTER LXXI.

And it came to pass after this that my spirit was translated And it ascended into the heavens: And I saw the holy sons of God. They were stepping on flames of fire: Their garments were white [and their raiment], And their faces shone like snow. 2. And I saw two streams of fire, And the light of that fire shone like hyacinth, And I fell on my face before the Lord of Spirits. 3. And the angel Michael [one of the archangels] seized me by my right hand, And lifted me up and led me forth into all the secrets. And he showed me all the secrets of righteousness. 4. And he showed me all the secrets of the ends of the heaven. And all the chambers of all the stars, and all the luminaries, Whence they proceed before the face of the holy ones. 5. And he translated my spirit into the heaven of heavens. And I saw there as it were a

SECTION II - PARABLES OF THE ELECT AND THE COMING JUDGMENT

structure built of crystals. And between those crystals tongues of living fire. 6. And my spirit saw the girdle which girt that house of fire. And on its four sides were streams full of living fire. And they girt that house. 7. And round about were Seraphin, Cherubin, and Ophannin: And these are they who sleep not And guard the throne of His glory. 8. And I saw angels who could not be counted, A thousand thousands, and ten thousand times ten thousand, Encircling that house, And Michael, and Raphael, and Gabriel, and Phanuel, And the holy angels who are above the heavens. Go in and out of that house. 9. And they came forth from that house. And Michael and Gabriel, Raphael and Phanuel, And many holy angels without number. 10. And with them the Head of Days, His head white and pure as wool. And His raiment indescribable. 11. And I fell on my face. And my whole body became relaxed. And my spirit was transfigured; And I cried with a loud voice, . . . with the spirit of power. And blessed and glorified and extolled. 12. And these blessings which went forth out of my mouth were well pleasing before that Head of Days. 13. And that Head of Days came with Michael and Gabriel, Raphael and Phanuel, thousands and ten thousands of angels without number. [Lost passage wherein the Son of Man was described as accompanying the Head of Days, and Enoch asked one of the angels (as in 46') concerning the Son of Man as to who he was.] 14. And he came to me and greeted me with His voice, and said unto me: 'This is the Son of Man who is born unto righteousness. And righteousness abides over him, And the righteousness of the Head of Days forsakes him not.' 15. And he said unto me: 'He proclaims unto thee peace in the name of the world to come; For from hence has proceeded peace since the creation of the world, And so shall it be unto thee for ever and for ever and ever. 16. And all shall walk in his ways since righteousness never forsaketh him: With him will be their dwelling-places, and with him their heritage, And they shall not be separated from him for ever and ever and ever. 17. And so there shall be length of days with that Son of Man, And the righteous shall have peace and an upright way In the name of the Lord of Spirits for ever and ever.'

Section III (Chapters LXXII–LXXXII)

MYSTERIES OF CREATION AND THE HEAVENLY ORDER

This section investigates cosmic order, astronomy, and divine law through Enoch's celestial journeys. It presents a calendar based on solar and lunar cycles, emphasizing the divine harmony embedded in creation.

This part reflects ancient attempts to understand the natural world as a reflection of divine order, highlighting the interconnectedness of heaven and earth. It also explores the obedience of heavenly bodies as a metaphor for human alignment with divine will, encouraging readers to seek harmony in their spiritual lives.

THE BOOK OF THE COUKSES OF THE HEAVENLY LUMINARIES.

The Sun

CHAPTER LXXII.
The Book of the courses of the luminaries of the heaven, the relations of each, according to their classes, their dominion and their seasons, according to their names and places of origin, and according to their months, which Uriel, the holy angel, who was with me, who is their guide, showed me; and he showed me all their laws exactly as they are, and how it is with regard to all the years of the world and unto eternity, till the new creation is accomplished which dureth till eternity. 2. And this is the first law of the luminaries: the luminary the Sun has its rising in the eastern portals of the heaven, and its setting in the western portals of t 4. And first there goes forth the great luminary, named the Sun, and his circumference is like the circumference of the heaven, and he is quite filled with illuminating and heating fire. 5. The chariot on which he ascends, the wind drives, and the sun goes down from the heaven and returns through the north in order to reach the east, and is so guided that he comes to the appropriate portal and shines in the face of the heaven. 6. In this way he rises in the first month in the great portal, which is the fourth [those six portals in the east]. 7. And in that fourth portal from which the sun rises in the first month are twelve window-openings, from which proceed a flame when they are opened in their season. 8. When the sun rises in the heaven, he comes forth through that fourth portal thirty mornings he heaven. 3. And I saw six portals in which the sun rises, and six portals in which the sun sets : and the moon rises and sets in these portals, and the leaders of the stars and those whom they lead : six in the east and six in the west, and all following each other in accurately corresponding order: also many windows to the right and left of these portals. 4. And first there

SECTION III - MYSTERIES OF CREATION AND THE HEAVENLY ORDER

goes forth the great luminary, named the Sun, and his circumference is like the circumference of the heaven, and he is quite filled with illuminating and heating fire. 5. The chariot on which he ascends, the wind drives, and the sun goes down from the heaven and returns through the north in order to reach the east, and is so guided that he comes to the appropriate (lit. ^that') portal and shines in the face of the heaven. 6. In this way he rises in the first month in the great portal, which is the fourth [those six portals in the east]. 7. And in that fourth portal from which the sun rises in the first month are twelve window-openings, from which proceed a flame when they are opened in their season. 8. When the sun rises in the heaven, he comes forth through that fourth portal thirty mornings in succession and sets accurately in the fourth portal in the west of the heaven. 9. And during this period the day becomes daily longer and the night nightly shorter to the thirtieth morning. 10. On that day the day is longer than the night by a ninth part^ and the day amounts exactly to ten parts and the night to eight parts. 11. And the sun rises from that fourth portal, and sets in the fourth and returns to the fifth portal of the east thirty mornings, and rises from it and sets in the fifth portal. 12. And then the day becomes longer by two parts and amounts to eleven parts and the night becomes shorter and amounts to seven parts. 13. And it returns to the east and enters into the sixth portal, and rises and sets in the sixth portal one and thirty mornings on account of its sign. 14. On that day the day becomes longer than the night, and the day becomes double the night, and the day becomes twelve parts, and the night is shortened and becomes six parts. 15. And the sun mounts up to make the day shorter and the night longer, and the sun returns to the east and enters into the sixth portal, and rises from it and sets thirty mornings. 16. And when thirty mornings are accomplished, the day decreases by exactly one part, and becomes eleven parts, and the night seven. 17. And the sun goes forth from that sixth portal in the west, and goes to the east and rises in the fifth portal for thirty mornings, and sets in the west again in the fifth western portal. 18. On that day the day decreases by two parts, and amounts to ten parts and the night to eight parts. 19. And the sun goes forth from that fifth portal and sets in the fifth portal of the west, and rises in the fourth portal for one and thirty mornings on account of its sign, and sets in the west. 20. On that day the day is equalised with the night, [and becomes of equal length], and the night amounts to nine parts and the day to nine parts. 21. And the sun rises from that portal and sets in the west, and returns to the east and rises thirty mornings in the third portal and sets in the west in the third portal. 22. And on that day the night becomes longer than the day, and night becomes longer than night, and day shorter than day till the thirtieth morning, and the night amounts exactly to ten parts and the day to eight parts. 23. And the sun rises from that third portal and sets in the third portal in the west and returns to the east^ and for thirty mornings rises in the second portal in the east, and in like manner sets in the second portal in the west of the heaven. 24. And on that day the night amounts to eleven parts and the day to seven parts. 25. And the sun rises on that day from that second portal and sets in the west in the second portal, and returns to the east into the first portal for one and thirty mornings, and sets in the first portal in the west of the heaven. 26. And on that day the night becomes longer and amounts to the double of the day: and the night amounts exactly to twelve parts and the day to six. 27. And the sun has (therewith) traversed the divisions of his orbit and turns again on those divisions of his orbit, and enters that portal thirty mornings and sets also in the west opposite to it. 28. And on that night has the night decreased in length by a f ninth f part, and the night has become eleven parts and the day seven parts. 29. And the sun has returned and entered into the second port al in the east, and returns on those his divisions of his orbit for thirty mornings, rising and setting. 30. And on that day the night decreases in length, and the night amounts to ten parts and the day to eight. 31. And on that day the sun rises from that portal, and sets in the west, and returns to the east, and rises in the third portal for one and thirty mornings, and sets in the west of the heaven. 32. On that day the night decreases and amounts to nine parts, and the day to nine parts, and the night is equal to the day and the year is exactly as to its days three hundred and sixty-four. 33. And the length of the day and of the night, and the shortness of the day and of the night arise —through the course of the sun these distinctions are made (lit. 'they are separated'). 34. So it comes that its course becomes daily longer, and its course nightly shorter. 35. And this is the law and the course of the sun, and his return as often as he returns sixty times and rises, i. e. the great luminary which is named the Sun, for ever and ever. 36. And that which (thus) rises is the great luminary, and is so named according to its appearance, according as the Lord commanded. 37. As he rises, so he sets and decreases not, and rests not, but runs day and night, and his light is sevenfold brighter than that of the moon ; but as regards size they are both equal.

The Moon and its Phases.

CHAPTER LXXIII.

And after this law I saw another law dealing with the smaller luminary, which is named the Moon. 2. And her circumference is like the circumference of the heaven, and her chariot in which she rides is driven by the wind, and light is given to her in (definite) measure. 3. And her rising and setting changes every month : and her days are like the days of the sun, and when her light is uniform (i. e. full) it amounts to the seventh part of the light of the sun. 4. And thus she rises. And her first phase in the east comes forth on the thirtieth morning : and on that day she becomes visible, and constitutes for you the first phase of the moon on the thirtieth day together with the sun in the portal where the sun rises. 5. And the one half of her goes forth by a seventh part, and her whole circumference is empty, without light, with the exception of one-seventh part of it, (and) the fourteenth part of her light. 6. And when she receives one-seventh part of the half of her light, her light amounts to one-seventh part and the half thereof. 7. And she sets with the sun, and when the sun rises the moon rises with him and receives the half of one part of light, and in that night in the beginning of her morning [in the commencement of the lunar day] the moon sets with the sun, and is invisible

SECTION III - MYSTERIES OF CREATION AND THE HEAVENLY ORDER

that night with the fourteen parts and the half of one of them. 8. And she rises on that day with exactly a seventh part, and comes forth and recedes from the rising of the sun, and in her remaining days she becomes bright in the (remaining) thirteen parts.

The Lunar Year.

CHAPTER LXXIV.

And I saw another course, a law for her, (and) how according to that law she performs her monthly revolution. 2, And all these Uriel, the holy angel who is the leader of them all, showed to me, and their positions, and I wrote down the positions as he showed them to me, and I wrote down their months as they were, and the appearance of their lights till fifteen days were accomplished. 3. In single seventh parts she accomplishes all her light in the east, and in single seventh parts accomplishes all her darkness in the west, 4. And in certain months she alters her settings, and in certain months she pursues her own peculiar course. 5. In two months the moon sets with the sun in those two middle portals the third and the fourth. 6. She goes forth for seven days, and turns about and returns again through the portal where the sun rises, and accomplishes all her light : and she recedes from the sun, and in eight days enters the sixth portal from which the sun goes forth. 7. And when the sun goes forth from the fourth portal she goes forth seven days, until she goes forth from the fifth and turns back again in seven days into the fourth portal and accomplishes all her light: and she recedes and enters into the first portal in eight days. 8. And she returns again in seven days into the fourth portal from which the sun goes forth. 9. Thus I saw their position—how the moons rose and the sun set in those days. 10. And if five years are added together the sun has an overplus of thirty days, and all the days which accrue to it for one of those five years, when they are full, amount to 364 days. 11. And the overplus of the sun and of the stars amounts to six days: in 5 years 6 days every year come to 30 days: and the moon falls behind the sun and stars to the number of 30 days. 12. And the sun and the stars bring in all the years exactly, so that they do not advance or delay their position by a single day unto eternity; but complete the years with perfect justice in 364 days. 13. In 3 years there are 1092 days, and in 5 years 1820 days, so that in 8 years there are 2912 days. 14. For the moon alone the days amount in 3 years to 1062 days, and in 5 years she falls 50 days behind : [i. e. to the sum (of 1770) there is to be added (1000 and) 62 days]. 15. And in 5 years there are 1770 days, so that for the moon the days in 8 years amount to 2832 days. 16. [For in 8 years she falls behind to the amount of 80 days], all the days she falls behind in 8 years are 80. 17. And the year is accurately completed in conformity with their world-stations and the stations of the sun, which rise from the portals through which it (the sun) rises and sets 30 days.

CHAPTER LXXV.

And the leaders of the heads of the thousands, who are placed over the whole creation and over all the stars, have also to do with the four intercalary days, being inseparable from their office, according to the reckoning of the year, and these render service on the four days which are not reckoned in the reckoning of the year. 2, And owing to them men go wrong therein, for those luminaries truly render service on the world-stations, one in the first portal, one in the third portal of the heaven, one in the fourth portal, and one in the sixth portal, and the exactness of the year is accomplished through its separate three hundred and sixty-four stations. 3. For the signs and the times and the years and the days the angel Uriel showed to me, whom the Lord of glory hath set for ever over all the luminaries of the heaven, in the heaven and in the world, that they should rule on the face of the heaven and be seen on the earth, and be leaders for the day and the night, i. e. the sun, moon, and stars, and all the ministering creatures which make their revolution in all the chariots of the heaven. 4. In like manner twelve doors Uriel showed me, open in the circumference of the sun's chariot in the heaven, through which the rays of the sun break forth: and from them is warmth diffused over the earth, when they are opened at their appointed seasons. 5. [And for the winds and the spirit of the dew when they are opened, standing open in the heavens at the ends.] 6. As for the twelve portals in the heaven, at the ends of the earth, out of which go forth the sun, moon, and stars, and all the works of heaven in the east and in the west, 7. There are many windows open to the left and right of them, and one window at its (appointed) season produces warmth, corresponding (as these do) to those doors from which the stars come forth according as He has commanded them, and wherein they set corresponding to their number. 8. And I saw chariots in the heaven, running in the world, above those portals in which revolve the stars that never set. 9. And one is larger than all the rest, and it is that that makes its course through the entire world.

The Twelve Winds and their Portals.

CHAPTER LXXVI.

And at the ends of the earth I saw twelve portals open to all the quarters (of the heaven), from which the winds go forth and blow over the earth. 2. Three of them are open on the face (i. e. the east) of the heavens, and three in the west, and three on the right (i. e. the south) of the heaven, and three on the left (i. e. the north). 3. And the three first are those of the east, and three are of the north, and three [after those on the left] of the south f, and three of the west. 4. Through four of these come winds of blessing and prosperity, and from those eight come hurtful winds: when they are sent, they bring destruction on all the earth and on the water upon it, and on all who dwell thereon, and on everything which is in the water and on the land. 5. And the first wind from those portals, called the east wind, comes forth through the first portal which is in the east, inclining towards the south: from it come forth desolation, drought, heat, and destruction. 6. And through the second portal in the middle comes what is fitting, and from it there come rain and fruitfulness and prosperity and dew; and through the third portal which lies toward the north come cold and drought. 7. And after these come forth the south winds through three portals: through the first portal of them inclining to the east comes forth a hot wind. 8. And through the middle portal next to it there come forth fragrant smells, and dew and rain, and prosperity and health.

9. And through the third portal lying to the west come forth dew and rain, locusts and desolation. 10. And after these the north winds: from the seventh portal in the east come dew and rain, locusts and desolation. 11. And from the middle portal come in a direct direction health and rain and dew and prosperity; and through the third portal in the west come cloud and hoar-frost, and snow and rain, and dew and locusts. 12. And after these [four] are the west winds: through the first portal adjoining the north come forth dew and hoar-frost, and cold and snow and frost. 13. And from the middle portal come forth dew and rain, and prosperity and blessing; and through the last portal which adjoins the south come forth drought and desolation, and burning and destruction. 14. And the twelve portals of the four quarters of the heaven are therewith completed, and all their laws and all their plagues and all their benefactions have I shown to thee, my son Methuselah.

The Four Quarters of the World: the Seven Mountains, the Seven Rivers, &c.

CHAPTER LXXVII.

And the first quarter is called the east, because it is the first: and the second, the south, because the Most High will descend there, yea, there in quite a special sense will He who is blessed for ever descend. 2. And the west quarter is named the diminished, because there all the luminaries of the heaven wane and go down. 3. And the fourth quarter, named the north, is divided into three parts : the first of them is for the dwelling of men: and the second contains seas of water, and the abysses and forests and rivers, and darkness and clouds ; and the third part contains the garden of righteousness. 4. I saw seven high mountains, higher than all the mountains which are* on the earth: and thence comes forth hoar-frost, and days, seasons, and years pass away. 5. I saw seven rivers on the earth larger than all the rivers: one of them coming from the fest pours its waters into the Great Sea. 6. And these two come from the north to the sea and pour their waters into the Erythraean Sea in the east. 7. And the remaining four come forth on the side of the north to their own sea, (two of them to) the Erythraean Sea, and two into the Great Sea and discharge themselves there [and some say: into the desert]. 8. Seven great islands I saw in the sea and in the mainland: two in the mainland and five in the Great Sea.

The Sun and Moon: the Waxing and Waning of the Moon.

CHAPTER LXXVIII.

And the names of the sun are the following: the first Orjares, and the second Tomas. 2. And the moon has four names: the first name is Asonja, the second Ebla, the third Benase, and the fourth Erae. 3. These are the two great luminaries : their circumference is like the circumference of the heaven, and the size of the circumference of both is alike. 4. In the circumference of the sun there are seven portions of light which are added to it more than to the moon, and in definite measures it is transferred till the seventh portion of the sun is exhausted. 5. And they set and enter the portals of the west, and make their revolution by the north, and come forth through the eastern portals on the face of the heaven. 6. And when the moon rises one-fourteenth part appears in the heaven: [the light becomes full in her] : on the fourteenth day she accomplishes her light. 7. And fifteen parts of light are transferred to her till the fifteenth day (when) her light is accomplished, according to the sign of the year, and she becomes fifteen parts, and the moon grows by (the addition of) fourteenth parts. 8. And in her waning (the moon) decreases on the first day to fourteen parts of her light, on the second to thirteen parts of light, on the third to twelve, on the fourth to eleven, on the fifth to ten, on the sixth to nine, on the seventh to eight, on the eighth to seven, on the ninth to six, on the tenth to five, on the eleventh to four, on the twelfth to three, on the thirteenth to two, on the fourteenth to the half of a seventh, and all her remaining light disappears wholly on the fifteenth. 9. And in certain months the month has twenty-nine days and once twenty-eight. 10. And Uriel showed me another law: when light is transferred to the moon, and on which side it is transferred to her by the sun. 11. During all the period during which the moon is growing in her light, she is transferring it to herself when opposite to the sun during fourteen days [her light is accomplished in the heaven], and when she is illumined throughout, her light is accomplished in the heaven. 12. And on the first day she is called the new moon, for on that day the light rises upon her. 13. She becomes full moon exactly on the day when the sun sets in the west, and from the east she rises at night, and the moon shines the whole night through till the sun rises over against her and the moon is seen over against the sun. 14. On the side whence the light of the moon comes forth, there again she wanes till all the light vanishes and all the days of the month are at an end, and her circumference is empty, void of light. 15. And three months she makes of thirty days, and at her time she makes three months of twenty-nine days each, in which she accomplishes her waning in the first period of time, and in the first portal for one hundred and seventy-seven days. 16. And in the time of he going out she appears for three months (of) thirty days each, and for three months she appears (of) twenty-nine each. 17. At night she appears like a man for twenty days each time, and by day she appears like the heaven, and there is nothing else in her save her light.

<u>*Recapitulation of several of the Laws.*</u>

CHAPTER LXXIX.

And now, my son, I have shown thee everything, and the law of all the stars of the heaven is completed. 2. And he showed me all the laws of these for every day, and for every season of bearing rule, and for every year, and for its going forth, and for the order prescribed to it every month and every week: 3. And the waning of the moon which takes place in the sixth portal: for in this sixth portal her light is accomplished, and after that there is the beginning of the waning: 4. (And the waning) which takes place in the first portal in its season, till one hundred and seventy-seven days are accomplished: reckoned according to weeks, twenty-five (weeks) and two days. 5. She falls behind the sun and the order of the stars exactly five days in the course of one period, and when this place

SECTION III - MYSTERIES OF CREATION AND THE HEAVENLY ORDER

which thou seest has been traversed. 6. Such is the picture and sketch of every luminary which Uriel the archangel, who is their leader, showed unto me.

CHAPTER LXXX.

And in those days the angel Uriel answered and said to me: 'Behold, I have shown thee everything, Enoch, and I have revealed everything to thee that thou shouldest see this sun and this moon, and the leaders of the stars of the heaven and all those who turn them, their tasks and times and departures.

Perversion of Nature and the heavenly Bodies owing to the Sin of Men.

And in the days of the sinners the years shall be shortened, And their seed shall be tardy on their lands and fields, And all things on the earth shall alter, And shall not appear in their time : And the rain shall be kept back And the heaven shall withhold (it). 3. And in those times the fruits of the earth shall be backward, And shall not grow in their time And the fruits of the trees shall be withheld in their time. 4. And the moon shall alter her order. And not appear at her time. 5. [And in those days the sun shall be seen and he shall journey in the evening on the extremity of the great chariot inf the west] And shall shine more brightly than accords with the order of light. 6. And many chiefs of the stars shall transgress the order (prescribed). And these shall alter their orbits and tasks, And not appear at the seasons prescribed to them. 7. And the whole order of the stars shall be concealed from the sinners, And the thoughts of those on the earth shall err concerning them, [And they shall be altered from all their ways], Yea, they shall err and take them to be gods. 8. And evil shall be multiplied upon them. And punishment shall come upon them So as to destroy all.'

The Heavenly Tablets and the Mission of Enoch.

CHAPTER LXXXI.

And he said unto me: 'Observe, Enoch, these heavenly tablets. And read what is written thereon. And mark every individual fact.' 2. And I observed the heavenly tablets, and read everything which was written (thereon) and understood everything, and read the book of all the deeds of mankind, and of all the children of flesh that shall be upon the earth to the remotest generations. 3. And forthwith I blessed the great Lord, the King of glory for ever, in that He has made all the works of the world, And I extolled the Lord because of His patience. And blessed Him because of the children of men. 4. And after that I said: ' Blessed is the man who dies in righteousness and goodness. Concerning whom there is no book of unrighteousness written, And against whom no day of judgement shall be found.' 5. And those seven holy ones brought me and placed me on the earth before the door of my house, and said to me: 'Declare everything to thy son Methuselah, and show to all thy children that no flesh is righteous in the sight of the Lord, for He is their Creator. 6. One year we will leave thee with thy son, till thou givest thy (last) commands, that thou mayest teach thy children and record (it) for them, and testify to all thy children; and in the second year they shall take thee from their midst. 7. Let thy heart be strong, For the good shall announce righteousness to the good;

The righteous with the righteous shall rejoice, And shall offer congratulation to one another. 8. But the sinners shall die with the sinners, And the apostate go down with the apostate. 9. And those who practise righteousness shall die on account of the deeds of men. And be taken away on account of the doings of the godless.' 10. And in those days they ceased to speak to me, and I came to my people, blessing the Lord of the world.

Charge given to Enoch: the four Intercalary Days: the Stars which lead the Seasons and the Months.

CHAPTER LXXXII.

And now, my son Methuselah, all these things I am recounting to thee and writing down for thee, and I have revealed to thee everything, and given thee books concerning all these : so preserve, my son Methuselah, the books from thy father's hand, and (see) that thou deliver them to the generations of the world. 2. I have given wisdom to thee and to thy children, [And thy children that shall be to thee], That they may give it to their children for generations, This wisdom (namely) that passeth their thought. 3. And those who understand it shall not sleep. But shall listen with the ear that they may learn this wisdom. And it shall please those that eat thereof better than good food. 4. Blessed are all the righteous, blessed are all those who walk in the way of righteousness and sin not as the sinners, in the reckoning of all their days in which the sun traverses the heaven, entering into and departing from the portals for thirty days with the heads of thousands of the order of the stars, together with the four which are intercalated which divide the four portions of the year, which lead them and enter with them four days. 5. Owing to them men shall be at fault and not reckon them in the whole reckoning of the year: yea, men shall be at fault, and not recognize them accurately. 6. For they belong to the reckoning of the year and are truly recorded (thereon) for ever, one in the first portal and one in the third, and one in the fourth and one in the sixth, and the year is completed in three hundred and sixty-four days. 7. And the account thereof is accurate and the recorded reckoning thereof exact; for the luminaries, and months and festivals, and years and days, has Uriel shown and revealed to me, to whom the Lord of the whole creation of the world hath subjected' the host of heaven. 8. And he has power over night and day in the heaven to cause the light to give light to men—sun, moon, and stars, and all the powers of the heaven which revolve in their circular chariots. 9. And these are the orders of the stars, which set in their places, and in their seasons and festivals and months. 10, And these are the names of those who lead them, who watch that they enter at their times, in their orders, in their seasons, in their months, in their periods of dominion, and in their positions. 11. Their four leaders who divide the four parts of the year enter first; and after them the twelve leaders of the orders who divide the months; and for the three hundred and sixty (days) there are heads over thousands who divide the days; and for the four intercalary days there are the leaders which sunder the four parts of the year. 13. And these heads over thousands are intercalated between leader and leader, each behind a station, but their leaders make the division. 13. And these are the names of the leaders who divide the four parts of the year which are ordained: Milki'el, Hel'emmelek, and Mel'ejal^ and Narel. 14. And the names of those who lead them: Adnar'el, and Ijasusa'el, and 'Eome'el—these three follow the leaders of the orders, and there is one that follows the three leaders of the orders which follow those leaders of stations that divide the four parts of the year,

15. In the beginning of the year Melkejal rises first and rules, who is named Tam'aini, and sun and all the days of his dominion whilst he bears rule are ninety-one days. 16. And these are the signs of the days which are to be seen on earth in the days of his dominion: sweat, and heat, and calms; and all the trees bear fruit, and leaves are produced on all the trees, and the harvest of wheat, and the rose-flowers, and all the flowers which come forth in the field, but the trees of the winter season become withered. 17. And these are the names of the leaders which are under them: Berka'el, Zelebs'el, and another who is added a head of a thousand, called Hilujaseph: and the days of the dominion of this (leader) are at an end. 18. The next leader after him is He'emmelek, whom one names the shining sun, and all the days of his light are ninety-one days. 19. And these are the signs of (his) days on the earth: glowing heat and dryness, and the trees ripen their fruits and produce all their fruits ripe and ready, and the sheep pair and become pregnant, and all the fruits of the earth are gathered in, and everything that is in the fields, and the winepress : these things take place in the days of his dominion. 20. These are the names, and the orders, and the leaders of those heads of thousands: Gida'ijal, Ke'el, and He'el, and the name of the head of a thousand which is added to them, Asfa'el : and the days of his dominion are at an end.

Section IV (Chapters LXXXIII–XC)

PROPHETIC DREAMS AND THE FUTURE OF HUMANITY

Often called the *Book of Dreams*, this section uses symbolic visions to narrate the history of humanity from creation to final judgment. Enoch's dreams depict a series of allegorical events, including the rise and fall of nations and the struggles between the righteous and the wicked.

Through vivid imagery, such as animals representing nations and leaders, this section provides prophetic insights into the moral and spiritual trajectory of the world. Readers are invited to contemplate the cycles of corruption and restoration and to find inspiration in God's ultimate plan for redemption.

THE DREAM-VISIONS.

LXXXIII–LXXXIV. First Bream-Vision on the Deluge.

CHAPTER LXXXIII.

And now, my son Methuselah, I will show thee all my visions which I have seen, recounting them before thee. 2. Two visions I saw before I took a wife, and the one was quite unlike the other: the first when I was learning to write: the second before I took thy mother, (when) I saw a terrible vision. And regarding them I prayed to the Lord. 3. I had laid me down in the house of my grandfather Mahalalel, (when) I saw in a vision how the heaven collapsed and was borne off and fell to the earth. 4. And when it fell to the earth I saw how the earth was swallowed up in a great abyss, and mountains were suspended on mountains, and hills sank down on hills, and high trees were rent from their stems, and hurled down and sunk in the abyss. 5. And thereupon a word fell into my mouth, and I lifted up (my voice) to cry aloud, and said: 'The earth is destroyed.' 6. And my grandfather Mahalalel waked me as I lay near him, and said unto me: 'Why dost thou cry so, my son, and why dost thou make such lamentation? ' 7. And I recounted to him the whole vision which I had seen, and he said unto me: ' A terrible thing hast thou seen, my son, and of grave moment is thy dream-vision as to the secrets of all the sin of the earth: it must sink into the abyss and be destroyed with a great destruction. 8. And now, my son, arise and make petition to the Lord of glory, since thou art a believer, that a remnant may remain on the earth, and that He may not destroy the whole earth. 9. My son, from heaven all this will come upon the earth, and upon the earth there will be great destruction.' 10. After that I arose and prayed and implored and besought, and wrote down my prayer for the generations of the world, and I will show everything to thee, my son Methuselah. 11. And when I had gone forth below and seen the heaven, and the sun rising in the east, and the moon setting in the west, and a few stars, and the whole earth, and everything as He had known it in the beginning, then I blessed the Lord of judgement and extolled Him because He had made the sun to go forth from the windows of the east, and he ascended and rose on the face of the heaven, and set out and kept traversing the path shown unto him.

CHAPTER LXXXIV.

And I lifted up my hands in righteousness and blessed the Holy and Great One, and spake with the breath of my mouth, and with the tongue of flesh, which God has made for the children of the flesh of men, that they should speak therewith, and He gave them breath and a tongue and a mouth that they should speak therewith: 2. 'Blessed be Thou, O Lord, King, Great and mighty in Thy greatness, Lord of the whole creation of the heaven, King of kings and God of the whole world. And Thy power and kingship and greatness abide for ever and ever, And throughout all generations Thy dominion: And all the heavens are Thy throne for ever. And the whole earth Thy footstool for ever and ever. 3. For Thou hast made and Thou rulest all things. And nothing is too hard for Thee, Wisdom departs not from the place of Thy throne, Nor turns away from Thy presence. And Thou knowest and seest and hearest everything", And there is nothing hidden from Thee [for Thou seest everything]. 4. And now the angels of Thy heavens are guilty of trespass, And upon the flesh of men abideth Thy wrath until the great day of judgement. 5. And now, O God and Lord and Great King, I implore and beseech Thee to fulfil my prayer. To leave me a posterity on earth. And not to destroy all the flesh of man, And make the earth without inhabitant. So that there should be an eternal destruction. 6. And now, my Lord, destroy from the earth the flesh which has aroused Thy wrath. But the flesh of righteousness and uprightness establish as a plant of the eternal seed. And hide not Thy face from the prayer of Thy servant, O Lord.'

LXXXV—XC. The Second Bream-Vision of Enoch: the History of the World to the Founding of the Messianic Kingdom.

CHAPTER LXXXV.

And after this I saw another dream, and I will show the whole dream to thee, my son. 2. And Enoch lifted up (his voice) and spake to his son Methuselah: 'To thee, my son, will I speak : hear my words—incline thine ear to the dream-vision of thy father. 3. Before I took thy mother Edna, I saw in a vision on my bed, and behold a bull came forth from the earth, and that bull was white ; and after it came forth a heifer, and along with this (latter) came forth two bulls, one of them black and the other red; 4. And that black bull gored the red one and pursued him over the earth, and thereupon I could no longer see that red bull. 5. But that black bull grew and that heifer went with him, and I saw that many oxen proceeded from him which resembled and followed him. 6. And that cow, that first one, went from the presence of that first bull in order to seek that red one, but found him not, and lamented with a great lamentation over him and sought him. 7. And I looked till that first bull came to her and quieted her, and from that time onward she cried no more. 8. And after that she bore another white bull, and after him she bore many bulls and black cows. 9. And I saw in my sleep that white bull likewise grow and become a great white bull, and from him proceeded many white bulls, and they resembled him. 10. And they began to beget many white bulls, which resembled them, one following the other, (even) many.

The Fall of the Angels and the Demoralization of Mankind.

CHAPTER LXXXVI.

And again I saw with mine eyes as I slept, and I saw the heaven above, and behold a star fell from heaven, and it arose and eat and pastured amongst those oxen. 2. And after that I saw the large and the black oxen, and behold they all changed their stalls and pastures and their cattle, and began to live with each other. 3. And again I saw in the vision, and looked towards the heaven, and behold I saw many stars descend and cast themselves down from heaven to that first star, and they became bulls amongst those cattle and pastured with them [amongst them]. 4. And I looked at them and saw, and behold they all let out their privy members, like horses, and began to cover the cows of the oxen, and they all became pregnant and . bare elephants, camels, and asses. 5. And all the oxen feared them and were affrighted at them, and began to bite with their teeth and to devour, and to gore with their horns. 6. And they began moreover to devour those oxen ; and behold all the children of the earth began to tremble and quake before them and to flee from them.

The Advent of the Seven Archangels.

CHAPTER LXXXVII.

And again I saw how they began to gore each other and to devour each other, and the earth began to cry aloud. 2. And I raised mine eyes again to heaven, and I saw in the vision, and behold there came forth from heaven beings who were like white men: and four went forth from that place and three with them. 3. And those three that had last come forth grasped me by my hand and took me up, away from the generations of the earth, and raised me up to a lofty place, and showed me a tower raised high above the earth, and all the hills were lower. 4. And one said unto me: " Remain here till thou seest everything that befalls those elephants, camels, and asses, and the stars and the oxen, and all of them."

The Punishment of the Fallen Angels by the Archangels.

CHAPTER LXXXVIII.

And I saw one of those four who had come forth first, and he seized that first star which had fallen from the heaven, and bound it hand and foot and cast it into an abyss: now that abyss was narrow and deep, and horrible and dark. 2. And one of them drew a sword, and gave it to those elephants and camels and asses : then they began to smite each other, and the whole earth quaked because of them. 3. And as I was beholding in the vision, lo, one of those four who had come forth stoned (them) from heaven, and gathered and took all the great stars whose privy members were like those of horses, and bound them all hand and foot, and cast them in an abyss of the earth.

LXXXIX. 1-9. The Deluge and the Deliverance of Noah.

CHAPTER LXXXIX.
And one of those four went to that white bull and instructed him in a secret without his being- terrified: he was born a bull and became a man, and built for himself a great vessel and dwelt thereon; and three bulls dwelt with him in that vessel and they were covered in. 2. And again I raised mine eyes towards heaven and saw a lofty roof, with seven water torrents thereon, and those torrents flowed with much water into an enclosure. 3. And I saw again, and behold fountains were opened on the surface of that great enclosure, and that water began to swell and rise upon the surface, and I saw that enclosure till all its surface was covered with water. 4. And the water, the darkness, and mist increased upon it; and as I looked at the height of that water, that water had risen above the height of that enclosure, and was streaming over that enclosure, and it stood upon the earth. 5. And all the cattle of that enclosure were gathered together until I saw how they sank and were swallowed up and perished in that water. 6. But that vessel floated on the water, while all the oxen and elephants and camels and asses sank to the bottom with all the animals, so that I could no longer see them, and they were not able to escape, (but) perished and sank into the depths. 7. And again I saw in the vision till those water torrents were removed from that high roof, and the chasms of the earth were levelled up and other abysses were opened. 8. Then the water began to run down into these, till the earth became visible; but that vessel settled on the earth, and the darkness retired and light appeared. 9. But that white bull which had become a man came out of that vessel, and the three bulls with him, and one of those three was white like that bull, and one of them was red as blood, and one black: and that white bull departed from them.

LXXXIX. 10-27. From the Death of Noah to the Exodus.

And they began to bring forth beasts of the field and birds, so that there arose different genera; lions, tigers, wolves, dogs, hyenas, wild boars, foxes, squirrels, swine, falcons, vultures, kites, eagles, and ravens; and among them was born a white bull. 11. And they began to bite one another; but that white bull which was born amongst them begat a wild ass and a white bull with it, and the wild asses multiplied. 12. But that bull which was born from him begat a black wild boar and a white sheep; and the former begat many boars, but that sheep begat twelve sheep. 13. And when those twelve sheep had grown, they gave up one of them to the asses, and those asses again gave up that sheep to the wolves, and that sheep grew up among the wolves. 14. And the Lord brought the eleven sheep to live with it and to pasture with it among the wolves: and they multiplied and became many flocks of sheep. 15. And the wolves began to fear them, and they oppressed them until they destroyed their little ones, and they cast their young into a river of much water: but those sheep began to cry aloud on account of their little ones, and to complain unto their Lord. 16. And a sheep which had been saved from the wolves fled and escaped to the wild asses; and I saw the sheep how they lamented and cried, and besought their Lord with all their might, till that Lord of the sheep descended at the voice of the sheep from a lofty abode, and came to them and pastured them. 17. And He called that sheep which had escaped the wolves, and spake with it concerning the wolves that it should admonish them not to touch the sheep. 18. And the sheep went to the wolves according to the word of the Lord, and another sheep met it and went with it, and the two went and entered together into the assembly of those wolves, and spake with them and admonished them not to touch the sheep from henceforth. 19. And thereupon I saw the wolves, and how they oppressed the sheep exceedingly with all their power; and the sheep cried aloud. 20. And the Lord came to the sheep and they began to smite those wolves: and the wolves began to make lamentation; but the sheep became quiet and forthwith ceased to cry out. 21. And I saw the sheep till they departed from amongst the wolves; but the eyes of the wolves were blinded, and those wolves departed in pursuit of the sheep with all their power. 22. And the Lord of the sheep went with them, as their leader, and all His sheep followed Him: and His face was dazzling and glorious and terrible to behold. 23. But the wolves began to pursue those sheep till they reached a sea of water. 24. And that sea was divided, and the water stood on this side and on that before their face, and their Lord led them and placed Himself between them and the wolves. 25. And as those wolves did not yet see the sheep, they proceeded into the midst of that sea, and the wolves followed the sheep, and [those wolves] ran after them into that sea. 26. And when they saw the Lord of the sheep, they turned to flee before His face, but that sea gathered itself together, and became as it had been created, and the water swelled and rose till it covered those wolves. 27. And I saw till all the wolves who pursued those sheep perished and were drowned.

LXXXIX. 28-40. Israel m the Desert, the Giving of the Law, the Entrance into Palestine.

But the sheep escaped from that water and went forth into a wilderness, where there was no water and no grass; and they began to open their eyes and to see; and I saw the Lord of the sheep pasturing them and giving them water and grass, and that sheep going and leading them. 29. And that sheep ascended to the summit of that lofty rock, and the Lord of the sheep sent it to them. 30. And after that I saw the Lord of the sheep who stood before them, and His appearance was great and terrible and majestic, and all those sheep saw Him and were afraid before His face. 3L And they all feared and trembled, because of Him, and they cried to that sheep with them [which was amongst them]: " We are not able to stand before our Lord or to behold Him/^ 32. And that sheep which led them again ascended to the summit of that rock, but the sheep began to be blinded and to wander from the way which he had showed them, but that sheep wot not thereof. 33. And the Lord of the sheep was wrathful exceedingly against them,

SECTION IV – PROPHETIC DREAMS AND THE FUTURE OF HUMANITY

and that sheep discovered it, and went down from the summit of the rock, and came to the sheep, and found the greatest part of them blinded and fallen away. 34. And when they saw it they feared and trembled at its presence, and desired to return to their folds. 35. And that sheep took other sheep with it, and came to those sheep which had fallen away, and began to slay them; and the sheep feared its presence, and thus that sheep brought back those sheep that had fallen away, and they returned to their folds. 36. And I saw in this vision till that sheep became a man and built a house for the Lord of the sheep, and placed all the sheep in that house. 37. And I saw till this sheep which had met that sheep which led them fell asleep: and I saw till all the great sheep perished and little ones arose in their place, and they came to a pasture, and approached a stream of water, 38. Then that sheep, their leader which had become a man, withdrew from them and fell asleep, and all the sheep sought it and cried over it with a great crying. 39. And I saw till they left off crying for that sheep and crossed that stream or water, and there arose the two sheep as leaders in the place of those which had led them and fallen asleep (lit. " had fallen asleep and led them "). 40. And I saw till the sheep came to a goodly place, and a pleasant and glorious land, and I saw till those sheep were satisfied; and that house stood amongst them in the pleasant land.

LXXXIX. 41-50. From the Time of the Judges till the Building of the Temple.

And sometimes their eyes were opened, and sometimes blinded, till another sheep arose and led them and brought them all back, and their eyes were opened. 42. And the dogs and the foxes and the wild boars began to devour those sheep till the Lord of the sheep raised up [another sheep] a ram from their midst, which led them. 43. And that ram began to butt on either side those dogs, foxes, and wild boars till he had destroyed them fall. 44. And that sheep whose eyes were opened saw that ram, which was amongst the sheep, till it forsook its glory and began to butt those sheep, and trampled upon them, and behaved itself unseemly. 45. And the Lord of the sheep sent the lamb to another lamb and raised it to being a ram and leader of the sheep instead of that ram which had for-saken its glory. 46. And it went to it and spake to it alone, and raised it to being a ram, and made it the prince and leader of the sheep; but during all these things those dogs oppressed the sheep. 47. And the first ram pursued that second ram, and that second ram arose and fled before it; and I saw till those dogs pulled down the first ram. 48. And that second ram arose and led the [little] sheep. 49. And those sheep grew and multiplied; but all the dogs, and foxes, and wild boars feared and fled before it, and that ram butted and killed the wild beasts, and those wild beasts had no longer any power among the sheep and robbed them no more of aught. 48. And that ram begat many sheep and fell asleep; and a little sheep became ram in its stead, and became prince and leader of those sheep. 50. And that house became great and broad, and it was built for those sheep: (and) a tower lofty and great was built on the house for the Lord of the sheep, and that house was low, but the tower was elevated and lofty, and the Lord of the sheep stood on that tower and they offered a full table before Him.

LXXXIX. 51-67. The Two Kingdoms of Israel and Judah to the Destruction of Jerusalem

And again I saw those sheep that they again erred and went many ways, and forsook that their house, and the Lord of the sheep called some from amongst the sheep and sent them to the sheep, but the sheep began to slay them. 52. And one of them was saved and was not slain, and it sped away and cried aloud over the sheep; and they sought to slay it, but the Lord of the sheep saved it from the sheep, and brought it up to me, and caused it to dwell there. 53. And many other sheep He sent to those sheep to testify unto them and lament over them. 54. And after that I saw that when they forsook the house of the Lord and His tower they fell away entirely, and their eyes were blinded; and I saw the Lord of the sheep how He wrought much slaughter amongst them in their herds until those sheep invited that slaughter and betrayed His place. 55. And He gave them over into the hands of the lions and tigers, and wolves and hyenas, and into the hand of the foxes, and to all the wild beasts and those wild beasts began to tear in pieces those sheep. 56. And I saw that He forsook that their house and their tower and gave them all into the hand of the lions, to tear and devour them, into the hand of all the wild beasts. 57. And I began to cry aloud with all my power, and to appeal to the Lord of the sheep, and to represent to Him in regard to the sheep that they were devoured by all the wild beasts. 58. But He remained unmoved, though He saw it, and rejoiced that they were devoured and swallowed and robbed, and left them to be devoured in the hand of all the beasts. 59. And He called seventy shepherds, and cast those sheep to them that they might pasture them, and He spake to the shepherds and their companions: " Let each individual of you pasture the sheep henceforward, and everything that I shall command you that do ye. 60. And I will deliver them over unto you duly numbered, and tell you which of them are to be destroyed—and them destroy ye." And He gave over unto them those sheep. 61. And He called another and spake unto him: "Observe and mark everything that the shepherds will do to those sheep; for they will destroy more of them than I have commanded them. 62. And every excess and the destruction which will be wrought through the shepherds, record (namely) how many they destroy according to my command, and how many according to their own caprice : record against every individual shepherd all the destruction he effects. 63. And read out before me by number how many they destroy, and how many they deliver over for destruction, that I may have this as a testimony against them, and know every deed of the shepherds, that I may comprehend and see what they do, whether or not they abide by my command which I have commanded them. 64. But they shall not know it and thou shalt not declare it to them, nor admonish them, but only record against each individual all the destruction which the shepherds effect each in his time and lay it all before me." 65. And I saw till those shepherds pastured in their season, and they began to slay and to destroy more than they were bidden, and they delivered those sheep into the hand of the lions. 66. And the lions and tigers eat and devoured the greater part of those sheep, and the wild boars eat along with them; and they burnt that tower and demolished that house. 67. And I became exceedingly sorrowful over that tower because that house of the sheep was demolished, and afterwards I was unable to see if those sheep entered that house.

LXXXIX. 68-71. First Period of the Angelic Rulers—from the Destruction of Jerusalem to the Return from the Captivity.

And the shepherds and their associates delivered over those sheep to all the wild beasts, to devour them, and each one of them received in his time a definite number: it was written by the other in a book how many each one of them destroyed of them. 69. And each one slew and destroyed many more than was prescribed; and I began to weep and lament on account of those sheep. 70. And thus in the vision I saw that one who wrote how he wrote down every one that was destroyed by those shepherds, day by day, and carried up and laid down and showed actually the whole book to the Lord of the sheep—(even) everything that they had done, and all that each one of them had made away with, and all that they had given over to destruction. 71. And the book was read before the Lord of the sheep, and He took the book from his hand and read it and sealed it and laid it down.

LXXXIX. 72-77. Second Period—from the time of Cyrus to that of Alexander the Great.

And forthwith I saw how the shepherds pastured for twelve hours, and behold three of those sheep turned back and came and entered and began to build up all that had fallen down of that house; but the wild boars tried to hinder them, but they were not able. 73. And they began again to build as before, and they reared up that tower, and it was named the high tower; and they began again to place a table before the tower, but all the bread on it was polluted and not pure. 74. And as touching all this the eyes of those sheep were blinded so that they saw not, and (the eyes of) their shepherds likewise; and they delivered them in large numbers to their shepherds for destruction, and they trampled the sheep with their feet and devoured them. 75. And the Lord of the sheep remained unmoved till all the sheep were dispersed over the field and mingled with them (i. e. the beasts), and they (i. e. the shepherds) did not save them out of the hand of the beasts. 76. And this one who wrote the book carried it up, and showed it and read it before the Lord of the sheep, and implored Him on their account, and besought Him on their account as he showed Him all the doings of the shepherds, and gave testimony before Him against all the shepherds. 77. And he took the actual book and laid it down beside Him and departed.

XC. 1-5. Third Period—from Alexander the Great to the Graeco-Syrian Domination.

CHAPTER XC.

And I saw till that in this manner thirty-five shepherds undertook the pasturing (of the sheep), and they severally completed their periods as did the first;

and others received them into their hands to pasture them for their period each shepherd in his own period. 2. And after that I saw in my vision all the birds of heaven coming, the eagles, the vultures, the kites, the ravens; but the eagles led all the birds; and they began to devour those sheep, and to pick out their eyes and to devour their flesh. 3. And the sheep cried out because their flesh was being devoured by the birds, and as for me I looked and lamented in my sleep over that shepherd who pastured the sheep. 4. And I saw until those sheep were devoured by the dogs and eagles and kites, and they left neither flesh nor skin nor sinew remaining on them till only their bones stood there: and their bones too fell to the earth and the sheep became few. 5. And I saw until that twenty-three had undertaken the pasturing and completed in their several periods fifty-eight times.

XC. 6-12. Fourth Period— from the Graeco-Syrian Domination to the Maccabean Revolt.

But behold lambs were borne by those white sheep, and they began to open their eyes and to see, and to cry to the sheep. 7. Yea, they cried to them, but they did not hearken to what they said to them, but were exceedingly deaf, and their eyes were very exceedingly blinded. 8. And I saw in the vision how the ravens flew upon those lambs, and took one of those lambs, and dashed the sheep in pieces and devoured them. 9. And I saw till horns grew upon those lambs, and the ravens cast down their horns; and I saw till there sprouted a great horn of one of those sheep, and their eyes were opened. 10. And it looked at them [and their eyes opened], and it cried to the sheep, and the rams saw it and all ran to it. 11. And notwithstanding all this those eagles and vultures and ravens and kites still kept tearing the sheep and swooping down upon them and devouring them: still the sheep remained silent, but the rams lamented and cried out. 12. And those ravens fought and battled with it and sought to lay low its horn, but they had no power over it. XC. 13-19. The last Assault of the Gentiles on the Jews 13. And I saw till the shephei-ds and eagles and those vultures and kites came, and they cried to the ravens that they should break the horn of that ram, and they battled and fought with it, and it battled with them and cried that its help might come. 19. And I saw till a great sword was given to the sheep, and the sheep proceeded against all the beasts of the field to slay them, and all the beasts and the birds of the heaven fled before their face. 14. And I saw till that man, who wrote down the names of the shepherds [and] carried up into the presence of the Lord of the sheep [came and helped it and showed it everything: he had come down for the help of that ram]. 15. And I saw till the Lord of the sheep came unto them in wrath, and all who saw Him fled, and they all fell into His shadow f from before His face.

XC. 20-27. Judgement of the Fallen Angels, the Shepherds, and the Apostoles.

And I saw till a throne was erected in the pleasant land, and the Lord of the sheep sat Himself thereon, and the other took the sealed books and opened those books before the Lord of the sheep. 21. And the Lord called those men the seven first white ones, and commanded that they should bring before Him, beginning with the first star which led the way, all the stars whose privy members were like those of horses, and they brought them all before Him. 22. And He said to that man who wrote before Him, being one of those seven white ones, and said unto him: "Take those seventy shepherds to whom I delivered the sheep, and who taking them on their own authority slew more than I commanded them." 23. And behold they were all bound, I saw, and they all stood before Him. 24. And the judgement was held first over the stars, and they were judged and found guilty, and went to the place of condemnation, and they were cast into an abyss, full of fire and flaming, and full of pillars of fire. 25. And those seventy shepherds were judged and found guilty, and they were cast into that fiery abyss. 26. And I saw at that time how a like abyss was opened in the midst of the earth, full of fire, and they brought those blinded sheep, and they were all judged and found guilty and cast into this fiery abyss, and they burned; now this abyss was to the right of that house. 27. And I saw those sheep burning and their bones burning.

XC. 28-38. The New Jerusalem, tie Conversion of the surviving Gentiles, the Resurrection of the Righteous, the Messiah.

And I stood up to see till they folded up that old house; and carried off all the pillars, and all the beams and ornaments of the house were at the same time folded up with it, and they carried it off and laid it in a place in the south of the land. 29. And I saw till the Lord of the sheep brought a new house greater and loftier than that first, and set it up in the place of the first which had been folded up : all its pillars were new, and its ornaments were new and larger than those of the first, the old one which He had taken away, and all the sheep were within it.

30. And I saw all the sheep which had been left, and all the beasts on the earth, and all the birds of the heaven, falling down and doing homage to those sheep and making petition to and obeying them in every thing. 31. And thereafter those three who were clothed in white and had seized me by my hand [who had taken me up before], and the hand of that ram also seizing of me, they took me up and set me down in the midst of those sheep f before the judgement took place. 32. And those sheep were all white, and their wool was abundant and clean. 33. And all that had been destroyed and dispersed, and all the beasts of the field, and all the birds of the heaven, assembled in that house, and the Lord of the sheep rejoiced with great joy because they were all good and had returned to His house. 34. And I saw till they laid down that sword, which had been given to the sheep, and they brought it back into the house, and it was sealed before the presence of the Lord, and all the sheep were invited into that house, but it held them not. 35. And the eyes of them all were opened, and they saw the good, and there was not one among them that did not see. 36. And I saw that that house was large and broad and very full. 37. And I saw that a white bull was born, with large horns and all the beasts of the field and all the birds of the air feared him and made petition to him all the time. 38. And I saw till all their generations were transformed, and they all became white bulls; and the first among them became

a lamb;, and that lamb became a great animal and had great black horns on its head; and the Lord of the sheep rejoiced over it and over all the oxen. 39. And I slept in their midst: and I awoke and saw everything. 40. This is the vision which I saw while I slept, and I awoke and blessed the Lord of righteousness and gave Him glory. 41. Then I wept with a great weeping, and my tears stayed not till I could no longer endure it: when I saw, they flowed on account of what I had seen; for everything shall come and be fulfilled, and all the deeds of men in their order were shown to me. 42. On that night I remembered the first dream, and because of it I wept and was troubled—because I had seen that vision.'

Section V (Chapters XCI–CIV)

THE PATH OF RIGHTEOUSNESS AND DIVINE WARNINGS

This section combines moral exhortations and prophetic blessings with warnings for sinners. It serves as a spiritual guide, calling readers to repentance, humility, and faithfulness. Themes of judgment and redemption dominate this part, reinforcing God's commitment to reward the righteous and punish the wicked. The emphasis on ethical living and divine justice makes it particularly relevant for readers seeking moral clarity in an age of uncertainty.

XCII. XCI. 1-10, 18-19. Enoch's Book of Admonition for his Children.

CHAPTER XCII.

The book written by Enoch—[Enoch indeed wrote this complete doctrine of wisdom, (which is) praised of all men and a judge of all the earth] for all my children who shall dwell on the earth. And for the future generations who shall observe uprightness and peace. 2. Let not your spirit be troubled on account of the times; For the Holy and Great One has appointed days for all things. 3. And the righteous one shall arise from sleep, [Shall arise] and walk in the paths of righteousness, And all his path and conversation shall be in eternal goodness and grace. 4. He will be gracious to the righteous and give him eternal uprightness. And He will give him power so that he shall be (endowed) with goodness and righteousness. And he shall walk in eternal light. 5. And sin shall perish in darkness for ever, And shall no more be seen from that day for evermore.

XCI. 1-11, 18-19. Enoch's Admonition to his Children.

CHAPTER XCI.

And now, my son Methuselah, call to me all thy brothers And gather together to me all the sons of thy mother. For the word calls me. And the spirit is poured out upon me. That I may show you everything That shall befall you for ever.' 2. And thereupon Methuselah went and summoned to him all his brothers and assembled his relatives. 3. And he spake unto all the children of righteousness and said: ' Hear, ye sons of Enoch, all the words of your father. And hearken aright to the voice of my mouth; For I exhort you and say unto you, beloved: Love uprightness and walk therein. 4. And draw not nigh to uprightness with a double heart. And associate not with those of a double heart, But walk in righteousness, my sons. And it shall guide you on good paths, And righteousness shall be your companion. 5. For I know that violence must increase on the earth, And a great chastisement be executed on the earth. And all unrighteousness come to an end: Yea, it shall be cut off from its roots, And its whole structure be destroyed. 6. And unrighteousness shall again be consummated on the earth. And all the deeds of unrighteousness and of violence And transgression shall prevail in a twofold degree. 7. And when sin and unrighteousness and blasphemy And violence in all kinds of deeds increase. And apostasy and transgression and uncleanness increase, A great chastisement shall come from heaven upon all these. And the holy Lord will come forth with wrath and chastisement To execute judgement on earth. 8. In those days violence shall be cut off from its roots, And the roots of unrighteousness together with deceit. And they shall be destroyed from under heaven, 9 And all the idols of the heathen shall be abandoned. And the temples burned with fire, And they shall remove them from the whole earth, And they (i. e. the heathen) shall be cast into the judgement of fire, And shall perish in wrath and in grievous judgement for ever. 10. And the righteous shall arise from their sleep, And wisdom shall arise and be given unto them. [11. And after that the roots of unrighteousness shall be cut off, and the sinners shall be destroyed by the sword ... shall be cut off from the blasphemers in every place, and those who plan violence and those who commit blasphemy shall perish by the sword.] 18. And now I tell you, my sons, and show yon The paths of righteousness and the paths of violence. Yea, I will show them to you again That ye may know what will come to pass. 19. And now, hearken unto me, my sons. And walk in the paths of righteousness, And walk not in the paths of violence; For all who walk in the paths of unrighteousness shall perish for ever.'

<u>XCIII, XCI. 12-17. The Apocalypse of Weeks.</u>

CHAPTER XCIII.

And after that Enoch both gave and began to recount from the books. 2. And Enoch said 'Concerning the children of righteousness and concerning the elect of the world, And concerning the plant of uprightness, I will speak these things, Yea, I Enoch will declare (them) unto you, my sons: According to that which appeared to me in the heavenly vision, And which I have known through the word of the holy angels. And have learnt from the heavenly tablets/ 3. And Enoch began to recount from the books and said : ' I was born the seventh in the first week. While judgement and righteousness still endured. 4. And after me there shall arise in the second week great wickedness. And deceit shall have sprung up; And in it there shall be the first end. And in it a man shall be saved; And after it is ended unrighteousness shall grow up, And a law shall be made for the sinners. 5. And after that in the third week at its close A man shall be elected as the plant of righteous judgement, And his posterity shall become the plant of righteousness for evermore. 6. And after that in the fourth week, at its close, Visions of the holy and righteous shall be seen, And a law for all generations and an enclosure shall be made for them. 7. And after that in the fifth week, at its close, The house of glory and dominion shall be built for ever. 8. And after that in the sixth week all who live in it shall be blinded, And the hearts of all of them shall godlessly forsake wisdom. And in it a man shall ascend; And at its close the house of dominion shall be burnt with fire. And the whole race of the chosen root shall be dispersed. 9. And after that in the seventh week shall an apostate generation arise, And many shall be its deeds. And all its deeds shall be apostate. 10. And at its close shall be elected The elect righteous of the eternal plant of righteousness. To receive sevenfold instruction concerning all His creation. [11. For who is there of all the children of men that is able to hear the voice of the Holy One without being troubled? And who can think His thoughts? and who is there that can behold all the works of heaven? 12. And how should there be one who could behold the heaven, and who is there that could understand the things of heaven and see a soul or a spirit and could tell thereof, or ascend and see all their ends and think them or do like them? 13. And who is there of all men that could know what is the breadth and the length of the earth, and to whom has been shown the measure of all of them? 14. Or is there any one who could discern the length of the heaven and how great is its height, and upon what it is founded, and how great is the number of the stars, and where all the luminaries rest?]

XCI. 12-17. The Last Three Weeks.

And after that there shall be another, the eighth week, that of righteousness. And a sword shall be given to it that a righteous judgement may be executed on the oppressors, And sinners shall be delivered into the hands of the righteous. 13. And at its close they shall acquire houses through their righteousness, And a house shall be built for the Great King in glory for evermore, 14d. And all mankind shall look to the path of uprightness. 14a. And after that, in the ninth week, the righteous judgement shall be revealed to the whole world, b. And all the works of the godless shall vanish from all the earth, c. And the world shall be written down for destruction. 15. And after this, in the tenth week in the seventh part, There shall be the great eternal judgement. In which He will execute vengeance amongst the angels. 16. And the first heaven shall depart and pass away, And a new heaven shall appear, And all the powers of the heavens shall give sevenfold light. 17. And after that there will be many weeks without number for ever, And all shall be in goodness and righteousness, And sin shall no more be mentioned for ever.

XCIV. 1-5. Admonitions to the Righteous.

CHAPTER XCIV.

And now I say unto you, my sons, love righteousness and walk therein; For the paths of righteousness are worthy of acceptation, But the paths of unrighteousness shall suddenly be destroyed and vanish. 2. And to certain men of a generation shall the paths of violence and of death be revealed, And they shall hold themselves afar from them, And shall not follow them. 3. And now I say unto you the righteous: Walk not in the paths of wickedness, nor on the paths of death, And draw not nigh to them, lest ye be destroyed. 4. But seek and choose for yourselves righteousness and an elect life, And walk in the paths of peace, And ye shall live and prosper. 5. And hold fast my words in the thoughts of your hearts, And suffer them not to be effaced from your hearts; For know that sinners will tempt men to evilly-entreat wisdom, So that no place may be found for her, And no manner of temptation may minish.

XCIV. 6-11. Woes for the Sinners.

Woe to those who build unrighteousness and oppression And lay deceit as a foundation; For they shall be suddenly overthrown, And they shall have no peace. 7. Woe to those who build their houses with sin; For from all their foundations shall they be overthrown, And by the sword shall they fall. [And those who acquire gold and silver in judgement suddenly shall perish.] 8. Woe to you, ye rich, for ye have trusted in your riches. And from your riches shall ye depart, Because ye have not remembered the Most High in the days of your riches. 9. Ye have committed blasphemy and unrighteousness. And have become ready for the day of slaughter. And the day of darkness and the day of the great judgement. 10. Thus I speak" and declare unto you : He who hath created you will overthrow you, And for your fall there shall be no compassion, And your Creator will rejoice at your destruction. 11. And your righteous ones in those days shall be A reproach to the sinners and the godless. Enoch's Grief: fresh Woes against the Sinners.

CHAPTER XCV.

Oh that mine eyes were [a cloud of] waters That I might weep over you. And pour down my tears as a cloud f of f waters: That so I might rest from my trouble of heart 2.fWho has permitted you to practise reproaches and wickedness? And so judgement shall overtake you, sinners. 3. Fear not the sinners, ye righteous; For again will the Lord deliver them into your hands, That ye may execute judgement upon them according to your desires. 4. Woe to you who fulminate anathemas which cannot be reversed: Healing shall therefore be far from you because of your sins. 5. Woe to you who requite your neighbour with evil; For ye shall be requited according to your works. 6. Woe to you, lying witnesses, And to those who weigh out injustice, For suddenly shall ye perish. 7. Woe to you, sinners, for ye persecute the righteous; For ye shall be delivered up and persecuted because of injustice. And heavy shall its yoke be upon you.

Grounds of Hopefulness for the Righteous: Woes for the Wicked.

CHAPTER XCVI.

Be hopeful, ye righteous; for suddenly shall the sinners perish before you, And ye shall have lordship over them according to your desires. [2. And in the day of the tribulation of the sinners, Your children shall mount and rise as eagles, And higher than the vultures will be your nest, And ye shall ascend and enter the crevices of the earth, And the clefts of the rock for ever as coneys before the unrighteous. And the sirens shall sigh because of you and weep.] 3. Wherefore fear not, ye that have suffered; For healing shall be your portion, And a bright light shall enlighten you, And the voice of rest ye shall hear from heaven. 4. Woe unto you, ye sinners, for your riches make you appear like the righteous. But your hearts convict you of being sinners, And this fact shall be a testimony against you for a memorial of (your) evil deeds. 5. Woe to you who devour the finest of the wheat. And drink wine in large bowls,

And tread under foot the lowly with your might. 6. Woe to you who drink water from every fountain, For suddenly shall ye be consumed and wither away, Because ye have forsaken the fountain of life. 7. Woe to you who work unrighteousness And deceit and blasphemy: It shall be a memorial against you for evil. 8. Woe to you, ye mighty, Who with might oppress the righteous; For the day of your destruction is coming. In those days many and good days shall come to the righteous—in the day of your judgement.

The Evils in Store for Sinners and the Possessors of unrighteous Wealth.

CHAPTER XCVII.

Believe, ye righteous, that the sinners will become a shame And perish in the day of unrighteousness. 2. Be it known unto you (ye sinners) that the Most High is mindful of your destruction. And the angels of heaven rejoice over your destruction. 3. What will ye do, ye sinners, And whither will ye flee on that day of judgement, When ye hear the voice of the prayer of the righteous? 4. Yea, ye shall fare like unto them, Against whom this word shall be a testimony: " Ye have been companions of sinners" 5. And in those days the prayer of the righteous shall reach unto the Lord, And for you the days of your judgement shall come. 6. And all the words of your unrighteousness shall be read out before the Great Holy One, And your faces shall be covered with shame. And He will reject every work which is grounded on unrighteousness. 7. Woe to you, ye sinners, who live on the mid ocean and on the dry land, Whose remembrance is evil against you. 8. Woe to you who acquire silver and gold in unrighteousness and say: " We have become rich with riches and have possessions; And have acquired everything we have desired. 9. And now let us do what we purposed: For we have gathered silver, 9d And many are the husbandmen in our houses, 9e And our granaries are (brim) full as with water" 10. Yea and like water your lies shall flow away; For your riches shall not abide But speedily ascend from you; For ye have acquired it all in unrighteousness. And ye shall be given over to a great curse.

Self-indulgence of Sinners: Sin originated by Man: all Sin recorded in Heaven: Woes for the Sinners.

CHAPTER XCVIII.

And now I swear unto you, to the wise and to the foolish, For ye shall have manifold experiences on the earth. 2. For ye men shall put on more adornments than a woman, And coloured garments more than a virgin: In royalty and in grandeur and in power, And in silver and in gold and in purple. And in splendour and in food they shall be poured out as water. 3. Therefore they shall be wanting in doctrine and wisdom, And they shall perish thereby together with their possessions; And with all their glory and their splendour, And in shame and in slaughter and in great destitution, Their spirits shall be cast into the furnace of fire. 4. I have sworn unto you, ye sinners, as a mountain has not become a slave, And a hill does not become the handmaid of a woman, Even so sin has not been sent upon the earth, But man of himself has created it, And under a great curse shall they fall who commit it. 5. And barrenness has not been given to the woman. But on account of the deeds of her own hands she dies without children. 6. I have sworn unto you, ye sinners, by the Holy Great One, That all your evil deeds are revealed in the heavens. And that none of your deeds of oppression are covered and hidden. 7. And do not think in your spirit nor say in your heart that ye do not know and that ye do not see that every sin is every day recorded in heaven in the presence of the Most High. 8. From henceforth ye know that all your oppression wherewith ye oppress is written down every day till the day of your judgement. 9. Woe to you, ye fools, for through your folly shall ye perish: and ye transgress against the wise, and so good hap shall not be your portion. 10. And now, know ye that ye are prepared for the day of destruction: wherefore do not hope to live, ye sinners, but ye shall depart and die; for ye know no ransom; for ye are prepared for the day of the great judgement, for the day of tribulation and great shame for your spirits. 11. Woe to you, ye obstinate of heart, who work wickedness and eat blood; Whence have ye good things to eat and to drink and to be filled From all the good things which the Lord the Most High has placed in abundance on the earth; therefore ye shall have no peace. 12. Woe to you who love the deeds of unrighteousness: wherefore do ye hope for good hap unto yourselves? know that ye shall be delivered into the hands of the righteous, and they shall cut off your necks and slay you, and have no mercy upon you. 13. Woe to you who rejoice in the tribulation of the righteous; for no grave shall be dug for you. 14. Woe to you who set at nought the words of the righteous; for ye shall have no hope of life. 15. Woe to you who write down lying and godless words ; for they write down their lies that men may hear them and act godlessly towards (their) neighbour. 16. Therefore they shall have no peace but die a sudden death.

Woes pronounced on the Godless, the Lawbreakers: evil Plight of Sinners in the last Days: further Woes.

CHAPTER XCIX.

Woe to you who work godlessness, And glory in lying, and extol them : Ye shall perish, and no happy life shall be yours. 2. Woe to them who pervert the words of uprightness, And transgress the eternal law, And transform themselves into what they were not [into sinners]: They shall be trodden under foot upon the earth. 3. In those days make ready, ye righteous, to raise your prayers as a memorial. And place them as a testimony before the angels. That they may place the sin of the sinners for a memorial before the Most High. 4. In those days the nations shall be stirred up, And the families of the nations shall arise on the day of destruction. 5. And in those days the destitute shall go forth and carry off their children. And they shall abandon them, so that their children shall perish through them: Yea, they shall abandon their children (that are still) sucklings, and not return to them, And shall have no pity on their beloved ones. 6. And again I swear to you, ye sinners, that sin is prepared for a day of unceasing bloodshed. 7. And they who worship stones, and grave images of gold and silver and wood (and stone) and clay, and those who worship impure spirits and demons, and all kinds of idols not according to knowledge, shall get no manner of help from them. 8. And they shall become godless by reason of the folly of their hearts, And their eyes shall be blinded through the fear of their hearts And through visions in their dreams. 9. Through these they shall become godless and fearful; For they shall have wrought all their work in a lie. And shall have worshipped a stone: Therefore in an instant shall they perish. 10. But in those days blessed are all they who accept the words of wisdom, and understand them. And observe the paths of the Most High, and walk in the path of His righteousness. And become not godless with the godless; For they shall be saved. 11. AVoe to you who spread evil to your neighbours; For you shall be slain in Sheol. 12. Woe to you who make deceitful and false measures. And (to them) who cause bitterness on the earth; For they shall thereby be utterly consumed. 13. Woe to you who build your houses through the grievous toil of others, And all their building materials are the bricks and stones of sin; I tell you ye shall have no peace. 14. Woe to them who reject the measure and eternal heritage of their fathers And whose souls follow after idols; For they shall have no rest. 15. Woe to them who work unrighteousness and help oppression, And slay their neighbours until the day of the great judgement. 16. For He shall cast down your glory, And bring affliction on your hearts, And shall arouse His fierce indignation, And destroy you all with the sword; And all the holy and righteous shall remember your sins.

Th Sinners destroy each other: Judgement of the fallen Angels: the Safety of the Righteous: further Woes for the Sinners.

CHAPTER C.

And in those days in one place the fathers together with their sons shall be smitten, And brothers one with another shall fall in death Till the streams flow with their blood. 2. For a man shall not withhold his hand from slaying his sons and his sons' sons And the sinner shall not withhold his hand from his honoured brother: From dawn till sunset they shall slay one another. 3. And the horse shall walk up to the breast in the blood of sinners, And the chariot shall be submerged to its height. 4. In those days the angels shall descend into the secret places And gather together into one place all those who brought down sin, And the Most High will arise on that day of judgement To execute great judgement amongst sinners. 5. And over all the righteous and holy He will appoint guardians from amongst the holy angels To guard them as the apple of an eye, Until He makes an end of all wickedness and all sin, And though the righteous sleep a long sleep, they have nought to fear. 6. And (then) the children of the earth shall see the wise in security. And shall understand all the words of this book, And recognize that their riches shall not be able to save them In the overthrow of their sins. 7. Woe to you, sinners, on the day of strong anguish, Ye who afflict the righteous and burn them with fire: Ye shall be requited according to your works. 8. Woe to you, ye obstinate of heart, Who watch in order to devise wickedness: Therefore shall fear come upon you And there shall be none to help you. 9. Woe to you, ye sinners, on account of the words of your mouth. And on account of the deeds of jour hands which your godlessness has wrought. In blazing flames burning worse than fire shall ye burn. 10. And now, know ye that from the angels He will inquire as to your deeds in heaven, from the sun and from the moon and from the stars in reference to your sins because upon the earth ye execute judgement on the righteous. 11. And He will summon to testify against you every cloud and mist and dew and rain; for they shall all be withheld because of you from descending upon you, and they shall be mindful of your sins. 12. And now give presents to the min that it be not withheld from descending upon you, nor yet the dew, when it has received gold and silver from you that it may descend. 13. When the hoar-frost and snow with their chilliness, and all the snow-storms with all their plagues fall upon you, in those days ye shall not be able to stand before them.

Exhortation to the Fear of God: all Nature feasr Him but not the Sinners.

CHAPTER CI.

Observe the heaven, ye children of heaven, and every work of the Most High, and fear ye Him and work no evil in His presence. 2. If He closes the windows of heaven, and withholds the rain and the dew from descending on the earth on your account, what will ye do then? 3. And if He sends His anger upon you because of your deeds, ye cannot petition Him; for ye spake proud and insolent words against Hii righteousness: therefore ye shall have no peace. 4. And see ye not the sailors of the ships, how their ships are tossed to and fro by the waves, and are shaken by the winds, and ai in sore trouble? 5. And therefore do they fear because al their goodly possessions go upon the sea with them, and the; have evil forebodings of heart that the sea will swallow them and they will perish therein. 6. Are not the entire sea and all its waters, and all its movements, the work of the Most High, and has He not set limits to its doings, and confined it throughout by the sand? 7. And at His reproof it is afraid and dries up, and all its fish die and all that is in it; but ye sinners that are on the earth fear Him not. 8. Has He not made the heaven and the earth, and all that is therein? Who has given understanding and wisdom to every thing that moves on the earth and in the sea? 9. Do not the sailors of the ships fear the sea? Yet sinners fear not the Most High. Terrors of the Bay of Judgement: the adverse Fortunes of the Righteous on the Earth.

CHAPTER CII.

In those days when He hath brought a grievous fire upon you, Whither will ye flee, and where will ye find deliverance? And when He launches forth His word against you, Will you not be affrighted and fear? 2. And all the luminaries shall be affrighted with great fear, And all the earth shall be affrighted and tremble and be alarmed. 3. And all the angels shall execute their commands And shall seek to hide themselves from the presence of the Great Glory, And the children of earth shall tremble and quake; And ye sinners shall be accursed for ever. And ye shall have no peace. 4. Fear ye not, ye souls of the righteous. And be hopeful ye that have died in righteousness. 5. And grieve not if your soul into Sheol has descended in grief, And that in your life your body fared not according to your goodness. But wait for the day of the judgement of sinners And for the day of cursing and chastisement. 6. And yet when ye die the sinners speak over you: " As we die, so die the righteous, And what benefit do they reap for their deeds? 7. Behold, even as we, so do they die in grief and darkness, And what have they more than we? From henceforth we are equal. 8. And what will they receive and what will they see for ever? Behold, they too have died, And henceforth for ever shall they see no light." 9. I tell you, ye sinners, ye are content to eat and drink, and rob and sin, and strip men naked, and acquire wealth and see good days. 10. Have ye seen the righteous how their end falls out, that no manner of violence is found in them till their death? 11. " Nevertheless they perished and became as though they had not been, and their spirits descended into Sheol in tribulation."

Different Destination of the Righteous and the Sinners: fresh Objections of the Sinners.

CHAPTER CIII.

Now, therefore, I swear to you, the righteous, by the glory of the Great and Honoured and Mighty One in dominion, and by His greatness I swear to you. 2. I know a mystery And have read the heavenly tablets. And have seen the holy books. And have found written therein and inscribed regarding them: 3. That all goodness and joy and glory are prepared for them. And written down for the spirits of those who have died in righteousness, And that manifold good shall be given to you in recompense for your labours, And that your lot is abundantly beyond the lot of the living. 4. And the spirits of you who have died in righteousness shall live and rejoice, And their spirits shall not perish, nor their memorial from before the face of the Great One Unto all the generations of the world: wherefore no longer fear their contumely. 5. Woe to you, ye sinners, when ye have died, If ye die in the wealth of your sins, And those who are like you say regarding you: "Blessed are the sinners : they have seen all their days. 6. And now they have died in prosperity and in wealth, And have not seen tribulation or murder in their life And they have died in honour. And judgement has not been executed on them during their life.' 7. Know ye, that their souls will be made to descend into Sheol And they shall be wretched in their great tribulation. 8. And into darkness and chains and a burning flame where there is grievous judgement shall your spirits enter; And the great judgement shall be for all the generations of the world. Woe to you, for ye shall have no peace. 9. Say not in regard to the righteous and good who are in life: "In our troubled days we have toiled laboriously and experienced every trouble, And met with much evil and been consumed, And have become few and our spirit small. 10. And we have been destroyed and have not found any to help us even with a word: We have been tortured [and destroyed], and not hoped to see life from day to day. 11. We hoped to be the head and have become the tail: We have toiled laboriously and had no satisfaction in our toil; And we have become the food of the sinners and the unrighteous, And they have laid their yoke heavily upon us. 12. They have had dominion over us that hated us fand smote us; And to those that hated us f we have bowed our necks But they pitied us not. 13. We desired to get away from them that we might escape and be at rest, But found no place whereunto we should flee and be safe from them. 14. And we complained to the rulers in our tribulation. And cried out against those who devoured us. But they did not attend to our cries And would not hearken to our voice. 15. And they helped those who robbed us and devoured us and those who made us few; and they concealed their oppression, and they did not remove from us the yoke of those that devoured us and dispersed us and murdered us, and they concealed their murder, and remembered not that they had lifted up their hands against us."

<u>Assurances given to the Righteous: Admonitions to Sinners and the Falsifiers of the Words of Uprightness.</u>

CHAPTER CIV.

I swear unto you, that in heaven the angels remember you for good before the glory of the Great One: and your names are written before the glory of the Great One. 2. Be hopeful; for aforetime ye were put to shame through ill and affliction; but now ye shall shine as the lights of heaven, ye shall shine and ye shall be seen, and the portals of heaven shall be opened to you. 3. And in your cry, cry for judgement, and it shall appear to you; for all your tribulation shall be visited on the rulers, and on all who helped those who plundered you. 4. Be hopeful, and cast not away your hope; for ye shall have great joy as the angels of heaven. 5. What shall ye be obliged to do? Ye shall not have to hide on the day of the great judgement and ye shall not be found as sinners, and the eternal judgement shall be far from you for all the generations of the world. 6. And now fear not, ye righteous, when ye see the sinners growing strong and prospering in their ways: be not companions with them, but keep afar from their violence; for ye shall become companions of the hosts of heaven. 7. And, although ye sjnners say: "All our sins shall not be searched out and written down/' nevertheless they shall write down all your sins every day. 8. And now. [show unto you that light and darkness, day and night, see all your sins. 9. Be not godless in your hearts, and lie not and alter not the words of uprightness, nor charge with lying the words of the Holy Great One, nor take account of your idols; for all your lying and all your godlessness issue not in righteousness but in great sin. 10. And now I know this mystery, that sinners will alter and pervert the words of righteousness in many ways, and will speak wicked words, and lie, and practise great deceits, and write books concerning their words. 11. But when they write down truthfully all my words in their languages, and do not change or minish ought from my words but .write them all down truthfully—all that I first testified concerning them, 12. Then, I know another mystery, that books shall be given to the righteous and the wise to become a cause of joy and uprightness and much wisdom. 13. And to them shall the books be given, and they shall believe in them and rejoice over them, and then shall all the righteous who have learnt therefrom all the paths of uprightness be recompensed.'

SECTION V - THE PATH OF RIGHTEOUSNESS AND DIVINE WARNINGS

God and the Messiah to dwell with Man.

CHAPTER CV.

In those days the Lord bade (them) to summon and testify to the children of earth concerning their wisdom: Show (it) unto them; for ye are their guides, and a recompense over the whole earth. 2. For I and My Son will be united with them for ever in the paths of uprightness in their lives; and ye shall have peace: rejoice, ye children of uprightness. Amen.

FRAGMENT OF THE BOOK OF NOAH

CHAPTER VI.

And after some days my son Methuselah took a wife for his son Lamech, and she became pregnant by him and bore a son, 2. And his body was white as snow and red as the blooming of a rose, and the hair of his head f and his long locks were white as wool, and his eyes beautiful. And when he opened his eyes, he lighted up the whole house like the sun, and the whole house was very bright. 3. And thereupon he arose in the hands of the midwife, opened his mouth, and conversed with the Lord of righteousness.

4. And his father Lamech was afraid of him and fled, and came to his father Methuselah. 5. And he said unto him: 'I have begotten a strange son, diverse from and unlike man, and resembling the sons of the God of heaven; and his nature is different and he is not like us, and his eyes are as the rays of the sun, and his countenance is glorious. 6. And it seems to me that he is not sprung from me but from the angels, and I fear that in his days a wonder may be wrought on the earth. 7. And now, my father, I am here to petition thee and implore thee that thou mayest go to Enoch, our father, and learn from him the truth, for his dwellingplace is amongst the angels.' 8. And when Methuselah heard the words of his son, he came to me to the ends of the earth; for he had heard that I was there, and he cried aloud, and I heard his voice and I came to him. And I said unto him: 'Behold, here am I, my son, wherefore hast thou come to me?

9. And he answered and said: 'Because of a great cause of anxiety have I come to thee, and because of a disturbing vision have I approached. 10. And now, my father, hear me: unto Lamech my son there hath been born a son, the like of whom there is none, and his nature is not like man's nature, and the colour of his body is whiter than snow and redder than the bloom of a rose and the hair of his head is whiter than white wool, and his eyes are like the rays of the sun, and he opened his eyes and hereupon lighted up the whole house. 11. And he arose in the hands of the midwife, and opened his mouth and blessed the Lord of heaven.

12. And his father Lamech became afraid and fled to me, and did not believe that he was sprung from him, but that he was in the likeness of the angels of heave ; and behold I have come to thee that thou mayest make known to me the truth.' 13. And I, Enoch, answered and said unto him: 'The Lord will do a new thing on the earth, and this I have already seen in a vision, and make known to thee that in the generation of my father Jared some of the angels of heaven transgressed the word of the Lord. 14. And behold they commit sin and transgress the law, and have united themselves with women and commit sin with them, and have married some of them, and have begot children by them. 17. And they shall produce on the earth giants not according to the spirit, but according to the flesh, and there shall be a great punishment on the earth, and the earth shall be cleansed from all impurity.

15. Yea, there shall come a great destruction over the whole earth, and there shall be a deluge and a great destruction for one year. 16. And this son who has been born unto you shall be left on the earth, and his three children shall be saved with him : when all mankind that are on the earth shall die [he and his sons shall be saved]. 18. And now make known to thy son Lamech that he who has been born is in truth his son, and call his name Noah; for he shall be left to you, and he and his sons shall be saved from the destruction, which shall come upon the earth on account of all the sin and all the unrighteousness, which shall be consummated on the earth in his days. 19. And after that there shall be still more unrighteousness than that which was first consummated on the earth; for I know the mysteries of the holy ones; for He, the Lord, has showed me and informed me, and I have read (them) in the heavenly tablets.

CHAPTER CVII.

And I saw written on them that generation upon generation shall transgress, till a generation of righteousness arises, and transgression is destroyed and sin passes away from the earth, and all manner of good comes upon it. 2. And now, my son, go and make known to thy son Lamech that this son, which has been born, is in truth his son, and that (this) is no lie' 3. And when Methuselah had heard the words of his father Enoch— for he had shown to him everything in secret— he returned and showed (them) to him and called the name of that son Noah; for he will comfort the earth after all the destruction.

CHAPTER CVIII.

Another book which Enoch wrote for his son Methuselah and for those who will come after him, and keep the law in the last days. 2. Ye who have done good shall wait for those days till an end is made of those who work evil, and an end of the might of the transgressors. 3. And wait ye indeed till sin has passed away, for their names shall be blotted out of the book of life and out of the holy books. and their seed shall be destroyed for ever, and their spirits shall be slain, and they shall cry and make lamentation in a place that is a chaotic wilderness, and in the fire shall they burn; for there is no earth there. 4. And I saw there something like an invisible cloud ; for by reason of its depth I could not look over, and I saw a flame of fire blazing brightly, and things like shining mountains circling and sweeping to and from. 5. And I asked one of the holy angels who was with me and said unto him: ' What is this shining thing? for it is not a heaven but only the flame of a blazing fire, and the voice of weeping and crying and lamentation and strong pain.' 6. And he said unto me: ' This place which thou seest—here are cast the spirits of sinners and blasphemers, and of those who work wickedness, and of those who pervert every thing that the Lord hath spoken through the mouth of the prophets—(even) the things that shall be. 7. For some of them are written and inscribed above in the heaven, in order that the angels may read them and know that which shall befall the sinners, and the spirits of the humble, and of those who have afflicted their bodies, and been recompensed by God ; and of those who have been put to shame by wicked men : 8. Who love God and loved neither gold nor silver nor any of the good things which are in the world, but gave over their bodies to torture. 9. "Who, since they came into being, longed not after earthly food, but regarded everything as a passing breath, and lived accordingly, and the Lord tried them much, and their spirits were found pure so that they should bless His name. 10. And all the blessings destined for them I have recounted in the books. And He hath assigned them their recompense, because they have been found to be such as loved heaven more than their life in the world, and though they were trodden under foot of wicked men, and experienced abuse and reviling from them and were put to shame, yet they blessed Me. 11. And now I will summon the spirits of the good who belong to the generation of light, and I will transform those who were born in darkness, who in the flesh were not recompensed with such honour as their faithfulness deserved. 12. And I will bring' forth in shining light those who have loved My holy name, and I will seat each on the throne of his honour. 13. And they shall be resplendent for times without number; for righteousness is the judgement of God; for to the faithful He will give faithfulness in the habitation of upright paths. 14. And they shall see those who were born in darkness led into darkness, while the righteous shall be resplendent. 15. And the sinners shall cry aloud and see them resplendent, and they indeed shall go where days and seasons are prescribed for them.'

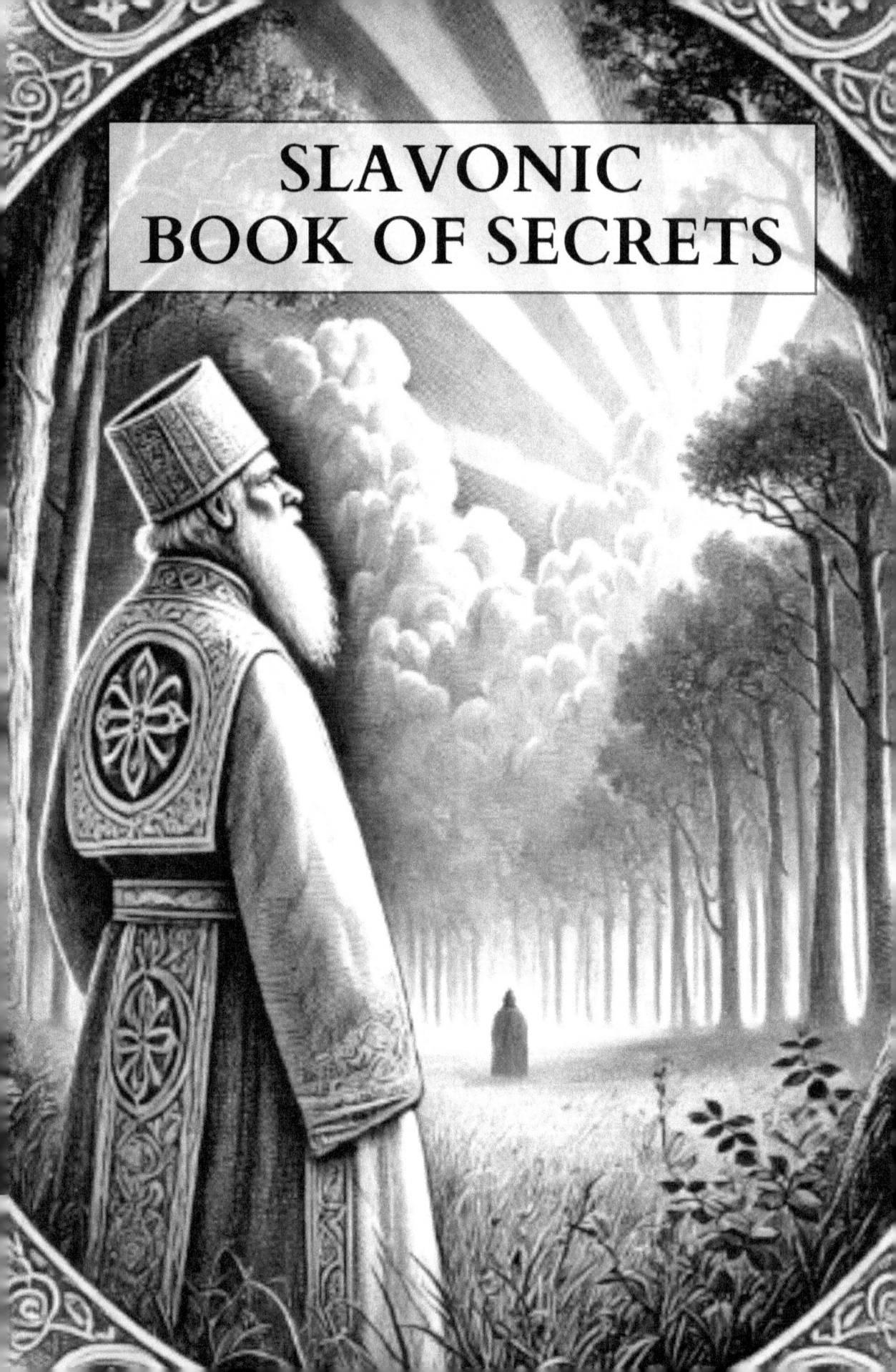

2 ENOCH

INTRODUCTION

HISTORICAL CONTEXT

The Second Book of Enoch, also known as Slavonic Enoch or 2 Enoch, is an enigmatic apocryphal text attributed to Enoch, the great-grandfather of Noah. Scholars generally place its composition between the 1st century BCE and the 1st century CE, situating it within the intellectually and theologically dynamic period of Second Temple Judaism. This era was characterized by apocalyptic speculation, mystical traditions, and heightened eschatological expectations, all of which are reflected in the themes of 2 Enoch. As Jewish communities grappled with foreign domination, socio-political upheavals, and internal religious debates, there was a growing fascination with celestial wisdom, divine judgment, and cosmic order, themes that resonate deeply throughout this text.

Unlike 1 Enoch, which was preserved in Ge'ez and canonized within the Ethiopian Orthodox Church, 2 Enoch survived primarily in Old Church Slavonic manuscripts. This linguistic transition suggests that the text was likely translated from an earlier Hebrew or Greek version, although no copies in these original languages have been discovered. Its preservation within Slavonic Christian traditions indicates its broad cultural and theological appeal, as it was transmitted beyond Jewish circles and absorbed into Eastern Orthodox mystical thought. The movement of 2 Enoch across linguistic and geographic boundaries reflects its enduring significance, not only within Jewish mysticism but also within later Christian esoteric traditions.

The text presents a highly mystical worldview, with a strong emphasis on angelology, divine wisdom, celestial hierarchies, and cosmological revelations. These themes align with broader trends in Second Temple apocalyptic literature, which sought to explain the hidden workings of the cosmos and the divine plan. The narrative of Enoch's heavenly journey, during which he receives revelations about creation, divine justice, and moral law, places 2 Enoch within the same literary tradition as texts like the Apocalypse of Abraham, the Book of Jubilees, and the Qumranic writings. The book's concerns with purity, ethical conduct, and divine law also suggest a possible connection to priestly traditions, reinforcing the idea that righteousness and adherence to divine decrees were essential for achieving spiritual elevation.

Although 2 Enoch exhibits certain Hellenistic influences, particularly in its descriptions of cosmic structures and divine governance, its core theological framework remains deeply rooted in Jewish traditions. The text reflects an understanding of priestly purity, mystical ascension, and angelic mediation, concepts that are also central to the Hekhalot and Merkabah mysticism that later emerged in Jewish esoteric traditions. These elements indicate that 2 Enoch was part of a broader mystical movement, concerned with revealing hidden wisdom and guiding the soul toward divine enlightenment.

As with many other apocryphal writings, 2 Enoch was excluded from Jewish and Christian biblical canons, yet it was still widely circulated and had a lasting impact on mystical traditions and Gnostic thought. The text is categorized as part of the Pseudepigrapha, a collection of writings attributed to biblical patriarchs and prophets, often expanding upon canonical narratives to provide additional theological insights. Within Slavonic Christian traditions, 2 Enoch found a particular home, where it was preserved alongside other apocalyptic and mystical writings. Its survival within these traditions underscores its role in bridging Jewish apocalyptic thought with early Christian eschatology, particularly in its discussions of divine judgment, resurrection, and the heavenly ascent of the soul.

One of the key differences between 2 Enoch and 1 Enoch is its shift in focus from the rebellion of the Watchers to themes of creation, divine order, and moral instruction. While 1 Enoch dedicates much of its narrative to angelic transgression and cosmic warfare, 2 Enoch presents Enoch as a recipient of divine revelation, a scribe of wisdom, and a lawgiver, expanding upon his role as a mediator between God and humanity. This text does not merely describe visions of judgment but also offers ethical guidance, reinforcing the idea that righteousness is not only about avoiding divine wrath but about aligning oneself with divine wisdom and cosmic balance.

The manuscript tradition of 2 Enoch reveals evidence of textual variation, with two primary recensions—a longer and a shorter version—suggesting that the text underwent editorial revision over time. The existence of multiple versions complicates efforts to reconstruct its original form, but it also highlights its adaptability and enduring transmission across different religious and cultural contexts. The absence of an original Hebrew or Greek manuscript continues to present challenges for scholars, yet its survival in Slavonic translations attests to the text's lasting significance and theological relevance.

As a whole, 2 Enoch stands as a testament to the evolving landscape of Jewish mysticism and early Christian theology, providing profound insights into the nature of creation, divine governance, and human moral responsibility. Its intricate visions, theological depth, and symbolic richness make it a cornerstone for understanding angelology, cosmic hierarchies, and the soul's journey toward eternal reward or judgment. Though its origins remain shrouded in mystery, its influence persists, offering both scholars and spiritual seekers a glimpse into the hidden dimensions of divine wisdom and eschatological prophecy.

KEY THEMES

The Second Book of Enoch delves into profound spiritual and philosophical ideas, blending apocalyptic visions, cosmology, and moral teachings to guide readers in their search for divine wisdom. Each theme explores a different aspect of humanity's relationship with God and offers insights into the cosmic and ethical order of creation.

Heavenly Ascent and Revelation

The central narrative of 2 Enoch begins with Enoch's ascent to heaven, where he is guided by angels through ten celestial levels. Each level unveils a deeper layer of divine mysteries, from the governance of heavenly beings to the architecture of creation.

This journey symbolizes spiritual elevation and emphasizes the hierarchical nature of the cosmos, with God enthroned at the pinnacle. Enoch's transformation into a heavenly scribe highlights his role as a mediator between heaven and earth, entrusted with divine knowledge to pass on to humanity.

The visions also provide cosmic insights, such as the structure of the heavens, angelic hierarchies, and the mechanics of time, inviting readers to reflect on the relationship between the physical and spiritual realms.

Divine Judgment and Justice

A recurring theme in 2 Enoch is the portrayal of God as the ultimate judge who rewards the righteous and punishes the wicked. The text describes the weighing of souls and the book of deeds, reflecting ancient Jewish beliefs in accountability and moral reckoning.

This focus on divine justice reassures readers of God's sovereignty, affirming that evil will not go unpunished and that the faithful will be vindicated. The text emphasizes that judgment is both personal and collective, extending to nations and generations.

The descriptions of heavenly courts and angelic record-keepers underscore the idea that moral choices are eternally recorded, reinforcing themes of accountability and moral vigilance.

Creation and Cosmology

2 Enoch offers a theological interpretation of creation, blending scientific observations with spiritual insights. It explores the ordering of celestial bodies, cycles of time, and the structure of the universe, portraying creation as a reflection of divine order and harmony.

Through detailed accounts of the sun, moon, and stars, the text establishes a sacred calendar, emphasizing the predictability and balance of creation. This serves as both a spiritual metaphor for alignment with divine will and a practical guide for measuring time and festivals.

The creation narrative highlights God's wisdom and intentionality, contrasting the chaos of sin with the order of divine law. Readers are encouraged to recognize the sacredness of time and the cosmic rhythm as a model for moral and spiritual discipline.

Moral Instruction

As Enoch ascends through the heavens, he receives ethical teachings that emphasize righteous living, charity, and devotion to God's laws. These instructions serve as a spiritual guide, addressing both personal morality and communal ethics.

Key teachings include:

- Repentance and Humility: Encouraging self-reflection and rejection of pride.
- Justice and Charity: Advocating fairness and compassion toward others.
- Obedience to Divine Law: Promoting faithfulness to God's commandments as the foundation for holiness and purity.

Enoch's role as a prophet and teacher reinforces the importance of moral leadership, calling readers to live in alignment with divine principles and to prepare for spiritual transformation.

Prophecy and Eschatology

2 Enoch concludes with prophecies about future events, including the coming flood, the final judgment, and the role of future generations in fulfilling God's plan. These prophecies emphasize the cyclical nature of divine intervention, presenting history as a series of judgments and renewals.

The text foreshadows Noah's story and the preservation of the righteous, linking Enoch's revelations to later biblical narratives. Its eschatological focus highlights God's mercy in offering redemption and warnings to prepare humanity for end-times accountability.

Readers are encouraged to view history through the lens of divine purpose, trusting in God's sovereignty while embracing their role as stewards of faith and morality.

THEOLOGICAL AND SYMBOLIC INSIGHTS

The *Second Book of Enoch* serves as a theological bridge between early Jewish mysticism and later Christian theology, reflecting a worldview that emphasizes God's transcendence, divine order, and moral accountability. At its core, the book portrays God as an all-powerful and sovereign Creator who governs the heavens and Earth through a meticulously structured hierarchy of angels and celestial beings. This depiction underscores the divine order of creation, presenting a universe where each element operates in obedience to God's will, mirroring the harmony and balance that humans are called to emulate in their spiritual lives.

One of the most striking theological themes in 2 Enoch is the transformation of Enoch into a heavenly being, a process that symbolizes the potential for spiritual elevation and communion with God. This transformation foreshadows later beliefs about the glorification of saints, resurrection, and the afterlife, offering readers a vision of divine reward and eternal fellowship with God. Enoch's ascension represents not only his personal elevation but also humanity's capacity for spiritual growth and moral perfection through faith and obedience.

The book also reinforces the foundational principles of monotheism, vehemently condemning idolatry and affirming God's sovereignty as the only divine authority. Through Enoch's encounters with angelic beings, the text emphasizes the importance of recognizing divine authority and rejecting false worship, positioning God as the ultimate source of wisdom, justice, and redemption. This theological framework mirrors the struggles faced by ancient Jewish communities against Hellenistic influences and offers reassurance that God's dominion transcends human corruption and cultural pressures.

Symbolically, Enoch's heavenly ascent serves as a profound metaphor for spiritual transformation and divine communion. His journey through the ten levels of heaven mirrors the believer's path toward moral purification and spiritual enlightenment, encouraging readers to pursue righteousness as a means of drawing closer to God. Each level of heaven reveals greater insights into cosmic mysteries, reflecting the layered nature of divine wisdom and the gradual process of spiritual awakening. This journey ultimately leads Enoch to God's throne, where he receives revelations that reaffirm God's justice, mercy, and glory, providing a vision of ultimate harmony and restoration.

The angelic hierarchies described in 2 Enoch also carry symbolic significance, illustrating the interconnectedness between heaven and earth and portraying angels as divine intermediaries who execute God's will. Their roles highlight the cosmic order governing the universe and emphasize the spiritual discipline required to align with God's plan. These celestial beings serve as models of obedience and devotion, reinforcing the moral teachings delivered to Enoch throughout his journey.

2 Enoch uses its symbolic framework to address the themes of judgment and redemption, presenting Enoch as a prophet and intercessor who warns humanity about the consequences of sin and calls them to repentance. The visions of divine justice and future judgment reflect a theology rooted in accountability and hope, encouraging readers to prepare for the end times by living righteous and faithful lives.

Through its rich theological and symbolic imagery, the *Second Book of Enoch* challenges readers to reflect on their spiritual journey, contemplate the mysteries of divine governance, and embrace their role as caretakers of moral order in preparation for eternal communion with God.

MODERN APPLICATIONS

The *Second Book of Enoch* continues to captivate readers and scholars alike, offering profound insights into questions of divine justice, moral accountability, and cosmic order that remain deeply relevant in modern times. Its exploration of the heavenly realms and the hierarchies of angels appeals to those interested in angelology and apocalyptic literature, while its emphasis on ethics and righteousness speaks directly to contemporary struggles with morality and spiritual growth. The text's vivid depictions of divine judgment and cosmic harmony invite readers to reflect not only on their place within creation but also on the enduring struggle between good and evil that shapes human experience.

As both a spiritual guide and a historical artifact, 2 Enoch offers modern readers an opportunity to explore timeless themes of faith, obedience, and redemption. Its teachings on moral purity and charity challenge individuals to live with integrity, while its symbolic imagery encourages deeper contemplation of life's spiritual dimensions. For those pursuing a closer connection to God, Enoch's journey serves as a model of transformation, illustrating the possibilities of spiritual ascent and divine enlightenment through devotion and humility.

Academically, 2 Enoch provides a valuable lens for studying the development of Jewish mysticism, Second Temple theology, and early Christian eschatology. Its insights into creation, angelic hierarchies, and judgment align with broader themes found in biblical texts like Genesis, Daniel, and Revelation, allowing scholars to trace the evolution of apocalyptic thought and cosmological frameworks. It also serves as an essential resource for understanding comparative religious traditions, particularly those that emphasize mystical experiences and divine visions.

The book's narrative structure, which weaves together creation myths, moral teachings, and prophetic warnings, resonates with modern audiences grappling with questions about existence, purpose, and redemption. Its portrayal of divine justice encourages readers to examine their own lives, emphasizing the importance of moral vigilance and spiritual preparedness in a world marked by uncertainty and moral decay.

2 Enoch challenges readers to think beyond their immediate circumstances, urging them to reflect on the larger cosmic plan and their role within it. It inspires hope by portraying a universe governed by divine wisdom and justice, while also cautioning against complacency by highlighting the consequences of sin and rebellion. Its emphasis on repentance, moral discipline, and faithfulness makes it a timeless guide for those seeking personal transformation and spiritual renewal.

Through its mystical vision of heavenly realms, its ethical exhortations, and its cosmological insights, the *Second Book of Enoch* remains a powerful text that speaks to both the spiritual seeker and the scholar, bridging the ancient and modern worlds in a unified quest for divine truth and moral integrity.

EDITORIAL NOTE ON STRUCTURE AND INTRODUCTIONS

To facilitate a deeper understanding of The Second Book of Enoch, this edition has been structured with thematic divisions, each accompanied by a contextual introduction. While the original text does not contain such structured sections, these introductions have been included to provide historical background, theological insights, and interpretative guidance, ensuring that readers—whether scholars or those new to apocryphal literature—can engage more fully with the text.

The introductions to each section have been newly written for this edition, serving as a bridge between the mystical traditions of Second Temple Judaism and contemporary readers seeking insight into early Jewish cosmology, angelology, and moral instruction. These additions do not alter the core text of 2 Enoch but rather enhance its readability, allowing for a more structured reflection on its narratives of heavenly ascension, divine wisdom, and eschatological themes.

By presenting 2 Enoch in this format, this edition aims to preserve its historical integrity while offering modern readers a guided exploration of its profound mystical and theological concepts.

STRUCTURE OF THE BOOK

The *Second Book of Enoch* is organized into 68 chapters in its traditional form and is divided into four thematic sections, each offering unique theological insights and spiritual guidance.

1. Section I: The Heavenly Journey (Chapters 1–20)

This section recounts Enoch's ascent through the layers of heaven, guided by angelic beings who reveal the mysteries of the celestial realm. Enoch encounters divine thrones, angelic orders, and cosmic wonders, witnessing the structure and hierarchy of creation.

The journey serves as both a spiritual transformation and an educational experience, preparing Enoch to receive divine revelations. The celestial realms are portrayed as ordered and hierarchical, reflecting the sovereignty of God and the harmony of divine creation.

Readers are introduced to angelology, including the roles of archangels as messengers and guardians, and are invited to reflect on the connection between heaven and earth. This section sets the stage for Enoch's deeper exploration of creation and moral law in later chapters.

2. Section II: Divine Creation and Wisdom (Chapters 21–37)

In this section, Enoch receives divine revelations about the creation of the universe, the foundations of the cosmos, and the origins of humanity. God reveals cosmological secrets, explaining the purpose of the stars, planets, and celestial cycles.

The text offers a theological framework for creation, blending scientific observation with spiritual meaning. It describes the seven days of creation, the role of angels in governing the elements, and the sacred rhythms of time, encouraging readers to contemplate the order and intentionality of God's design.

Enoch is shown the Book of Secrets, where divine wisdom is recorded, underscoring the theme of knowledge as a divine gift entrusted to the righteous. This section highlights the interconnectedness of creation, divine law, and moral order, emphasizing humanity's role as caretakers of God's creation.

3. Section III: Ethics and Righteous Living (Chapters 38–63)

This section shifts focus to moral and ethical teachings, presenting Enoch as a teacher and lawgiver who delivers divine instructions to his children and followers. The text emphasizes justice, humility, and devotion as the foundation for righteous living.

Key teachings include:

- Repentance and Forgiveness: Encouraging readers to seek God's mercy and turn away from sin.

- Charity and Compassion: Promoting kindness and justice as expressions of faith.

- Obedience and Worship: Highlighting the importance of honoring God's commandments and maintaining spiritual purity.

This section mirrors Wisdom Literature found in other ancient texts, providing a moral framework for navigating daily life. Enoch's role as a spiritual guide reinforces the timeless relevance of his teachings, making this section particularly meaningful for readers seeking personal growth and moral clarity.

4. Section IV: Enoch's Legacy and Prophecies (Chapters 64–68)

The final section chronicles Enoch's return to earth and his final blessings to his descendants. He delivers prophecies about future generations, including warnings about divine judgment and promises of restoration.

Enoch's ascension to heaven and transformation into an angelic being symbolize spiritual completion and divine favor. This section highlights his enduring legacy as a mediator between heaven and earth, inspiring future generations to seek righteousness and remain faithful to God's laws.

The narrative ends with visions of judgment, emphasizing themes of accountability, moral vigilance, and hope for redemption. It challenges readers to view history through the lens of divine purpose and trust in the sovereignty of God over creation and destiny.

SLAVONIC BOOK OF SECRETS

THE SON OF ARED: A MAN WISE AND BELOVED OF GOD

Section I - The Heavenly Journey

In this opening section, *2 Enoch* transports readers into a celestial narrative where the boundaries between heaven and earth dissolve. Enoch's extraordinary journey begins with his divine calling and ascension through the **ten levels of heaven**, guided by angelic beings. Along the way, he encounters visions of **heavenly thrones**, **angelic orders**, and **cosmic mysteries** that unveil the structure and governance of the universe.

This ascent is more than a physical journey; it represents a **spiritual transformation**, as Enoch transitions from mortal man to **divine scribe**. Each level of heaven reveals profound truths about **God's sovereignty**, **creation**, and **moral law**, preparing Enoch—and by extension, the reader—for deeper revelations about the universe and humanity's place within it. This section sets the foundation for the **divine wisdom** and **moral teachings** that follow, inviting readers to reflect on their own spiritual ascent and relationship with the divine.

I. - Concerning the Life and the Dream of Enoch.

At that time he said: 'Hardly had I aecomplished 165 years, when I begat my son Methusal: after that I lived 200 years and accomplished all the years of my life, 365 years. 2. On the first day of the first month! I was alone in my house, and I rested on my bed and slept. 3. And as I slept a great grief came upon my heart, and I wept with mine eyes? *in my dream, and I could not understand what this grief meant, or what would happen to me 3. 4. And there appeared to me two men very tall, such as I have never seen on earth. 5. And their faces shone like the sun 4, and their eyes were like burning lamps; and fire came forth from their lips. Their dress had the appearance of feathers: their feet were purple, *their wings were brighter than gold'; their hands whiter than snow. They stood at the head of my bed and called me by my name. 6. I awoke from my sleep and saw clearly these men standing in front of me. 7. 1 hastened and made obeisance to them and was terrified, and the appearance of my countenance was changed from fear. 8. And these 1! men said to me: "Be of good cheer, Enoch, be not afraid; the everlasting God hath sent us to thee, and lo! to-day thou shalt ascend with us into heaven.

9. And tell thy sons and thy servants, all who work in thy house, and let no one seek thee, till the Lord bring thee back to them." 10. And I *hastened to obey them, and went out of my house 5. And I called my sons Methusal, Regim [and Gaidal], and told them what wonderful' things the two men had said to me.'.

II. - The Instruction: how Enoch taught his Sons

Hear me, my children, for I do not know whither Tam going, or what awaits me. 2. Now, my children, IT say unto you: turn not aside from God: walk before the face of the Lord and keep his judgements and do not worship vain gods, who did not make heaven and earth, for these will perish, and also those who worship them 3. But may God make confident your hearts in the fear of Him'. 4. And now, my children, let no one seek me till the Lord brings me back to you.

III. - Of the taking up of Enoch how the Angels took him up into the first heaven.

It came to pass when I had spoken to my sons, these men summoned me and took me on their wings and placed me on the clouds. And lo! the clouds moved. 2. And again (going) higher I saw the air and (going still) higher I saw the ether, and they placed me in the first heaven. 3.And they showed me a very great sea, greater than the earthly sea.

VI. - Of the Angels who rule the Stars.

And they brought before my face the elders, and the rulers of the orders of the stars, and they showed me the two hundred angels who rule the stars and their heavenly service; 2. And they fly with their wings and go round all (the stars) as they float.

V. - How the Angels guard the Habitations of the Snow.

And then I looked and saw the treasuries of the snow and ice and the angels who guard their terrible store-places; 2. And the treasuries of the clouds from which they come forth and into which they enter.

VI. - Concerning the Dew and the Oil, and different Colours.

And they showed me the treasuries of the dew, like oil for anointing, and its form was in appearance like that of all earthly colours: also many angels keeping their treasuries, and they shut and open them.

VII. - How Enoch was taken into the second Heaven.

And the men took me and brought me to the second heaven, and showed me the darkness, and there I saw the prisoners suspended, reserved for (and) awaiting the eternal judgement. 2. And these angels were gloomy in appearance, more than the darkness of the earth. And they unceasingly wept every hour, and I said to the men who were with me: 'Why are these men continually? 3. And the men answered me: 'These are they who apostatized from the Lord: who obeyed not the commandments of God, and took counsel of their own will and transgressed together with their prince and have been already confined to the second heaven. 4. And I felt great pity for them. And lo! the angels made obeisance to me, and said to me: "O man of God! pray-for us to the Lord."- 5. And I answered them: "Who am I, a mortal man, that I should pray for angels? Who knows whither I go, or what awaits me: or who prays for me!?".'

VIII. - Of the taking of Enoch to the third Heaven.

And these men took me from thence, and brought me to the third heaven, and placed me in the midst of a garden a place such as has never been known for the goodliness of its appearance. 2. And saw all the trees of beautiful colours and their fruits ripe and fragrant, and all kinds of food which they produced, springing up with delightful fragrance 3. And in the midst (there is) the tree of life, in that place, on which God rests, when He comes into Paradise. And this tree cannot be described for its excellence and sweet odour. 4. And it is beautiful more than any created thing. And on all sides in appearance it is like gold and crimson and transparent as fire, and it covers everything. 5. From its root in the garden! there go forth four streams which pour honey and milk, oil and wine, and are separated in four directions, and go about with a soft course. 6. And they go down to the Paradise of Eden, between corruptibility and incorruptibility. And thence they go along the earth, and have a revolution in their circle like also the other elements, 7. And there is another tree, an olive tree always distilling oil. And there is no tree there without fruit, and every tree" is blessed. 8. And there are three hundred angels very glorious, who keep the garden, and with never ceasing voices and blessed singing, they serve the Lord every day. And I said: 'What a very blessed place is this!' And those men spake unto me.

IX. - The showing to Enoch of the Righteous, and the Place of Prayers.

This place, Q Enoeh, is prepared for the righteous who endure every kind of attack in their lives from those who afflict their souls: who turn away their eyes from unrighteousness, and accomplish a righteous judgement, and also give bread to the hungry, and clothe the naked, and raise the fallen, and assist the orphans who are oppressed, and who walk without blame before the face of the Lord, and serve him only. For them this place is prepared as an eternal inheritance.'

X. - Here they showed Enoch the terrible Places, and various Tortures

And the men then led me to the Northern region, and showed me there a very terrible place. 2. And there are all sorts of tortures in that place. Savage darkness and impenetrable gloom; and there is no light there, but a gloomy fire is always burning, and a fiery river goes forth. And all that place has fire on all sides, and on all sides cold and ice, thus it burns and freezes. 3. And the prisoners are very savage. And the angels terrible and without pity, carrying savage weapons, and their torture was unmerciful. 4. And I said: 'Woe, woe! How terrible is this place!' And the men said to me: ' This place, Enoch, is prepared for those who do not honour God; who commit evil deeds on earth, vitium sodomiticum, witchcraft, enchantments, devilish magic; and who boast of their evil deeds, stealing, lying, calumnies, envy, evil thoughts, fornication, and murder 5. Who steal the souls of wretched men, oppressing the poor and spoiling them of their possessions, and themselves grow rich by the taking of other men's possessions, injuring them. Who when they might feed the hungry, allow them to die of famine; who when they might clothe them, stip them naked. 6. Who do not know their Creator and have worshipped gods without life; who can neither see nor hear, being vain gods, and have fashioned the forms of idols, and bow down to a contemptible thing, made with hands for all these this place is prepared cation, and murder for an eternal inheritance.

XI. - Here they took Enoch to the fourth Heaven, where is the Course of the Sun and Moon.

And the men took me and conducted me to the fourth heaven, and showed me all the comings and goings forth and all the rays of the light of the sun and moon. And I measured their goings, and computed their light. 2. And I saw that? the sun has a light seven times greater than the moon. I beheld their circle, and their chariot on which each goes like a wind advancing with astonishing swiftness, and they have no rest day or night coming or going. 3. There are four great stars; each star has under it a thousand stars at the right of the chariot of the sun; and four at the left, each having under it a thousand stars, altogether eight thousand 4. Fifteen myriads of angels go out with the sun and attend him during the day, and by night one thousand. Each angel has six wings. They go before the chariot of the sun. 5. And a hundred angels keep warm and light up the sun.

XII. - Of the wonderful Creatures of the Sun.

And I looked and saw other flying creatures, their names phoenixes and chalkadri wonderful and strange in appearance, with the feet and tails of lions, and the heads of crocodiles! their appearance was of a purple colour, like the rainbow; their size nine hundred measures. 2. Their wings were like those of angels, each with twelve, and they attend the chariot of the sun, and go with him, bringing heat and dew as they are ordered by God. 3. So the sun makes his revolutions, and goes under the heavens, and goes under the earth with the light of his beams unceasingly.

XIII. - The Angels took Enoch, and placed him on the East at the Gates of the Sun.

These men brought me to the East and showed me the gates* by which the sun goes forth® at the appointed seasons, and according to the revolution of the months of the whole year, and according to the number of the hours, day and night. 2. And I saw the six great cates open, each gate having sixty-one stadia and a quarter of one stadium; and I truly measured them and understood their size to be so much, by which the sun goes forth; and he goes to the west and makes his course correspond. And he proceeds through all the months. 3. And by the first gates he goes out forty-two days; by the second gates thirty-five days; by the fourth gates thirty-five; by the fifth gates thirty-five; by the sixth gates forty-five. 4. And so he returns from the sixth gates in the course of time: and he enters by the fifth gates during thirty-five days, by the fourth gates thirty-five, by the third gates during thirty-five days; by the second gates thirty-five. 5. And so the days of the whole year! are finished according to the alternation of the four seasons.

XIV. - They took Enoch to the West

And then these men took me to the West of the heavens and showed me six great gates open, corresponding to the Eastern gates, opposite to which the sun goes out by the Eastern gates, according to the number of the days three hundred and sixty-five, and the quarter of a day. 2. So he sets by the Western gates. When he goes out by the Western gates four hundred angels take his crown and bring it to the Lord. 3. And the sun revolves in his chariot and goes without light for seven complete hours in the night. And when he comes near the East at the eighth hour of the night, the four hundred angels bring his crown and crown him.

XV. - The Creatures of the Sun; the Phoenines and Chalkidri sang.

Then sang the creatures called the Phoenixes and the Chalkidri. On this account every bird claps its wings, rejoicing at the giver of light, and they sang a song at the command of the Lord. 2. The giver of light comes to give his brightness to the whole world. 3. And they showed me the calculation of the going of the sun. And the gates by which he enters and goes out are great gates, which God made for the computation of the year. 4. On this account the sun is great.

XVI. - The Men took Enoch and placed him at the East, at the Course of the Moon.

The other, the computation of the moon these men showed me; all the goings and revolutions". And they pointed out the gates to me, twelve great gates extending from the West to the East°, by which the moon enters and goes out at the customary times. 2. She enters the first gate when the sun is in the West thirty-one days exactly; by the second gate thirty-one days exactly; by the third gate thirty days exactly; by the fourth gate thirty days exactly; by the fifth gate thirty-one days exactly; by the sixth gate thirty-one days exactly; by the seventh gate thirty days exactly; by the eighth gate thirty-one days exactly; by the ninth gate thirty-one days exactly; by the tenth gate thirty days exactly; by the eleventh gate thirty-one days exactly; by the twelfth gate twenty-eight days exactly. 3. And so by the Western gates in her revolutions, and corresponding to the number of the Eastern gates she goes, and accomplishes the year. 4.And unto the sun there are three hundred and sixty-five days and a quarter of one day, 5. But in the lunar year there are three hundred and fifty-four days, making twelve months of twenty-nine days; and there remain eleven days over, which belong to the solar circle of the whole year, and are lunar epacts of the whole year and thirty-two years. [Thus the great circle has five hundred and thirty-two years.] 6. The fourth part (of one day) is neglected during three years and the fourth year completes it exactly. On account of this they are omitted from the heavens during three years, and are not added to the number of the days, on which account these change the seasons of the year in two new months, to make the number complete and there are two others to diminish. 7. And when she has gone through the Western gates, she returns and goes to the Eastern, with her high, and so she goes day and night in the heavenly circles, below all the circles more quickly than the winds of the heavens, and there are spirits and creatures, and angels flying, with six wings to each of the angels. 8. And seven (months) are computed to the circle of the moon during a revolution of nineteen years.

XVII. - Of the singing of the Angels, which cannot be described.

In the middle of the heavens I saw an armed host serving the Lord with cymbals, and organs, and unceasing voice. I was delighted at hearing it.

XVIII. - Of the taking up of 'Enoch into the fifth Heaven.

The men took and brought me up into the fifth heaven, and I saw there many hosts not to be counted called Grigori; and their appearance was like men, and their size was greater than that of the giants. 2. And their countenances were withered, and their lips are always silent. And there was no service in the fifth heaven. And I said to the men who were with me: ' Why are these men very withered, and their faces melancholy, and their lips silent, and there 1s no service in this heaven?' 3. And they said to me: 'These are the Grigori, who, with their prince Satanail, rejected the holy! Lord' 4. And in consequence of these things they are kept in great darkness in the second heaven; and of them there went three to the earth from the throne of God to the place Ermon; and they entered into dealings on the side of Mount Iermon, and they saw the daughters of men, that they were fair, and took unto themselves wives. 5. And they made the earth foul with their deeds. And they acted lawlessly in all times of this age, and wrought confusion, and the giants were born, and the strangely tall men, and there was much wickedness. 6. And on account of this God judged them with a mighty judgement. And they lament for their brethren, and they will be punished at the great day of the Lord. 7. And I said to the Grigori: 'I have seen your brethren and their works, and their great torments. And I have prayed for them, but God has condemned them (to be) under the earth, till the heaven and earth are ended for ever. 8. And I said: 'Why do ye wait, brethren, and not serve before the face of the Lord? and perform your duties before the face of the Lord, and do not anger your Lord to the end, 9. And they listened to my rebuke. And they stood in the four orders in this heaven, and lo! as I was standing with these men, four trumpets resounded together with a loud voice, and the Grigori sang with one voice, and their voices went forth before the Lord with sadness and tenderness.

XIX. - The taking up of Enoch into the sixth Heaven.

And these men took me thence and brought me to the sixth heaven, and I saw there seven bands of angels, very bright and glorious, and their faces shining more than the rays of the sun. is no difference in their countenances, or their manner, or the style of their clothing. 2. And these orders arrange and study the revolutions of the stars, and the changes of the moon, and revolutions of the sun, and superintend the good or evil condition of the world. 3. And they arrange teachings, and instructions, and sweet speaking, and singing, and all kinds of glorious praise. These are the archangels who are appointed over the angels! They hold in subjection all living things both in heaven and earth 4. And there are the angels who are over seasons and years, and the angels who are over rivers and the sea, and those who are over the fruits of the earth, and the angels over every herb, giving all kinds of nourishment to every living thing, 5. And the angels over all souls of men, who write down all their works and their lives before the face of the Lord. 6. In the midst of them are seven phoenixes and seven cherubins, and seven six-winged creatures, being as one voice and singing with one voice; and it is not possible to describe their singing, and they rejoice before the Lord at His footstool.

XX. - Thence Enoch is taken into the seventh Heaven.

And these men took me thence and brought me to the seventh heaven, and I saw there a very great light and all the fiery hosts of great archangels, and incorporeal powers and lordships, and principalities, and powers; cherubim and seraphim, thrones and the watchfulness of many eyes. There were ten troops, a station of brightness, and I was afraid, and trembled with a great terror. 2. And those men took hold of me and brought me into their midst and said to me: 'Be of good cheer, Enoch, be not afraid.'. And they showed me the Lord from afar sitting on His lofty throne And all the heavenly hosts having approached stood! on the ten! steps, according to their rank: and} made obeisance to the Lord. 4. And so they proceeded to their places in joy and mirth, and in boundless light singing songs with low and gentle voices, and gloriously serving Him.

Section II – Divine Creation and Wisdom

Building upon Enoch's heavenly journey, this section shifts focus to **divine creation** and the **origins of the cosmos**, presenting God as the ultimate architect of existence. Through revelations imparted to Enoch, readers gain insights into the **foundations of creation**, including the **ordering of time**, the **movement of celestial bodies**, and the **cycles of nature** that sustain life.

The narrative explores not only the physical universe but also the **spiritual dimensions** that govern it, emphasizing **divine wisdom** as the guiding force behind creation. Enoch is shown the **Book of Secrets**, a symbolic repository of divine knowledge that underscores humanity's role as **caretakers of creation**. This section highlights the intricate relationship between **cosmology** and **spirituality**, encouraging readers to see the natural world as a reflection of **God's purpose** and order.

In preparation for the **moral teachings** that follow, this section reinforces the idea that knowledge of creation carries with it a **moral responsibility**, urging readers to align their lives with the **rhythms and laws** established by God.

XXI. – *How the Angels placed Enoch there at the limits of the seventh Heaven, and departed from him invisibly.*

They leave not nor depart day or night standing before the face of the Lord, working His will, cherubim and seraphim, standing round His throne. And the six-winged creature overshadow all His throne, singing with a soft voice before the face of the Lord: 'Holy, Holy, Holy: Lord God of Sabaoth! heaven and earth are full of Thy glory' 2. When I had seen all these things, these men said unto me: 'Enoch, up to this time we have been ordered to accompany thee. 'And those men departed from me, and I saw them ne more. And I remained alone at the extremity of the heaven, and was afraid, and fell on my face, and said within myself: 'Woe is me! what has come upon me! 3. And the Lord sent one of His glorious archangels, Gabriel, and he said to me: 'Be of good cheer, Enoch, be not afraid, stand up, come with me, and stand up before the face of the Lord for ever. 4. And I answered him, and said: 'Oh! Lord, my spirit has departed from me with fear *and trembling call to me the men? who have brought me to this place: upon them I have relied, and with them I would go before the face of the Lord.' 5. And Gabriel hurried me away like a leaf carried off by the wind, and he took me! and set me before the face of the Lord.

CHAPTER XXII.

I fell down and worshipped the Lord. 5. And the Lord spake with His lips to me: 'Be of good cheer, Enoch, be not afraid: rise up and stand before my face for ever. 6. And Michael, the chief captain, lifted me up, and bronght me before the face of the Lord, and the Lord said to His servants making trial of them: 'Let Enoch come to stand before My face for ever! 7. And the glorious ones made obeisance *to the Lord, and said: 'Let Enoch proceed according to Thy word! 8. And the Lord said to Michael: 'Go and take from Enoch his earthly robe, and anoint him with My holy oil, and clothe him with the raiment of My glory' 9. And so Michael did as the Lord spake unto him. He anointed me and clothed me, and the appearance of that oil was more than a great light, and its anointing was like excellent dew; and its fragrance like myrrh, shining like a ray of the sun. 10. And I gazed upon myself, and I was like one of His glorious ones, And there was no difference, and fear and trembling departed from me'. 11. And the Lord called one of His archangels, by name Vretil, who was more wise than the other archangels, and wrote down all the doings of the Lord. 12, And the Lord said to Vretil, 'Bring forth the books from my store-places, and give a reed to Enoch, and interpret to him the books.' And Vretil made haste and brought me the books, fragrant with myrrh, and gave me a reed from his hand.

XXIII. - Of the Writing of Enoch how he wrote about his wonderful Goings and the heavenly Visions, and he himself wrote 366 Books.

And he told me all the works of the heaven and the earth and the sea, and their goings and comings, the noise of the thunder; the sun and moon and the movement of the stars; their changings; the seasons and years; days and hours; and goings of the winds; and the numbers of the angels; the songs of the armed hosts. 2. And everything relating to man, and every language of their songs, and the lives of men, and the precepts and instructions, and sweet-voiced singings, and all which it is suitable to be instructed in. 3. And Vretil instructed me thirty days and thirty nights, and his lips never ceased speaking; and I did not cease thirty days and thirty nights writing all the remarks'. 4. And Vretil said to me: 'All the things which I have told thee, thou hast written down. Sit down and write all about the souls of men, those of them which are not born, and the places prepared for them for ever. 5. For every soul was created eternally before the foundation of the world.' 6. And I wrote all out continuously during thirty days and thirty nights, and I copied all out accurately, and I wrote 366 books.

XXIV. - Of the great Secrets of God, which God revealed and told to Enoch, and spoke with him Face to Face.

And the Lord called me and said to me: 'Enoch, sit thou on My left hand with Gabriel.' And I made obeisance to the Lord. 2. And the Lord spake to me: 'Enoch, the things which thou seest at rest and in motion were completed by me I will tell thee now, even from the first, what things I created from the non-existent, and what visible things from the invisible. 3. Not even to My angels have I told My secrets, nor have I informed them of their origin, nor have they understood My infinite creation which I tell thee of to-day. 4. For before anything which is visible existed, I alone held my course among the invisible things, like the sun from the east to the west, and from the west to the east. 5. But even the sun has rest in himself, but I did not find rest, because I was creating every thing. And I planned to lay the foundations and to make the visible creation.

XXV. - God tells Enoch how out of the lowest Darkness, there comes forth the visible and the invisible.

And I commanded .in the depths that visible things should come out of invisible. And out came Adoil very great, and I gazed upon him. And lo! his colour was red, of great brightness. 2. And I said unto him: "Burst asunder, Adoil, and let that which comes from thee be visible." 3. And he burst asunder, and there came forth a great light, and I was in the midst of a great light, and as the light came forth from the light, there came forth the great world, revealing all the creation, which I had purposed to make, and I saw that it was good. 4. And I made for Myself a throne, and sat upon it, and I said to the light: "Go forth on high and be established above My throne, and be the foundation for things on high.' 5. And there was nothing higher than the light, and as I reclined, I saw it from My throne.

XXVI. - God again calls from the Depths and there came forth Arkhas, Tazhis, and one who is very red.

And I summoned a second time from the depths, and said: 'Let the solid thing which is visible come forth from the invisible'" And Arkhas came forth firm and heavy and very red. 2. And I said: 'Be thou divided, O Arkhas, and let that be seen which is produced from thee.' And when he was divided, the world came forth, very dark and great, bringing the creation of all things below. 3. And I saw that it was good. And I said to him: 'Go thou down and be thou established. And be a foundation for things below'; and it was so. And it came forth and was established, and was a foundation for things below. And there was nothing else below the darkness'.

XXVII. - How God established the Water, and surrounded it with Light, and established upon it Seven Islands.

And I ordered that there should be a separation between the light and the darkness, and I said: 'Let there be a thick substance,' and it was sol. 2. And I spread this out and there was water, and I spread it over the darkness, below the light. 3. And thus I made firm the waters, that is, the depths, and I surrounded the waters with light, and I created seven circles and I fashioned them like crystal, moist and dry, that is to say, like glass and ice, and as for the waters, and also the other elements, I showed each of them their paths, (viz.) to the seven stars, each of them in their heaven, how they should go; and I saw that it was good. 4. And I separated between the light and the darkness; that is to say, between the waters here and there. And I said to the light: 'Let it be day®'; and to the darkness, 'Let it be night.' And the evening and the morning were the first day.

CHAPTER XXVIII.

And thus I made firm the circles of the heavens, and caused the waters below, which are under the heavens to be gathered into one place, and that the waves should be dried up, and it was so. 2. Out of the waves I made firm and great stones, and out of the stones I heaped together a dry substance, and I called the dry substance earth. 3. And in the midst of the earth I appointed a pit, that is to say an abyss. 4. I gathered the sea into one place, and I restrained it with a yoke. And I said to the sea: 'Lo! I give thee an eternal portion and thou shalt not move from thy established position.' So I made fast the firmament and fixed it above the water. 5. This I called the first day of the creation. Then it was evening, and again morning, and it was the second day.

XXIX.

And for all the heavenly hosts I fashioned a nature like that of fire, and My eye gazed on the very firm and hard stone. And from the brightness of My eye the lightning received its wonderful nature. 2. And fire is in the water and water in the fire, and neither is the one quenched, nor the other dried up. On this account lightning is brighter than the sun, and soft water is stronger than hard stone. 3. And from the stone I cut the mighty fire. And from the fire I made the ranks of the spiritual hosts, ten thousand angels, and their weapons are fiery, and their garment is a burning flame, and I ordered them to stand each in their ranks.

Here Satana was hurled from the Heights with his Angels.

One of these in the ranks of the Archangels, having turned away with the rank below him, entertained an impossible idea, that he should make his throne higher than the clouds over the earth, and should be equal in rank to My power. 5. And I hurled him from the heights with his angels. And he was flying in the air continually, above the abyss.

CHAPTER XXX.

And so I created all the heavens, and it was the third day. On the third day I ordered the earth to produce great: trees, such as bear fruit, and mountains, and every sort of herb and every seed that is sown, and I planted Paradise, and enclosed it, and placed fiery angels armed, and so I made a renewing. 2. Then it was evening, and it was morning, being the fourth day® On the fourth day I ordered that there should be great lights in the circles of the heavens. 3. In the first and highest circle I placed the star Kruno; and on the second" Aphrodite; on the third Ares; on the fourth the Sun; on the fifth Zeus; on the sixth Hermes; on the seventh the moon. 4. And the lower air I adorned with the lesser stars. 5. And I placed the sun to give light to the day, and the moon and the stars to give light to the night; the sun that he should go according to each sign of the Zodiac and the course of the moon through the twelve signs of the Zodiac. 6. And I fixed their names and existence, the thunders, and the revolutions of the hours, how they take place. 7. Then it was evening and the morning, the fifth day. On the fifth day I commanded the sea to produce fish, and winged fowls of all kinds, and all things that creep upon the earth, and four-footed things that go about the earth, and the things that fly in the air, male and female, and every living thing breathing with life. 8. And it was evening and morning the sixth day. On the sixth day I ordered My Wisdom to make man? of seven substances. His flesh from the earth; his blood from the dew; his eyes from the sun; his bones from the stones; his thoughts from the swiftness of the angels, and the clouds; his veins and hair from the grass of the earth; his spirit from My spirit and from the wind. 9. And I gave him seven natures: hearing to his body, sight to his eyes, smell to the perception, touch to the veins, taste to the blood, the bones for endurance, sweetness for thought. 10. I purposed a subtle thing: from the invisible and visible nature I made man. From both are his death and life, and his form and the word was like a deed both small in a great thing *, and great in a small thing. 11. And I placed him upon the earth; like a second angel, in an honourable, great, and glorious way. 12. And I made him a ruler *to rule upon the earth, and to have My wisdom. And there was no one like him upon the earth of all My creations. 13. And I gave him a name from the four substances: the East, the West, the North, and the South. 14. And I appointed for him four special stars, and I gave him the name Adam. 15. And I gave him his will, and I showed him the two ways, the light and the darkness. And I said unto him: 'This is good and this is evil; that I should know whether he has love for Me or hate: that he should appear in his race as loving Me. I knew his nature, he did not know his nature. 16. Therefore his ignorance is a woe to him that he should sin, and I appointed death on account of his sin. 17. And I caused him to sleep, and he slumbered. And I took from him a rib, and I made him a wife. 18. And by his wife death came, and I received his last word. And I called her by a name, the mother; that is Eve.

XXXI. - God gives Paradise to Adam, and gives him Knowledge, so as to see the Heavens open, and that he should see the Angels singing a Song of Triumph.

Adam had a life on earth,... and I made a garden in Eden in the East, and (I ordained) that he should observe the law and keep the instruction. 2. I made for him the heavens open that he should perceive the angels singing the song of triumph. And there was light without 3. And the devil took thought, as if wishing to make another world, because things were subservient to Adam on earth, to rule it and have lordship over it. 4. The devil is to be the evil spirit of the lowest places; he became Satan, after he left the heavens. 5. And then, though he became different from the angels in nature, he did not change his understanding of just and sinful thoughts. He understood the judgement upon him, and the former sin which he had sinned. 6, And on account of this, he conceived designs against Adam; in such a manner he entered and deceived Eve. But he did not touch Adam. 7. But I cursed him for (his) ignorance: but those I previously blessed, them I did not curse. 8. nor man did I curse, nor the earth, nor any other things created, but the evil fruit of man, and then his works.

XXXII. - On account of the Sin of Adam, God sends him to the Earth, 'From which I took thee, but He does not wish to destroy him in the Life to come.

I said to him: 'Earth thou art, and to earth also from whence I took thee shalt thou return. I will not destroy thee, but will send thee whence I took thee. Then IT can also take thee in My second coming'; and I have blessed all My creation, visible and invisible. 2. And I blessed the seventh day, which is the Sabbath, for in it I rested from all My labours.

XXXIII. – God shows Enoch the Duration of this World, 7000 Years, and the eighth Thousand is the End. (There will be) no Years, no Months, no Weeks, no Days.

Then also I established the eighth day. Let the eighth be the first after My work, and let the days be after the fashion of seven thousand. 2. Let there be at the beginning of the eighth thousand a time when there is no computation, and no end; neither years, nor months, nor weeks, nor days, nor hours. 3. And now Enoch, what things I have told thee, and what thou hast understood, and what heavenly things thou hast seen, and what thou hast seen upon the earth, and what thou hast written in books, by My wisdom all these things I devised so as to create them, and I made them from the highest foundation to the lowest, and to the end. 4. And there is no counsellor nor inheritor of My works. I am the eternal One, and the One not made with hands: My thought is without change, My wisdom is My counsellor and My word is reality; and My eyes see all things, if I look to all things they stand fast. If I turn away My face, all are mm need of Me. 5. And now pay attention, Enoch, and know thou who is speaking to thee, and do thou take the books which thou thyself hast written. 6. And I give thee Samuil and Raguil who brought thee to Me. And go with them upon the earth, and tell thy sons what things I have said to thee, and what thou hast seen from the lowest heaven up to My throne. 7. For I have created all the hosts, and all the powers, and there is none that opposes Me, or is disobedient to Me. For all are obedient to My sole power, and labour for My rule alone. 8. Give them the works written ont by thee, and they shall read them, and know Me to be the Creator of all; and shall understand that there is no other God beside Me. 9. They shall distribute the books of thy writing to their children's children, and from generation to generation, and from nation to nation. 10. And I will give thee, Enoch, My messenger, the great captain Michael, for thy writings and for the writings of thy fathers, Adam, Seth, Enos, Kainan, Malaleel, and Jared, thy father. 11. And I shall not require them till the last age, for I have instructed My two angels, Arinkh and Parinkh, whom I have put upon the earth as their guardians. 12. And I have ordered them in time to guard them that the account of what I shall do in thy family may not be lost in the deluge to come.

XXXIV. – God accuses the Idolators; the Workers of Iniquity, such as Sodom, and on this account He brings the Deluge upon them.

For I know the wickedness of men that they will not bear the yoke which I have put upon them, nor sow the seeds which J have given them, but will cast off My yoke and accept another, and sow vain seeds and bow to vain gods, and deny Me the only God. 2. And they will fill all the world with wickedness and iniquity, and foul impurities with one another, sodomy and all other impure practices, which it is foul to speak about. 3. And on this account I will bring a deluge upon the earth and I will destroy all, and the earth shall be destroyed in great corruption.

XXXV. - God leaves one Just Man from the Family of Enoch, with all his House, which pleased God according to His Will.

And I will leave a righteous man of thy race, with all his house who shall act according to My will. From their seed after some time will be raised up a numerous generation, but of these, many will be! very insatiable. 2. Then on the extinction of that family, I will show them the books of thy writings, and of thy fathers, and the guardians of them on earth will show them to the men who are true, and please Me, who do not take My name in vain. 3. And they shall tell to another generation, and these having read them, shall be glorified at last more than before.

XXXVI. - God ordered Enoch to live on the Earth thirty Days, so as to teach his Sons, and his Sons Sons. After thirty Days he was thus taken up into Heaven.

And now, Enoch, I give thee a period of thirty days to work in thy house. And tell thou thy sons, and all thy household before Me; that they may listen to what is spoken to them by thee; that they read and understand, how there is no other God beside Me; and let them always keep My commandments, and begin to read and understand the books written out by thee. 2. And after thirty days, I will send My angels for thee, and they shall take thee from the earth, and from thy sons, according to My will.

XXXVII. - Here God summons an Angel

And God called one of His greatest angels, terrible and awful, and placed him by me, and the appearance of that angel was like snow, and his hands were like ice; he had a very cold appearance, and my face was chilled because I could not endure the fear of the Lord; just as it is not possible to endure the mighty fire and heat of the sun, and the frost of the air. 2. And the Lord said to me, 'Enoch, if thy face is not chill here, no man can look upon thy face.'

Section III - Ethics and Righteous Living

In this pivotal section, the focus shifts from **cosmic mysteries** to **moral instruction**, as Enoch delivers **ethical teachings** to his children and followers. Having witnessed the **divine order** of the heavens, Enoch now shares **practical guidance** for living in harmony with God's will.

Readers encounter teachings on **justice**, **humility**, **repentance**, and **charity**, emphasizing the importance of **righteousness** in maintaining both **personal integrity** and **spiritual balance**. Enoch acts as a **divine mediator**, translating heavenly wisdom into actionable lessons, encouraging his audience to prepare for **divine judgment** through acts of **faithfulness** and **obedience**.

This section challenges readers to view **ethical living** not as an obligation but as a path to **spiritual transformation**, reflecting the harmony seen in the heavens. It also serves as a bridge between the **revelations of creation** and the **prophecies** in the final section, showing that adherence to **divine laws** is essential for preparing one's soul for the **final judgment** and the fulfillment of God's plan.

XXXVIII. - Mathusal hal Hope, and awaited his Father Enoch by his Bed, Day and Night.

And the Lord said to those men who first took me: 'Take Enoch with you to the earth, and wait for him till the appointed day.' 2. And at night they placed me upon my bed, and Mathusal, expecting my coming by day and by night, was a guard at my bed. 3. And he was terrified when he heard my coming, and I gave him directions that all my household should come, that I might tell them everything.

XXXIX. - The mournful Admonition of Enoch to his Sons, with Weeping and great Sorrow, speaking to them.

Listen, my children, what things are according to the will of the Lord. I am sent to-day to you to tell you from the lips of the Lord, what was and what is happening now, and what will be before the day of judgement. 2. Hear, my children, for I do not speak to you to-day from my lips, but from the lips of the Lord who has sent me to you. For you hear the words of my lips, a mortal man like yourselves. 3. I have seen the face of the Lord as it were iron that is heated in the fire, and when brought out sends forth sparks and burns. 4. Look at the eyes of me, a man laden with a sign for you. I have seen the eyes of the Lord shining like a ray of the sun and striking with terror human eyes. 5. You, my children, see the right hand of a man made like yourselves assisting you. I have seen the right hand of the Lord assisting me, and filling the heavens. 6. You see the compass of my actions, like to your own. I have seen the measureless and harmonious' form of the Lord. To Him there is no end. 7. You therefore hear the words of my lips, but I have heard the words of the Lord, like great thunder, with continual agitation of the clouds. 8. And now, my children, listen to the discourses of your earthly father. It is terrible and awful to stand before the face of an earthly prince— terrible and very awful because the will of the prince is death and the will of the prince is life; how much more is it terrible and awful to stand before the face of the Lord of lords, and of the earthly and the heavenly hosts. Who can endure this never-ending terror?

XL. - Enoch instructs faithfully his Children about all Things from the Mouth of the Lord; how he saw, and heard and wrote them down.

And now, my children, I know all things? from the lips of the Lord; for? my eyes have seen from the beginning to the end. 2. I know all things and have written all things in the books, both the heavens and the end of them, and their fulness, and all the hosts, and I have measured their goings, and written down the stars and their innumerable quantity. 3. What man has seen their alternations and their goings? Not even the angels know their number; I have written down the names of all. 4. And I have measured the circle of the sun, and I have measured his rays; and his coming in and going out, through all the months, and all his courses, and their names I have written down. 5. I have measured the circle of the moon, and its waning which occurs during every day, and the secret places in which it hides every day and ascends according to all the hours. 6. I have Jaid down the four seasons, and from the seasons I made four circles, and in the circles I placed the years; I placed the months, and from the months I calculated the days, and from the days! I have calculated the hours. 7, Moreover, I have written down all things moving upon the earth I have written down all things that are nourished, all seed sown and unsown, which grows on the earth, and all things belonging to the garden, and every herb and every flower, and their fragrance and their names. 8. And the dwellings of the clouds, *and their conformations and their wings, how they bring rain and the rain-drops, I investigated all. 9. And I wrote down the course of the thunder and lightning, and they showed me the keys, and their guardians and their path by which they go. They are brought forth in bonds, in measured degree, and are let go in bonds, lest by their heavy course and vehemence they should overload the clouds of wrath and destroy everything on earth. to. 10.I have written down the treasuries of the snow, and the store-houses of the hail, and the cool breezes. And I observed the holder of the keys of them during the season: and how he fills the clouds with them, and yet does not exhaust their treasuries. 11. I wrote down he abodes of the winds, and I observed and saw how those who hold their keys bear balances and measures, and in the first place they put them on a balance, in the second they let them go in measure moderately, with care over the whole earth, so that with their heavy breathing they should not shake the whole earth. 12. For I have measured the whole earth, its mountains and all hills, fields, trees, stone, rivers; all things that exist I have written down, the height from earth to the seventh heaven, and down to the lowest hell, the place of judgement and the mighty hell laid open, and full of lamentation. And I saw how! the prisoners suffer, awaiting the immeasurable judgement. 13. And I wrote out all of those who are being judged by the judge, and all the judgement they receive, and all their deeds.

XLI. - How Enoch wept for the Sins of Adam.

And I saw all our forefathers from the beginning with Adam and Eve, and I sighed and wept, and spake of the ruin (caused by) their wickedness: Woe is me for my infirmity and that of my forefathers. 9. And I meditated in my heart and said: Blessed is the man who was not born, or, having been born, has never sinned before the face of the Lord, so that he should not come into this place, to bear the yoke of this place!

XLII - How Enoch saw those who keep the Keys, and the Guardians of the Gates of Hades standing by.

I saw those who keep the keys, and are the guardians of the gates of hell, standing, like great serpents, and their faces were like quenched lamps, and their eyes were fiery, and their teeth were sharp. And they were stripped to the waist. 2. And I said before their faces, 'Would that I had not seen you, nor heard of your doings, and that those of my race had never come to you! Now they have only sinned a little in this life, and always suffer in the eternal life' 3. I went out to the East, to the paradise of Eden, where rest bas been prepared for the just, and it is open to the third heaven, and shut from this world. 4. And guards are placed at the very great gates of the east of the sun, i.e. fiery angels, singing triumphant songs, that never cease rejoicing in the presence of the just. 5. At the last coming they will lead forth Adam with our forefathers, and conduct them there, that they may rejoice, as a man calls those whom he loves to feast with him; and they having come with joy hold converse, before the dwelling of that man', with joy awaiting his feast, the enjoyment and the immeasurable wealth, and joy and merriment in the light, and eternal life. 6. Then I said, 'I tell you, my children: blessed is he who fears the name of the Lord, and serves continually before His face, and brings his gifts with fear continually in this life", and lives all his life justly, and dies. 7. Blessed is he who executes a just judgement, not for the sake of recompense, but for the sake of righteousness, expecting nothing in return: a sincere judgement shall afterwards come to him 8. Blessed is he who clothes the naked with a garment, and gives his bread to the hungry. 9. Blessed is he who gives a just judgement for the orphan and the widow, and assists every one who is wronged. 10. Blessed is he who turns from the unstable path of this vain world, and walks by the righteous path which leads to eternal life. 11. Blessed is he who sows just seed, he shall reap sevenfold. 12. Blessed is he in whom is the truth, that he may speak the truth to his neighbour. 13. Blessed is he who has love upon his lips, and tenderness in his heart. 14. Blessed is he who understands every work of the Lord, and glorifies the Lord God; for the works of the Lord are just, and of the works of man some are good, and others evil, and by their works those who have wrought them are known.

XLIII. - Enoch shows his Children how he measured and wrote out the Judgements of God.

Lo! my children, the things which I have gained on the earth and meditated upon from the Lord God I have written down both winter and summer. I have compiled the account of all, and concerning the years I have calculated each hour; I have measured the hours and written out the lists of them and I have ascertained all their differences. 2. As one year is more honourable than another, so is one man more honourable than another. This man on account of many possessions, that man on account of the wisdom! of the heart; this man on account of understanding, another on account of cunning; this man for the silence of the lips; this man on account of purity, that on account of strength; this man on account of comeliness, another on account of youth; this man on account of sharpness of mind, another on account of quick sightedness of body, and another for the perception of many things. 3. Let it be heard everywhere; there is no one greater than he who fears God. He shall be the most glorious for ever.

XLIV. - Enoch instructs his Sons that they should not revile the Persons of Men, whether they are great or small.

God made man with His own hands, in the likeness of His countenance, both small and great the Lord created him. He who reviles the countenance of man, reviles the countenance of the Lord. 2. He who shows wrath against another without injury, the great wrath of the Lord shall consume him. 3. If a man spits at the face of another insultingly, he shall be consumed in the great judgement of the Lord. 4. Blessed is the man who does not direct his heart with malice against any man, and who assists the man who is injured, and under judgement, and raises up the oppressed, and accomplishes the prayer of him who asks 5. For in the day of the great judgement, every measure and standard and weight, which is for traffic, namely, that which is hung on a balance and stands for traffic, knows its own measure, and shall receive its reward by measure.

.XLV. - God shows that He does not wish Sacrifices from Man, nor Burnt-Offerings, but pure and contrite Hearts

He who hastens and brings his offering before the face of the Lord, then the Lord will hasten the accomplishment of his work, and will execute a just judgement for him. 2. He who increases his lamp before the face of the Lord, the Lord increases greatly his treasure in the heavenly kingdom. 3. God does not require bread, nor a light, nor an animal, nor any other sacrifice, for it is as nothing 4. But God requires a pure heart, and by means of all this, He tries the heart of man.

XLVI. - How an earthly Prince will not receive Gifts from Man which are contemptible and impure. How much more does God loath impure Gifts, and rejects them with Wrath, and will not receive the

Gifts of such a Man.

Hear, my people, and pay attention to the words of my lips. If any one brings gifts to an earthly prince, but having unfaithfulness in his heart: if the prince knows it, will he not be angry with him on account of that, and he will not take his gifts, and will hand him over to condemnation? 2. Or if a man flatters another in his language, but (plans) evil against him in his heart, will not the other understand the craft of his heart, and he himself will be condemned, so that his unrighteousness will be evident to all? 3. But when God shall send a great light, by means of that there will be judgement to the just and unjust, and nothing will be concealed.

XLVII. - Enoch instructs his Sons from the Lips of God, and gives them the Manuscripts of this Book.

Now, my children, put my thoughts in your hearts; pay attention to the words of your father, which have come to you from the mouth of the Lord. 2. Take these books of the writings of your father, and read them, and in them ye shall learn all the works of the Lord. There have been many books from the beginning of creation, and shall be to the end of the world, but none shall make things known to you like my writings. 3. But if you shall preserve my writings, you will not sin against God. For there is no other besides the Lord, neither in heaven nor on earth, nor the depths below, nor the solitary foundations. 4. God established the foundations upon things that are unknown, and stretched out the visible and invisible heavens, and made firm the earth upon the waters, and established the waters on things that are not fixed. 4. Who has created all the innumerable works of creation? 5. Who has numbered the dust of the earth, and the sand of the sea, and the drops of rain, and the dew of the morning, and the breath of the wind? Who has bound earth and sea with bonds that cannot be broken up: and has cut the stars out of fire, and beautified® the heavens, and placed the sun in the midst of them so that).

XLVIII. - Of the course of the Sun throughout the seven Circles.

The sun goes in the seven circles of the heavens, and I gave him! 182 thrones when he goes on a short day, and also 182 thrones when he goes on a long day. 2. And he has two great thrones on which he rests, returning hither and thither above the monthly thrones. From the month Tsivan after seventeen days he descends to the month Thevan, and from the seventeenth day of Thevad he ascends. 3. And so the sun goes through all the courses of the heaven; when he goes near the earth, then the earth rejoices and produces its fruit; when he departs, then the earth is sad, and the trees and all the fruits have no development. 4. All this by measure and minute arrangement of time He has arranged by His wisdom, both in the case of things visible and invisible. 5. He has made all things visible out of invisible, Himself being invisible. 6. Thus I tell you, my children, distribute the books to your children, in all your families, and among the nations. 7. Those who are wise let them fear God, and let them receive them and let them love them more than any kind of food, and read them 8. But those who are senseless and have no thought of the Lord and do not fear God will not receive them but turn away, and keep themselves from them, the terrible judgement shall await them. 9. Blessed is the man who bears their yoke, and puts it on, for he shall be set free in the day of the great judgement.

XLIX. - Enoch instructs his Sons not to swear either by the Heaven or the Earth; and shows the Promise of God to a Man even in the Womb of his Mother.

For I swear to you my children, but I will not swear by a single oath, neither by heaven, nor by earth, nor by any other creature which God made. God said: 'There is no swearing in me, nor injustice, but truth. If there is no truth in men, let them swear by a word, yea, yea, or nay, nay. 2. But I swear to you, yea, yea, that there has not been even a man in his mother's womb, for whom a place has not been prepared for every soul; and a measure is fixed how long a man shall be tried in this world. O! my children, be not deceived! there is a place prepared there for every soul of man.

L. - How Nobody born upon the Earth can hide himself, nor are his Deeds concealed. (God) commands that he should be on the Earth a short time, endure Temptation, and Annoyance, and not injure the Widow and Orphan.

I have laid down in the writings the actions of every man, * and no one born on the earth can hide himself, nor can his deeds he concealed; I see all. 2. Now, therefore, my children, in patience and meekness accomplish the number of your days, and ye shall inherit the endless life which is to come. 3. Every wound, and every affliction, and every evil word, and attack! endure for the sake of the Lord. 4. And when you might have vengeance do not repay, either your neighbour or your enemy. For God will repay as our avenger in the day of the great judgement. Let it not be for you to take vengeance. 5. Whoever of you shall spend gold or silver for the sake of a brother, shall receive abundant treasure in the day of judgement and stretch up your hands to the orphan, the widow, and the stranger.

LI. - Enoch instructs his Sons, not to hide their Treasures upon Earth, but lids them give Alms to the Needy.

Stretch out your hands to the poor man according to your powers. 2. Do not hide your silver in the earth: assist the honest man in his affliction, and affliction shall not come upon you, in the time of your labour. 3. And whatever violent and grievous yoke shall be put upon you, endure all for the Lord's sake, and so you will receive your reward in the day of judgement. 4. Morning, afternoon, and evening, it is good to go into the house of the Lord to glorify the Creator of all. 5. Wherefore let every thing that hath breath glorify Him, and let every creature visible and invisible give forth praise.

LII. – God instructs His faithful Servants how they are to praise his Name.

Blessed is the man who opens his lips to praise the God of Sabaoth, and praises the Lord with his heart. 2. Cursed is every man who opens his lips to abuse and to calumniate his neighbour. 3. Blessed is he who opens his lips to the blessing and praise of God! 4. Cursed is he who opens his lips to swearing and blasphemy before the face of the Lord all his days. 5. Blessed is he who blesses all the works of the Lord. 6. Cursed is he who speaks ill of the works of the Lord. 7. Blessed is he who looks to raise his own hand for labour. 8. Cursed is he who looks to make use of another man's labour. 9. Blessed is he who preserves the foundations of his fathers from the beginning. 10. Cursed is he who breaks the enactments^ of his fathers. 11, Blessed is he who establishes peace and love. 12. Cursed is he who troubles those who are at peace. 13. Blessed is he who does not speak peace with his tongue, but in his heart there is peace to all! 14. Cursed is he who speaks peace with his tongue, but in his heart there is no peace. 15. For all these things in measures and in books will be revealed in the day of the great judgement.

LIII. – Let us not say that our Father is with God, and will plead for us at the Day of Judgement. For I know that a Father cannot help his Son, nor a Son a Father.

And now, my children, do not say; Our father stands before God, and prays for us (to be released) from sin; for there is no person there to help any man who has sinned. 2. You see how I have written down all the works of every man before his creation, which is done in the case of all men for ever. 3. And no man can say or unsay what I have written with my hand. For God sees all things, even the thoughts of wicked men, which lie in the storeplaces of the heart. 4. And now, my children, pay attention to all the words of your father which I say to you: that ye may not grieve afterwards and say: Our father for some cause or other, never told them to us, in the time of this folly.

LIV. – Enoch admonishes his Sons that they should give the Books to Others.

Let these books which I have given you be the inheritance of your peace: do not conceal them? but tell them to all desiring them and admonish them that they may know the works of the Lord which are very wonderful.

LV. – Here Enoch makes a Declaration to his Sons: and speaks to them with Tears: 'My children, my Hour draws near, that I should go to Heaven. Lo! Angels stand before me!'

My children, the appointed day and time have drawn near and constrain me to depart. The angels will come and stand before me on the earth awaitmg what has been ordered them. 2. In the morning I shall go to the highest heavens to my eternal habitation. 3. Therefore I tell you to do all that is good before the face of the Lord.

LVI. - Methosalem asks a Blessing of his Father; that he may give him Bread to eat.

Methosalem having answered his father Enoch said: 'If it is good in thine eyes, my father, let me put food before thy face and then, having blessed our houses and thy sons, and all thy family, let thy people be glorified by thee and then afterwards thou wilt depart, as God hath said 3. Enoch answered his son Methosalem and said: 'Hear, my child, since God has anointed me with the oil of his glory, there has been no food in me, and my soul remembers nothing of earthly pleasure nor do I desire anything earthly. [Enoch orders his Son Methosalem to call all his Brothers.

CHAPTER LVII.

But call all thy brothers, and all your families, and the elders of the people, that I may speak to them and depart as is appointed for me, 2. And Methosalem hastened, and called his brethren, Regim, Riman, Ukhan, Khermion, [Gaidal], and the elders of the people, and brought them all before the face of his father Enoch. And having blessed them, he spake to them.

LVIII. - The Instruction of Enoch to his Sons.

Listen to me, my sons. In those days when the Lord came upon the earth for the sake of Adam, and visited all his creation, which He Himself had made, 2. The Lord called all the cattle of the earth, and all creeping things, and all the fowls that fly in the air, and brought them all! before the face of our father Adam, and he gave names to all living things on the earth. 3. And the Lord made him lord over all, and put all things under his hands, and subdued (them) to submission and to all obedience to man. So the Lord created man as master over all His possessions. 4. The Lord will not judge any soul of beast on account of man, but he will judge the soul of man on account of the souls of beasts in the world to come'. 5. * For as there is a special place for mankind for all the souls of men according to their number, so there is also of beasts. And not one soul shall perish which God has made till the great judgement. 6, And every soul of beast shall bring a charge against man if he feeds them badly'.

LIX. - Enoch teaches all his Sons why they must not touch the Flesh of Cattle, because of what comes from it.

He, who acts lawlessly with regard to the souls of beasts, acts lawlessly with regard to his own soul. 2, For a man offers clean animals and makes his sacrifice that he may preserve his soul. And if he offer as a sacrifice from clean beasts and birds, he preserves his soul. 3. Everything that is given you for food, bind by the four feet: that is an atonement: he acts righteously (therein) and preserves his soul. 4. But he who kills a beast without a wonnd kills his own soul and sins against his own flesh. 5. And if any one does an injury to an animal secretly, it is an evil custom and he sins against his soul.

LX. - How we ought not to kill a Man, neither with Weapon nor with Tongue.

If he does an injury to the soul of man, he does an injury to his own soul and there is no salvation for his flesh, nor forgiveness for ever. 2. He who kills the soul of a man, kills his own soul, and destroys his own body, and there is no salvation for him for ever. 3. He who prepares a net for another man will fall into it himself and there is no salvation for him for ever. 4. He, who prepares a weapon against a man, shall not escape punishment in the great judgement for ever. 5. If a man acts crookedly or speaks evil against any soul, he shall have no righteousness for himself for ever.

LXI. - Enoch admonishes his Sons to preserve themselves from Unrighteousness, and to stretch out thew hands frequently to the Poor, and to give them something from their Labours

Now therefore, my children, preserve your hearts from every unrighteousness which the Lord hates. As a man asks his soul from God, so let him do to every living soul, 2. For in the world to come, I know all things how that! there. are many mansions prepared for men good for the good; evil for the evil many and without number. 3. Blessed are those who shall go to the mansions of the blessed for in the evil ones there is no rest nor any means of return from them. 4. Listen, my children, both small and great: When a man conceives a good thought in his heart and brings gifts before the Lord of his labours—if his hands have not wrought them then the Lord turns away His face from the labour of his hands, and he cannot gain advantage from® the work of his hand. 5. But if his hands have wrought, but his heart murmurs and he does not make an offering of his heart, but murmurs continually, he has no success.

LXII. - How it is proper to bring one's Gifts with Faith, and how there is no Repentance after Death.

Blessed is the man who in patience shall bring his gifts' before the face of the Lord, for he shall avert the recompense of his sin. 2. If he speaks words out of season there is no repentance for him: if he lets the appointed time? pass and does not perform the work, he is not' blessed; for there is no repentance after death. 3. For every deed which a man does unseasonably is an offence before men, and a sin before God.

LXIII. - How one must not despise the Humble, but give to them truly, so that thou mayest not be accursed before God.

When a man clothes the naked and feeds the hungry, he gets a recompense from God. 2. If his heart murmurs, he works for himself a double evil he works destruction to that which he gives and there shall be no reward for it: 3. And the poor man, when his heart is satisfied or his flesh is clothed and he acts contemptuously, he destroys the effect of all his endurance of poverty and shall not gain the blessing of a recompense. 4. For the Lord hates every contemptuous and proud-speaking man: and likewise every lying word: and that which is covered with unrighteousness. And it is cut with the sharpness of a deadly sword, and thrown into the fire, and burns for ever.

Section IV - Enoch's Legacy and Prophecies

The final section of 2 Enoch brings the narrative full circle, presenting Enoch's return to earth, his final words of wisdom, and prophecies for future generations. This section reflects on Enoch's transformation and the spiritual authority he has gained through his encounters with God and the angels. It portrays him not only as a visionary prophet but also as a spiritual patriarch, leaving behind a legacy of faith and moral instruction for humanity.

As Enoch prepares for his final ascension, he blesses his children and shares prophecies about the flood, divine judgment, and the destiny of the righteous and the wicked. These prophecies serve as both warnings and encouragement, calling readers to reflect on their spiritual preparedness and alignment with God's will.

This section ties together the themes of **creation, morality, and judgment**, emphasizing the **continuity of** God's plan across generations. It challenges readers to view history and prophecy as interconnected threads, reminding them of their responsibility to act as stewards of righteousness and bearers of divine truth.

LXIV. - How the Lord calls Enoch: the People take Counsel to go to kiss him in the Place called Achuzan.

When Enoch said these words to his sons, and the princes of the people, all the people far and near heard how the Lord called Enoch. And they took counsel, and they all said: 'Let us go and kiss Enoch!' 2. And the men assembled to the number of 20005, and came to the place Achuzan, where Enoch was, and his sons. 3. And the elders of the people came together and made obeisance and kissed Enoch, and said to him: 'Enoch, our father be thou blessed of the Lord, the eternal King!' 4. And now bless thy sons, and all the people, that we may be glorified before thee today. 5. For thou art glorified before the face of the Lord for ever; since God has chosen thee above all men upon the earth, and has appointed thee as the scribe of His creation of visible and invisible things, and an avenger of the sins of men, and a succour to thy family! And Enoch answered all his people saying.

LXV. - Of the Exhortation of Enoch to his Sons.

Listen, my children: before that anything existed and all creatures were made, the Lord made 1 all things both visible and invisible. 2. When the times of these things had come and were passed, understand how! after all these things He made man in His own image after His likeness, and placed in him eyes to see; and ears to hear; and a heart to understand, and reason to take counsel. 3. And the Lord contemplated the world for the sake of man, and made all the creation for his sake and divided it into times. And from the times He made years, and from the years He made months, and from the months He made days, and of the days He made seven. 4. And in these He made the hours and divided them into small portions, that a man should understand the seasons, and compute years and months, and hours; their alternations and beginnings and ends: and® that he should compute his life from the beginning till death, and should meditate upon his sin, and should write down his evil and good deeds. 5. For nothing done is concealed before the Lord. Let each man know his deeds, and not transgress the commandments and let him keep My writings securely from generation to generation'. 6. When all the creation of visible and invisible things comes to an end which the Lord has made; then every man shall come to the great judgement of the Lord. 7. Then the times shall perish, and there shall be no year, nor month, nor day, and there shall be no hours nor shall they be reckoned. 8. There shall be one eternity, and all the just who shall escape the great judgement of the Lord shall be gathered together in eternal life and for ever and ever the just shall be gathered together and they shall be eternal. 9. Moreover there shall be no labour, nor sickness, nor sorrow, nor anxiety, nor need*, nor night, nor darkness, but a great® light. 10. And there shall be to them a great wall that cannot be broken down; and bright and incorruptible paradise shall be their protection, and their eternal habitation. For all corruptible things shall vanish, and there shall be eternal life.

LXVI. - Enoch instructs his Sons, and all the Elders of the People: how with Fear and Trembling they ought to walk before the Lord, and serve Him alone, and not to worship Idols; for God made Heaven and Earth and every Creature and its form.

And now, my children, preserve your souls from all unrighteousness, which the Lord hates. Walk before His face with fear and trembling, and serve Him alone. Worship the true God, and not dumb idols. 2. But pay attention to His command, and bring every just offering before the face of the Lord. But the Lord hates that which is unrighteous. 3. For the Lord sees every thing; whatever man meditates in his heart, and what counsel he plans, and every thought is continually before the Lord. 4. If ye look at the heavens there is the Lord, as the Lord made the heavens. If ye look at the earth then the Lord is there since the Lord made firm the earth and established every creature in it. If ye scrutinize the depths of the sea, and every thing under the earth there also is the Lord. For the Lord created all things. 5. Do not bow down to the work of men, nor to the work of the Lord 4, leaving the Lord of all creation; for no deed is concealed before the face of the Lord. 6. Walk, my children, in long suffering, in humility, in spite of calumny, and insult; in faith, and truth: in the promises, and sickness, in abuse, in wounds, in temptation, in nakedness, in deprivation, loving one another, till ye depart from this world of sickness. Then ye shall be heirs of eternity. 7. Blessed are the just, who shall escape the great judgement! And they shall be seven times brighter than the sun, for in this age altogether the seventh part is separated. 8. (Now concerning) the light, the darkness, the food, the sweetnesses, the bitternesses, the paradise, the tortures, the fires, the frosts and other things; I have put all this down in writing, that ye may read and understand.

LXVII. – Ze Lord sent a Darkness upon the Earth, and covered the People and Enoch; and he was taken up on high; and there was Light in the Heavens.

When Enoch had discoursed with the people, the Lord sent a darkness upon the earth, and there was a gloom, and it hid those men standing? with Enoch. 2. And the angels hasted and took Enoch and carried him to the highest heaven where the Lord® received him, and set him before His face, and the darkness departed from the earth, and there was light. 3. And the people saw and did not understand, how Enoch was taken, and they glorified God. And they * who had seen such things departed to their houses.

CHAPTER LXVIII.

Enoch was born on the sixth day of the month Tsivan! he lived 365 years. He was taken up into heaven on the first day of the month Tsivan, and he was in heaven sixty days. 2. He wrote down the descriptions of all the creation which the Lord had made, and he wrote 366 books, and gave them to his sons. 3. And he was on earth thirty days, and thus he was taken to heaven in the same month Tsivan on the same day the sixth day; the day on which he was born, and the same hour. 4. As each man has but a dark existence in this life, so also is his beginning and birth, and departure from this life. In what hour he began ; in that he was born, and in that he departs 5. And Methusalem hasted, and all his brethren, the sons of Enoch, and built an altar in the place called Achuzan, whence and when Enoch was taken up to heaven. 6. And they took cattle, and invited all the people and sacrificed victims before the face of the Lord. 7. All the people came and the elders of the people; all the host of them to the festivity, and brought their gifts to the sons of Enoch, and made a great festivity, rejoicing and being merry for three days; praising God who had given such a sign by means of Enoch, who had found favour with Him. And that they should hand it down to their son's sons, from generation to generation, for ever. Amen.

CONCLUSION TO THE SECOND BOOK OF ENOCH

The *Second Book of Enoch* stands as a powerful and enduring exploration of divine mysteries, cosmic order, and moral responsibility. It weaves together elements of **apocalyptic vision, philosophical reflection**, and **ethical instruction**, offering readers a rich tapestry of themes that resonate across time and cultures. By chronicling Enoch's extraordinary journey through the **heavens**, the text not only provides a window into ancient Jewish mysticism but also challenges readers to reflect deeply on their own spiritual paths and moral convictions.

Through its portrayal of **Enoch's ascent to the heavenly realms**, the text serves as both a **spiritual allegory** and a **cosmic revelation**, demonstrating humanity's potential for divine communion. It presents Enoch as a model of faithfulness, humility, and obedience, qualities that enable his transformation from a mortal being to a **heavenly figure**, entrusted with divine secrets. His journey mirrors the universal quest for **wisdom and enlightenment**, reminding readers of the importance of seeking higher truths while remaining grounded in righteousness and integrity.

The themes of **creation and divine wisdom** highlight the intricacy of God's design and emphasize humanity's role as **caretakers of creation**. By exploring the **structure of the cosmos** and the **laws of time and nature**, the text encourages readers to contemplate the interconnectedness of **physical and spiritual realities**. This reflection serves as a reminder that understanding the world's order is not only an intellectual pursuit but also a **spiritual discipline** that draws us closer to the Creator.

In its **moral teachings**, *2 Enoch* provides timeless guidance for living a life of **justice, compassion, and humility**. It calls readers to embrace **ethical living**, resist **temptations**, and prepare for **divine judgment**, reinforcing the idea that righteousness is both a **personal commitment** and a **communal responsibility**. The book's emphasis on **accountability** and **repentance** offers hope for renewal and transformation, making it as relevant today as it was to its earliest readers.

The **final chapters**, focusing on **Enoch's legacy and prophecies**, leave readers with a profound sense of continuity in God's plan for creation. The text's vision of **judgment and redemption** underscores the enduring tension between **good and evil** and offers a roadmap for navigating this struggle with faith and perseverance. Enoch's legacy serves as a **bridge between heaven and earth**, inspiring generations to live in alignment with divine law while looking forward to the fulfillment of God's ultimate promises.

For readers who are captivated by the mysteries and insights of *2 Enoch*, the journey does not have to end here. The exploration of **angelic hierarchies, divine order**, and **mystical visions** continues in the *Third Book of Enoch* (*3 Enoch*), a text that expands upon themes of **heavenly transformation** and **angelology**. It offers further revelations about the **heavenly realms** and **Enoch's transformation into Metatron, the angelic scribe**. Those seeking a deeper understanding of **Jewish mysticism** and **apocalyptic thought** will find *3 Enoch* to be a compelling companion, enriching their exploration of divine mysteries.

In closing, the *Second Book of Enoch* leaves readers with a lasting impression of **divine majesty**, **cosmic harmony**, and **moral accountability**. It challenges us to look beyond the material world, to seek **spiritual elevation**, and to embrace the **wisdom of the heavens** as we navigate our own journeys of **faith and transformation**. Whether approached as a historical artifact, a theological exploration, or a spiritual guide, *2 Enoch* continues to inspire and enlighten, reminding us that the path to divine understanding is both **timeless** and **transformative**.

3 ENOCH
INTRODUCTION

HISTORICAL CONTEXT

The Third Book of Enoch, also known as 3 Enoch or Sefer Hekhalot, is a foundational text of early Jewish mysticism, attributed to Rabbi Ishmael, a high priest and visionary. Written between the 3rd and 6th centuries CE, it stands as one of the most significant works within the Merkabah (Chariot) tradition, which explores themes of heavenly ascension, angelology, and divine authority. Unlike 1 Enoch and 2 Enoch, which are rooted in apocalyptic prophecy and cosmic judgment, 3 Enoch focuses on mystical ascent and spiritual transformation, aligning closely with the Hekhalot literature, a corpus of Jewish texts that describe journeys through celestial palaces and encounters with angelic beings. The book presents a detailed account of Rabbi Ishmael's visionary experiences, chronicling his ascent through the heavens and his witness to the transformation of Enoch into Metatron, the Prince of the Presence and highest-ranking angelic being.

As a bridge between ancient Jewish apocalyptic traditions and emerging mystical theology, 3 Enoch provides a unique window into the esoteric dimensions of Jewish spirituality. It reflects the spiritual aspirations of Jewish mystics who, in the absence of the Temple in Jerusalem, sought a direct connection with God through visions, sacred names, and heavenly journeys. The text offers glimpses into divine secrets and celestial hierarchies, presenting a structured vision of the angelic order and the mechanisms of divine governance. While its origins are firmly rooted in Jewish tradition, its mystical themes influenced later Christian and Islamic esoteric thought, particularly in discussions of divine ascent, angelic mediation, and the role of hidden knowledge in spiritual transformation.

The historical period in which 3 Enoch emerged was marked by Roman rule, the dispersion of Jewish communities, and the development of rabbinic traditions. In this era, mystical experiences became an essential means for Jewish mystics to compensate for the loss of the Temple, allowing them to experience divine presence outside of ritual sacrifices. The text reflects this longing for spiritual intimacy through its vivid descriptions of heavenly realms, angelic orders, and cosmic mysteries. It also mirrors broader philosophical and religious influences, particularly Platonic cosmology and Gnostic thought, which emphasized hidden knowledge, divine emanations, and the ascent of the soul toward enlightenment. However, 3 Enoch remains distinctly Jewish in its theology, emphasizing monotheism, Torah-based wisdom, and covenantal faithfulness. The transformation of Enoch into Metatron symbolizes the human potential for divine elevation, reinforcing the belief that obedience, purity, and devotion lead to a higher spiritual state.

Unlike earlier Enochian texts, which center around prophetic visions and cosmic judgments, 3 Enoch introduces a new mystical paradigm—one in which the soul ascends through celestial spheres, encounters angelic guardians, and attains secret knowledge.

The journey through the seven heavenly palaces represents the progression of the soul toward divine enlightenment, where each stage of ascent is guarded by powerful angelic beings. Enoch's transformation into Metatron serves as both a theological revelation and a metaphor for spiritual elevation, demonstrating that through divine grace, the human soul can achieve transcendence. This mystical framework addresses complex theological questions about the relationship between God and humanity, presenting Metatron as a mediator—a figure who exists between the divine and the created world, facilitating spiritual ascent and divine revelation.

One of the key aspects of 3 Enoch is its emphasis on sacred names, ritual purity, and celestial worship, all of which play essential roles in accessing divine mysteries. The text repeatedly stresses that language holds intrinsic spiritual power, particularly in the use of divine names and angelic invocations, a concept that would later be expanded upon in Kabbalistic thought. The book also describes the angelic liturgies sung before the divine throne, reinforcing the idea that worship and praise are central to maintaining cosmic order. Through these descriptions, 3 Enoch provides a detailed vision of divine hierarchy, where angels are both messengers and cosmic functionaries, executing the divine will and guarding the celestial realms.

The influence of 3 Enoch extends far beyond early Jewish mysticism. Its themes and symbolic structures deeply shaped later Kabbalistic writings, particularly regarding the sefirot (divine emanations) and the angelic governance of creation. Its impact can also be seen in Christian and Islamic mystical traditions, where concepts of heavenly ascent, angelic hierarchies, and hidden knowledge continue to be central to mystical theology. The figure of Metatron, in particular, became a subject of fascination in later mystical traditions, often viewed as a divine scribe, a heavenly priest, or even a lesser manifestation of divine presence.

For contemporary readers, 3 Enoch offers both a historical insight into early mystical practices and a profound theological exploration of divine mysteries. Its descriptions of heavenly courts, celestial palaces, and angelic orders provide a structured vision of the divine realm, while its mystical ascent narrative offers a spiritual roadmap for seekers of hidden knowledge.

Through its intricate blend of cosmology, theology, and esotericism, 3 Enoch continues to inspire scholars, mystics, and those drawn to the deeper dimensions of faith, serving as a timeless testament to humanity's pursuit of transcendence and divine union.

INTRODUCTION

KEY THEMES

The Third Book of Enoch presents readers with profound insights into heavenly mysteries, divine authority, and the cosmic order governing creation. It delves into theological and mystical concepts that challenge human understanding and invite contemplation of the spiritual hierarchy that connects humanity to God. The key themes explored in this text build upon earlier apocalyptic traditions but push further into mystical exploration, offering new dimensions of insight into the heavenly realms and divine governance.

One of the central themes of 3 Enoch is Heavenly Ascension and Transformation. Rabbi Ishmael's visionary journey through the heavens reflects a profound spiritual ascent, symbolizing the soul's pursuit of divine closeness and ultimate transformation. The text recounts Ishmael's encounter with Enoch, who has been elevated to the rank of the angel Metatron, marking the transition from mortal prophet to heavenly being. This transformation emphasizes the concept of divine selection and glorification, portraying Enoch as a figure who embodies faithfulness, purity, and divine favor. His elevation prefigures theological concepts of resurrection, glorification, and eternal life, themes that resonate deeply within Jewish mysticism and later Christian eschatology.

Closely tied to this theme is the exploration of Divine Authority and Angelology. The text provides a detailed hierarchy of angels and celestial beings, each assigned specific roles in executing God's commands and maintaining cosmic order. Metatron, as the Prince of the Presence, exemplifies both submission and authority, reflecting God's sovereignty over creation while also acting as a mediator between heaven and earth. The book highlights the functions of angels as guardians, record-keepers, and worshippers, underscoring their role in facilitating divine will and enforcing moral and cosmic law. These descriptions offer readers a glimpse into the spiritual bureaucracy governing the universe, illustrating the harmony and precision with which divine authority operates.

The theme of Mystical Knowledge and Secrets permeates the narrative, as Metatron reveals the hidden truths of creation, the names of God, and the mechanisms of divine judgment. These revelations emphasize the importance of sacred knowledge in accessing divine mysteries, presenting language and symbols as powerful tools for understanding and influencing the spiritual realm. Through esoteric teachings, the text challenges readers to look beyond material existence and seek deeper, spiritual understanding, positioning knowledge as both a privilege and a responsibility granted to the righteous.

Another key theme is Judgment and Worship, which portrays heaven as a realm of perpetual praise and divine justice. The angels continuously glorify God, reinforcing the message that worship is central to maintaining cosmic order and expressing devotion. At the same time, the depiction of divine judgment reminds readers of their moral accountability and the consequences of sin. This focus on praise and submission highlights the relationship between obedience and harmony, teaching readers that true worship is both an act of reverence and a means of alignment with divine law.

3 Enoch explores The Power of Names and Language, presenting sacred words and divine names as keys to spiritual authority and creative power. The text describes how the names of God hold the essence of divine attributes, serving as conduits for creation, judgment, and spiritual transformation. By emphasizing the mystical significance of letters, names, and sounds, it illustrates how language itself functions as a bridge between heaven and earth, embodying the divine authority that sustains existence.

Through these interconnected themes, the Third Book of Enoch offers readers a theological framework for understanding the mysteries of creation, the hierarchy of spiritual beings, and the transformative power of divine encounters. It challenges readers to view heavenly ascent not just as a literal journey but as a symbolic process of spiritual growth, moral purification, and alignment with divine will. The text's emphasis on mystical knowledge, angelic order, and divine judgment ensures its enduring relevance, providing both spiritual guidance and philosophical insight for those seeking a deeper understanding of their place within God's creation.

THEOLOGICAL AND SYMBOLIC INSIGHTS

The Third Book of Enoch offers a profound theological meditation on both the transcendence and immanence of God, presenting a vision of the divine majesty that is simultaneously awe-inspiring and deeply personal. Unlike traditional apocalyptic texts that focus primarily on eschatological judgment and cosmic destruction, 3 Enoch instead reveals a structured and ordered universe, governed by angelic hierarchies, divine authority, and the mysteries of heavenly ascension. It emphasizes spiritual transformation, illustrating the potential for mortals to ascend to divine status through purity, faith, and obedience—a concept embodied in the transformation of Enoch into Metatron, the Prince of the Presence.

Metatron serves as the ultimate bridge between the human and divine realms, an exalted figure who transcends mortality yet remains distinct from the divine essence itself. His elevation from a righteous human to the highest angelic being mirrors the spiritual aspirations of Jewish mysticism, where the path to enlightenment involves an increasing alignment with divine will. His role as divine scribe and celestial mediator symbolizes not only authority but also intercession, reinforcing the belief that obedience and devotion can lead to direct communion with the divine. In this way, 3 Enoch does not merely depict the hidden structure of heaven, but also provides a spiritual roadmap for those who seek transformation.

The intricate hierarchies of angels described in the text illustrate a cosmic order in which every being has a purpose and role, reinforcing the notion that the universe operates according to divine precision and structured governance. This angelic framework, with its strict divisions of power, function, and responsibility, serves as a metaphor for spiritual refinement, where different levels of purity and enlightenment allow souls to ascend toward greater proximity to the divine throne. The portrayal of heavenly courts, celestial palaces, and the divine chariot (Merkabah) reflects not only the splendor of the divine realm, but also its meticulously maintained balance, where justice and harmony prevail over chaos.

Another key theme in 3 Enoch is the mystical power of language and sacred names, a concept deeply embedded in Jewish esoteric traditions. Divine speech is not merely a means of communication but a force of creation itself—the articulation of sacred names holds the power to shape reality, command angels, and reveal hidden knowledge. This linguistic mysticism, seen in the use of divine titles, angelic invocations, and secret utterances, underscores the belief that true wisdom is accessed not only through knowledge but through direct engagement with the sacred words of creation. Through its exploration of language as a transformative tool, 3 Enoch elevates the role of prayer, incantation, and divine revelation as essential pathways to spiritual elevation and enlightenment.

Beyond its mystical themes, the text reinforces the duality of judgment and redemption, offering a vision of divine justice that is both absolute and restorative. The celestial hierarchies function not only as guardians of divine order but also as agents of cosmic restoration, ensuring that righteousness is rewarded and transgression is punished. However, alongside these depictions of strict divine authority, 3 Enoch also conveys a sense of hope and renewal, portraying divine mercy as an ever-present force within the cosmic order. This delicate balance between judgment and redemption, authority and grace, reflects a theological vision where human destiny is not fixed but shaped by the pursuit of divine wisdom and spiritual purity.

Through its rich symbolism, intricate cosmology, and emphasis on mystical ascent, 3 Enoch provides not only a theological framework for understanding the divine realm but also a transformative vision of what it means to seek and embody divine presence. It challenges readers to consider their own place within this cosmic hierarchy, inviting them to reflect on the nature of spiritual refinement, the power of sacred language, and the possibility of ultimate union with the divine.

MODERN APPLICATIONS

The Third Book of Enoch continues to captivate readers today with its profound exploration of spiritual ascent, divine transformation, and mystical knowledge. Unlike purely prophetic or apocalyptic texts, 3 Enoch offers a structured vision of the celestial realms, presenting a detailed account of angelic hierarchies, sacred language, and the mechanisms of divine governance. Its intricate cosmology and emphasis on humanity's potential for spiritual elevation make it an essential text for those engaged in Jewish mysticism, angelology, and Kabbalistic studies. The text provides not only theological insights into the nature of divine authority but also practical guidance for those seeking to understand their place within the cosmic order. By portraying spiritual ascension as a transformative journey, 3 Enoch challenges its readers to explore the deeper dimensions of faith, divine favor, and the pursuit of higher wisdom.

For theologians and scholars of religious history, 3 Enoch serves as a critical link between early Jewish mysticism and later esoteric traditions, illuminating the development of Merkabah mysticism and its eventual influence on Kabbalistic thought. The text's depictions of heavenly ascent, angelic authority, and the role of sacred names reflect ideas that would later be expanded upon in medieval and Renaissance mystical traditions. By examining its portrayal of Metatron as the highest angelic being, scholars gain deeper insights into the evolution of theological concepts surrounding divine mediation and the human potential for spiritual transformation. Its reflections on cosmic order and moral accountability also provide valuable context for understanding the broader apocalyptic and mystical currents of Second Temple Judaism, as well as their impact on early Christian and Islamic mystical thought.

Beyond its academic significance, 3 Enoch remains an inspirational text for modern spiritual seekers, offering a framework for personal transformation and divine connection. It urges individuals to reflect on their relationship with God, the discipline of prayer, and the power of divine names, emphasizing that spiritual wisdom is not reserved for an elite few but is accessible to those who seek it with humility and devotion. The text reinforces the idea that spiritual ascent requires discipline, purification, and faith, encouraging readers to cultivate a deeper awareness of divine presence and the sacred structures governing the universe.

In an age where many seek spiritual meaning beyond institutional religion, 3 Enoch offers a pathway into the mystical dimensions of faith, reminding its readers that humanity is not bound by the material world alone but is invited to ascend toward divine knowledge and enlightenment. Whether studied as a historical document, a mystical manual, or a visionary guide, 3 Enoch continues to inspire intellectual curiosity, spiritual refinement, and the pursuit of hidden wisdom, ensuring its relevance across generations and diverse traditions.

EDITORIAL NOTE ON STRUCTURE AND INTRODUCTIONS

To enhance the accessibility and comprehension of The Third Book of Enoch, this edition has been structured with thematic divisions, each accompanied by a contextual introduction. While the original manuscript does not contain these structured sections, they have been introduced to provide historical background, theological insights, and interpretative context, helping readers navigate the complex mystical themes, angelic hierarchies, and celestial ascent narratives found within 3 Enoch.

The introductions to each section have been newly written for this edition, offering clarity and deeper engagement with the text. These additions aim to bridge the gap between early Jewish mysticism and modern readers, ensuring that both scholars and those new to apocryphal literature can explore the spiritual depth and esoteric wisdom of 3 Enoch. The core text remains unaltered, preserving its authenticity and theological significance while presenting it in a way that facilitates study and reflection.

By structuring the text in this way, this edition seeks to provide a guided exploration of 3 Enoch, allowing readers to engage more deeply with its mystical revelations, discussions of divine authority, and visions of spiritual transformation while maintaining its place as a cornerstone of Jewish esoteric tradition.

STRUCTURE OF THE BOOK

The Third Book of Enoch unfolds in four thematic parts, each offering readers profound insights into divine mysteries, angelic hierarchies, and cosmic order. These sections present a structured progression from heavenly visions to mystical revelations, providing a roadmap for spiritual transformation and exploration.

1. Section 1: The Revelation of Metatron (Chapters 1–7)

The opening section introduces readers to Rabbi Ishmael's ascent into the heavenly realms, guided by divine visions and angelic messengers. It sets the tone for the journey, revealing the transition of Enoch into Metatron, the most exalted of all angels. This transformation represents the culmination of faith, purity, and divine favor, establishing Enoch as the Prince of the Presence—a figure imbued with divine authority and tasked with overseeing the heavenly host. Through Rabbi Ishmael's encounters, readers gain insight into the hierarchical structure of the heavens, preparing them for deeper revelations about divine mysteries.

2. Section 2: Transformation into an Angelic Being (Chapters 8–15)

In this section, the narrative delves into Enoch's glorification and transformation as he takes on his new identity as Metatron. The text describes his radiant form, his robes of light, and his crown of glory, symbolic of his divine appointment. This part emphasizes themes of spiritual elevation, portraying Enoch's ascent as a metaphor for purity, obedience, and divine union. The transformation also raises theological questions about human potential for divinity and the path of righteousness required to achieve such exaltation. Readers are invited to reflect on their own spiritual journeys, aspiring to embody faithfulness and humility as pathways to transformation.

3. Section 3: Visions of the Divine Throne (Chapters 16–30)

This section shifts focus to the magnificence of God's Throne of Glory and the heavenly realms surrounding it. Rabbi Ishmael witnesses the angelic hosts, the worship of God, and the celestial order that sustains the universe. The visions highlight the majesty of God's sovereignty and the unwavering devotion of the angels, portraying heaven as a realm of eternal worship and justice. This part also explores the cosmic balance maintained by angelic beings, emphasizing themes of order, obedience, and divine harmony. The reader is drawn into the splendor of the divine throne room, reflecting on the majesty of creation and humanity's place within this divine order.

4. Section 4: Mystical Hierarchies and Heavenly Realms (Chapters 31–48)

The final section provides a detailed exploration of the heavenly hierarchies and the mechanisms of divine governance. It examines the roles of angels, their duties as messengers and enforcers of divine law, and the judgment processes that ensure cosmic justice. The text also delves into esoteric knowledge, revealing sacred names of God, the power of divine language, and the spiritual laws that govern creation. This section bridges the mystical and the theological, inviting readers to reflect on the sacredness of knowledge and the discipline required to approach divine mysteries.

Readers are left with an appreciation of the complexity of the divine order and a sense of wonder and awe at the mysteries revealed. The book concludes by affirming God's sovereignty and the eternal nature of divine justice, while challenging readers to pursue deeper spiritual understanding and personal transformation in their own journeys of faith.

HEBREW BOOK OF PALACES

THE ASCENT TO DIVINE MYSTERIES

Section I - The Revelation of Metatron

This first section draws readers into the heavenly realms through Rabbi Ishmael's mystical vision. As he embarks on his journey, the mortal world fades, and the spiritual dimensions of the universe are revealed. The encounter with Metatron establishes the framework for the exploration of divine authority and angelic transformation, preparing readers for deeper insights into heavenly hierarchies.

CHAPTER I

When I ascended on high to behold the vision of the Merkaba and had entered the six Halls, one within the other: as soon as I reached the door of the seventh Hall I stood still in prayer before the Holy One, blessed be He, and, lifting up my eyes on high, I said : " Lord of the Universe, I pray thee, that the merit of Aaron, the son of Amram, the lover of peace and pursuer of peace, who received the crown of priesthood from Thy Glory on the mount of Sinai, be valid for me in this hour, so that Qafsiel*, the prince, and the angels with him may not get power over me nor throw me down from the heavens ". Forthwith the Holy One, blessed be He, sent to me Metatron, his Servant the angel, the Prince of the Presence, and he, spreading his wings, with great joy came to meet me so as to save me from their hand. And he took me by his hand in their sight, saying to me: "Enter in peace before the high and exalted King3 and behold the picture of the Merkaba". Then I entered the seventh Hall, and he led me to the campof Shekina and placed me before 6the Holy One, blessed be He, to behold the Merkaba. As soon as the princes of the Merkaba and the flaming Seraphim perceived me, they fixed their eyes upon me. Instantly trembling and shuddering seized me and I fell down and was benumbed by the radiant image of their eyes and the splendid appearance of their faces; until the Holy One, blessed be He, rebuked them, saying: "My servants, my Seraphim, my Kerubim and my 'Ophanniml Cover ye your eyes before Ishmael, my son, my friend, my beloved one and my glory, that he tremble not nor shudder !" Forthwith Metatron the Prince of the Presence, came and restored my spiritand put me upon my feet. After that there was notin me strength enough to say a song before the Throne of Glory of the glorious King, the mightiest of all kings, the most excellent of all princes, until after the hour had passed. After one hour the Holy One, blessed be He, opened to me the gates of Shekina, the gates of Peace, the gates of Wisdom, the gates of Strength, the gates of Power, the gates of Speech, the gates of Song, the gates of Qedushsha, the gates of Chant.

And he enlightened my eyes and my heart by words of psalm, song, praise, exaltation, thanksgiving, extolment, glorification, hymn and eulogy. And as I opened my mouth, uttering a song before the Holy One, blessed be He, the Holy Chayyoth beneath and above the Throne of Glory answered and said : "HOLY " and "BLESSED BE THE GLORY OF YHWH FROM HIS PLACE !"

CHAPTER II

In that hour the eagles of the Merkaba, the flaming 'Ophannim and the Seraphim of consuming fire asked Metatron, saying to him: "Youth ! Why sufferest thou one born of woman to enter and behold the Merkaba? From which nation, from which tribe is this one? What is his character?" Metatron answered and said to them : "From the nation of Israel whom the Holy One, blessed be He, chose for his people from among seventy tongues, from the tribe of Levi, whom he set aside as a contribution to his name and from the seed of Aaron whom the Holy One, blessed be He, did choose for his servant and put upon him the crown of priesthood on Sinai". Forthwith they spake and said: "Indeed, this one is worthy to behold the Merkaba ". And they said: "Happy is the people that is in such a case!".

CHAPTER III

In that hour1 I asked Metatron, the angel, the Prince of the Presence: "What is thy name?" He answered me: "I have seventy names, corresponding to the seventy tongues of the world and all of them are based upon the name Metatron, angel of the Presence; but my King calls me 'Youth' "

CHAPTER IV

I asked Metatron and said to him: "Why art thou called by the name of thy Creator, by seventy names? Thou art greater than all the princes, higher than all the angels, beloved more than all the servants, honoured above all the mighty ones in kingship, greatness and glory : why do they call thee ' Youth ' in the high heavens ?" He answered and said to me: " Because I am Enoch, the son of Jared. For when the generation of the flood sinned and were confounded in their deeds, saying unto God: 'Depart from us, for we desire not the knowledge of thy ways', then the Holy One, blessed be He, removed me from their midst to be a witness against them in the high heavens to all the inhabitants of the world, that they may not say: 'The Merciful One is cruel". What sinned all those multitudes, their wives, their sons and their, daughters, their horses, their mules and their cattle and their property, and all the birds of the world, all of which the Holy One, blessed be He, destroyed from the world together with them in the waters of the flood? Hence the Holy One, blessed be He, lifted me up in their lifetime before their eyes to be a witness against them to the future world. And the Holy One, blessed be He, assigned me for a prince and a ruler among the ministering angels. In that hour three of the ministering angels, 'UZZA, 'AZZA and 'AZZAEL came forth and brought charges against me in the high heavens, saying before the Holy One, blessed be He: "Said not the Ancient Ones rightly before Thee: < Do not create man! ' " The Holy One, blessed be He, answered and said unto them: "I have made and I will bear, yea, I will carry and will deliver". As soon as they saw me, they said before Him: "Lord of the Universe! What is this one that he should ascend to the height of heights? Is not he one from among the sons of those who perished in the days of the Flood? "What doeth he in the Raqia'?" Again, the Holy One, blessed be He, answered and said to them: "What are ye, that ye enter and speak in my presence? I delight in this one more than in all of you, and hence he shall be a prince and a ruler over you in the high heavens." Forthwith all stood up and went out to meet me, prostrated themselves before me and said: "Happy art thou and happy is thy father for thy Creator doth favour thee". And because I am small and a youth among them in days, months and years, therefore they call me "Youth".

CHAPTER V

From the day when the Holy One, blessed be He, expelled the first Adam from the Garden of Eden, Shekina was dwelling upon a Kerub under the Tree of Life. And the ministering angels were gathering together and going down from heaven in parties, from the Raqia in companies and from the heavens in camps to do His will in the whole world. And the first man and his generation were sitting outside the gate of the Garden to behold the radiant appearance of the Shekina. For the silendour of the Shekina traversed the world from one end to the other 365,000 times of the globe of the sun. And everyone who made use of the splendour of the Shekina, on him no flies and no gnats did rest, neither was he ill nor suffered he any pain. No demons got power over him, neither were they able to injure him. When the Holy One, blessed be He, went out and went in: from the Garden to Eden, from Eden to the Garden, from the Garden to Raqia and from Raqia to the Garden of Eden then all and everyone beheld the splendour of His Shekina and they were not injured; until uthe time of the generation of Enosh who was the head of all idol worshippers of the world. And what did the generation of Enosh do? They went from one end of the world to the other, and each one brought silver, gold, precious stones and pearls in heaps like unto mountains and hills making idols out of them throughout all the world. And they erected the idols in every quarter of the world: the size of each idol was 1000 parasangs. And they brought down the sun, the moon, planets and constellations, and placed them before the idols on their right hand and on their left, to attend them even as they attend the Holy One, blessed be He, as it is written: "And all the host of heaven was standing by him on his right hand and on his left". What power was in them that they were able to bring them down? They would not have been able to bring them down but for 'Uzza, 'Azza and 'Azziel who taught them sorceries whereby they brought them down and made use of them In that time the ministering angels brought charges before the Holy One, blessed be He, saying before him: "Master of the World! What hast thou to do with the children of men? As it is written 'What is man that thou art mindful of him?' 'Mah Adam' is not written here, but 'Mah Enosh', for he is the head of the idol worshippers. Why hast thou left the highest of the high heavens, the abode of thy glorious Name, and the high and exalted Throne in 'Araboth Raqia' in the highest and art gone and dwellest with the children of men who worship idols and equal thee to the idols. Now thou art on earth and the idols likewise. What hast thou to do with the inhabitants of the earth who worship idols?" Forthwith the Holy One, blessed be He, lifted up His Shekina from the earth, from their midst. In that moment came the ministering angels, the troops of hosts and the armies of 'Araboth in thousand camps and ten thousand hosts: they fetched trumpets and took the horns in their hands and surrounded the Shekina with all kinds of songs. And He ascended to the high heavens, as it is written: "God is gone up with a shout, the Lord with the sound of a trumpet"

CHAPTER VI

When the Holy One, blessed be He, desired to lift me up on high, He first sent 'Anaphiel H the Prince, and he took me from their midst in their sight and carried me in great glory upon a a fiery chariot with fiery horses, servants of glory. And he lifted me up to the high heavens together with the Shekina. As soon as I reached the high heavens, the Holy Chayyoth, the 'Ophannim, the Seraphim, the Kerubim, the Wheels of the Merkaba, and the ministers of the consuming fire, perceiving my smell from a distance of 365,000 myriads of parasangs, said: "What smell of one born of woman and what taste of a white drop that ascends on high, and a gnat among those who 'divide flames'?" The Holy One, blessed be He, answered and spake unto them: "My servants, my hosts, my Kerubim, my 'Ophannim, my Seraphim! Be ye not displeased on account of this! Since all the children of men have denied me and my great Kingdom and are gone worshipping idols, I have removed my Shekina from among them and have lifted it up on high. But this one whom I have taken from among them is an ELECT ONE among the world and he is equal to all of them in faith, righteousness and perfection of deed and I have taken him fo a tribute from my world under all the heavens".

CHAPTER VII

When the Holy One, blessed be He, took me away from the generation of the Flood, he lifted me on the wings of the wind of Shekina to the highest heaven and brought me into the great palaces of the 'Araboth Raqia' on high, where are the glorious Throne of Shekina, the Merkaba, the troops of anger, the armies of vehemence, the fiery Shin'anim', the flaming Kerubim, and the burning 'Ophannim, the flaming servants, the flashing Chashmattim and the lightening Seraphim. And he placed me to attend the Throne of Glory day after day.

Section II - Trasformation Into an Angelic Being

This section expands upon Enoch's transformation into the radiant angel Metatron. It challenges readers to reflect on the possibility of spiritual elevation, exploring how obedience, faith, and divine favor lead to glorification. The narrative provides a template for transformation, encouraging introspection on personal growth and alignment with divine principles.

CHAPTER VIII

Before He appointed me to attend the Throne of Glory, the Holy One, blessed be He, opened to me three hundred thousand gates of Understanding three hundred thousand gates of Subtlety three hundred thousand gates of Life three hundred thousand gates of grace and loving-kindness three hundred thousand gates of love three hundred thousand gates of Tora three hundred thousand gates of meekness three hundred thousand gates of maintenance three hundred thousand gates' of mercy three hundred thousand gates of fear of heaven In that hour the Holy One, blessed be He, added in me wisdom unto wisdom, understanding unto understanding, subtlety unto subtlety, knowledge unto knowledge, mercy unto mercy, instruction unto instruction, love unto love, loving-kindness unto loving-kindness, goodness unto goodness, meekness unto meekness, power unto power, strength unto strength, might unto might, brilliance unto brilliance, beauty unto beauty, splendour unto splendour, and I was honoured and adorned with all these good and praiseworthy things more than all the children of heaven.

CHAPTER IX

After all these things the Holy One, blessed be He, put His hand upon me and blessed me with 5360 blessings. And I was raised and enlarged to the size of the length and width of the world. And He caused 72 wings to grow on me, 36 on each side. And each wing was as the whole world. And He fixed on me 365 eyes : each eye was as the great luminary. And He left no kind of splendour, brilliance, radiance, beauty in all the lights of the universe that He did not fix on me.

CHAPTER X

All these things the Holy One, blessed be He, made for me:He made me a Throne, similar to the Throne of Glory. And He spread over me a curtain of splendour and brilliant appearance, of beauty, grace and mercy, similar to the curtain of the Throne of Glory; and on it were fixed all kinds of lights in the universe. And He placed it at the door of the Seventh Hall and seated me on it. And the herald went forth into every heaven, saying:This is Metatron, my servant. I have made him into a prince and a ruler over all the princes of my kingdoms and over all the children of heaven, except the eight great princes, the honoured and revered ones who are called YHWH, by the name of their King. And every angel and every prince who has a word to speak in my presence shall go into his presence and shall speak to hi). And every command that he utters to you in

SECTION II – TRANSFORMATION INTO AN ANGELIC BEING

my name do ye observe and fulfil. For the Prince of Wisdom and the Prince of Understanding have I committed to him to instruct him in the wisdom of heavenly things and of earthly things, in the wisdom of this world and of the world to come. Moreover, I have set him over all the treasuries of the palapes of Araboih and over all the stores of life that I have in the high heavens.

CHAPTER XI

Henceforth the Holy One, blessed be He, revealed to me all the mysteries of Tora and all the secrets of wisdom and all the depths of the Perfect Law; and all living beings' thoughts of heart and all the secrets of the universe and all the secrets of Creation were revealed unto me even as they are revealed unto the Maker of Creation. And I watched intently to behold the secrets of the depth and the wonderful mystery. Before a man did think in secret, I saw and before a man made a thing I beheld it. And there was no thing on high nor in the deep hidden from me.

CHAPTER XII

By reason of the love with which the Holy One, blessed be He, loved me more than all the children of heaven, He made me a garment of glory on which were fixed all kinds of lights, and He clad me in it. And He made me a robe of honour on which were fixed all kinds of beauty, splendour, brilliance and majesty. And he made me a royal crown in which were fixed forty-nine costly stones like unto the light of the globe of the sun. For its splendour went forth in the four quarters of the 'Araboth Raqia', and in the seven heavens, and in the four quarters of the world. And he put it on my head. And He called me THE LESSER YHWH in the presence of all His heavenly household; as it is written: "For my name is in him".

CHAPTER XIII

Because of the great love and mercy with which the Holy One, blessed be He, loved and cherished me more than all the children of heaven, He wrote with his ringer with a flaming style upon the crown on my head the letters by which were created heaven and earth, the seas and rivers, the mountains and hills, the planets and constellations, the lightnings, winds, earthquakes and voices, the snow and hail, the storm- wind and the tempest; the letters by which were created all the needs of the world and all the orders of Creation. And every single letter sent forth time after time as it were lightnings, time after time as it were torches, time after time as it were flames of fire, time after time like the rising of the sun and the moon and the planets.

CHAPTER XIV

When the Holy One, blessed be He, put this crown on my head, trembled before me all the Princes of Kingdoms who are in the height of 'Araboth Raqiaf and all the hosts of every heaven; and even the princes thc 'Elim, the princes the 'Er'ellim and the princes the Tafsarim, who are greater than all the ministering angels who minister before the Throne of Glory, shook, feared and trembled before me when they beheld me. Even Sammael, the Prince of the Accusers, who is greater than all the princes of kingdoms on high; feared and trembled before me. And even the angel of fire, and the angel of hail, and the angel of the wind, and the angel of the lightning, and the angel of anger, and the angel of the thunder, and the angel of the snow, and the angel of the rain; and the angel of the day, and the angel of the night, and the angel of the sun and the angel of the moon, and the angel of the planets and the angel of the constellations who rule the world under their hands, feared and trembled and were affrighted before me, when they beheld me. These are the names of the rulers of the world: Gabriel, the angel of the fire, Baradiel, the angel of the hail, Ruchiel who is appointed over the wind, Baraqiel who is appointed over the lightnings, Za'amiel who is appointed over the vehemence, Ziqiel who is appointed over the sparks, Zi'iel who is appointed over the commotion, Zdaphiel who is appointed over the storm-wind, Ra'amiel who is appointed over the thunders, Rctashiel who is appointed over the earthquake, Shalgiel who is appointed over the snow, Matariel who is appointed over the rain, Shimshiel who is appointed over the day, Lailiel who is appointed over the night, Galgalliel who is appointed over the globe of the sun, 'Ophanniel who is appointed over the globe of the moon, Kokbiel who is appointed over the planets, Rahatiel who is appointed over the constellations. And they all fell prostrate, when they saw me. And they were not able to behold me because of the majestic glory and beauty of the appearance of the shining light of the crown of glory upon my head.

CHAPTER XV

As soon as the Holy One, blessed be He, took me in service to attend the Throne of Glory and the Wheels of the Merkaba and the needs of Shekina, forthwith my flesh was changed into flames, my sinews into flaming fire, my bones into coals of burning juniper, the light of my eye-lids into splendour of lightnings, my eye-balls into fire-brands, the hair of my head into dot flames, all my limbs into wings of burning fire and the whole of my body into glowing fire. And on my right were divisions 6 of fiery flames, on my left fire-brands were burning, round about me stormwind and tempest were blowing and in front of me and behind me was roaring of thunder with earthquake.

Section III - Visions of The Divine Throne

In this section, the focus shifts to God's Throne of Glory, a symbol of ultimate sovereignty and divine judgment. The imagery of angels in constant worship reinforces themes of reverence and cosmic order. Readers are invited to contemplate the grandeur of creation and reflect on their role in maintaining spiritual harmony within God's design.

CHAPTER XVI

At first I was sitting upon a great Throne at the door of the Seventh Hall and I was judging the children of heaven, the household on high by authority of the Holy One, blessed be He. And I divided Greatness, Kingship, Dignity, Rulership, Honour and Praise, and Diadem and Crown of Glory unto all the princes of kingdoms, while I was presiding in the Celestial Court, and the princes of kingdoms were standing before me, on my right and on my left by authority of the Holy One, blessed be He. But when Acher came to behold the vision of the Merkaba and fixed his eyes on me, he feared and trembled before me and his soul was affrighted even unto departing from him, because of fear, horror and dread of me, when he beheld me sitting upon a throne like a king with all the ministering angels standing by me as my servants and all the princes of kingdoms adorned with crowns surrounding me: in that moment he opened his mouth and said: "Indeed, there are two Divine Powers in heaven!" Forthwith Bath Qol went forth from heaven from before the Shekina and said: "Return, ye backsliding children, except Acher!" Then came 'Aniyel, the Prince, the honoured, glorified, beloved, wonderful, revered and fearful one, in commission from the Holy One, blessed be He and gave me sixty strokes with lashes of fire and made me stand on my feet.

CHAPTER XVII

Seven princes, the great, beautiful, revered, wonderful and honoured ones who are appointed over the seven heavens. And these are they: MIKAEL, GABRIEL, SHATQIEL, SHACHAQIEL, BAKARIEL, BADARIEL, PACHRIEL. And every one of them is the prince of the host of heaven. And each one of them is accompanied by 496,000 myriads of ministering angels. MIKAEL, the great prince, is appointed over the seventh heaven, the highest one, which is in the 'Araboth. GABRIEL, the prince of the host, is appointed over the sixth heaven which is in Makon. SHATAQIEL, prince of the host, is appointed over the fifth heaven which is in Ma'on. SHAHAQi'EL, prince of the host, is appointed over the fourth heaven which is in Zebul. BADARIEL, prince of the host, is appointed over the third heaven which is in Shehaqim. BARAKIEL, prince of the host, is appointed over the second heaven which is in the height of Raqia. PAZRIEL, prince of the host, is appointed over the first heaven which is in Wilon, which is in Shamayim. Under them is GALGALLIEL, the prince who is appointed over the globe of the sun, and with him are 96 great and honoured angels who move the sun in Raqia'. Under them is 'OPHANNIEL, the prince who is set over the globe of the moon. And with him are 88 angels who move the globe of the moon 354 thousand parasangs every night at the time when the moon stands in the East at its turning point. And when is the moon sitting in the East at its turning point? Answer: in the fifteenth day of every month. Under them is RAHATIEL, the prince who is appointed over the constellations. And he is accompanied by 72 great and honoured angels. And why is he called RAHATIEL? Because he makes the stars run in their orbits and courses 339 thousand parasangs every

night from the East to the West, and from the West to the East. For the Holy One, blessed be He, has made a tent for all of them, for the sun, the moon, the planets and the stars in which they travel at night from the West to the East. Under them is KOKBIEL, the prince who is appointed over all the planets. And with him are 365,000 myriads of ministering angels, great and honoured ones who move the planets from city to city and from province to province in the Raqia' of heavens. And over them are SEVENTY-TWO PRINCES OF KINGDOMS on high corresponding to the 72 tongues of the world. And all of them are crowned with royal crowns and clad in royal garments and wrapped in royal cloaks. And all of them are riding on royal horses and they are holding royal sceptres in their hands. And before each one of them when he is travelling in Raqia', royal servants are running with great glory and majesty even as on earth they are travelling in chariot with horsemen and great armies and in glory and greatness with praise, song and honour.

CHAPTER XVIII

THE ANGELS OF THE FIRST EAVEN, when they see their prince, they dismount from their horses and fall on their faces. And THE PRINCE OF THE FIRST HEAVEN, when he sees the prince of the second heaven, he dismounts, removes the crown of glory from his head and falls on his face. And THE PRINCE OF THE SECOND HEAVEN, when he sees the Prince of the third heaven, he removes the crown of glory from his head and falls on his face. And THE PRINCE OF THE THIRD HEAVEN, when he sees the prince of the fourth heaven, he removes the crown of glory from his head and falls on his face. And THE PRINCE OF THE FOURTH HEAVEN, when he sees the prince of the fifth heaven, he removes the crown of glory from his head and falls on his face. And THE PRINCE OF THE FIFTH HEAVEN, when he sees the prince of the sixth heaven, he removes the crown of glory from his head and falls on his face. And THE PRINCE OF THE SIXTH HEAVEN, when he sees the prince of the eventh heaven, he removes the crown of glory from his head and falls on his face. And THE PRINCE OF THE SEVENTH HEAVEN, when he sees THE SEVENTY- TWO PRINCES OF KINGDOMS, he removes the crown of glory from his head and falls on his face. And the seventy-two princes of kingdoms, when they see THE DOOR KEEPERS OF THE FIRST HALL IN THE ARABOTH RAQIA in the highest, they remove the royal crown from their head and fall on their faces.

SECTION III - VISIONS OF THE DIVINE THRONE

And THE DOOR KEEPERS OF THE FIRST HALL, when they see the door keepers of the second Hall, they remove the crown of glory from their head and fall on their faces. And THE DOOR KEEPERS OF THE SECOND HALL, when they see the door keepers of the third Hall, they remove the crown of glory from their head and fall on their faces. And THE DOOR KEEPERS OF THE THIRD HALL, when they see the door keepers of the fourth Hall, they remove the crown of glory from their head and fall on their faces. And THE DOOR KEEPERS OF THE FOURTH HALL, when they see the door keepers of the fifth Hall, they remove the crown of glory from their head and fall on their faces. And THE DOOR KEEPERS OF THE FIFTH HALL, when they see the door keepers of the sixth Hall, they remove the crown of glory from their head and fall on their faces. And THE DOOR KEEPERS OF THE SIXTH HALL, when they see the DOOR KEEPERS OF THE SEVENTH HALL, they remove the crown of glory from their head and fall on their faces. And the door keepers of the seventh Hall, when they see THE FOUR GREAT PRINCES, the honoured ones, WHO ARE APPOINTED OVER THE FOUR CAMPS OF SHEKINA, they remove the crown of glory from their head and fall on their faces. And the four great princes, when they see TAG'AS, the prince, great and honoured with song praise, at the head of all the children of heaven, they remove the crown of glory from their head and fall on their faces. And Tag'as, the great and honoured prince, when he sees BARATTIEL, the great prince of three fingers in the height of 'Araboth, the highest heaven, he removes the crown of glory from his head and falls on his face. And Barattiel, the great prince, when he sees HAMON, the great prince, the fearful and honoured, pleasant and terrible one who maketh all the children of heaven to tremble, when the time draweth nigh for the saying of the 'Holy', as it is written: "At the noise of the tumult the peoples are fled; at the lifting up of thyself the nations are scattered" he removes the crown of glory from his head and falls on his face. And Hamon, the great prince, when he sees TUTRESIEL, the great prince, he removes the crown of glory from his head and falls on his face. And Tutresiel H', the great prince, when he sees ATRUGIEL, the great prince, he removes the crown of glory from his head and falls on his face. And Atrugiel the great prince, when he sees NA'ARIRIEL H', the great prince, he removes the crown of glory from his head and falls on his face. And Na'aririel H', the great prince, when he sees SASNIGIEL H', the great prince, he removes the crown of glory from his head and falls on his face. And Sasnigiel H', when he sees ZAZRIEL H', the great prince, he removes the crown of glory from his head and falls on his face. And Zazriel H', the prince, when he sees GEBURATIEL H', the prince, he removes the crown of glory from his head and falls on his face. And Geburatiel H', the prince, when he sees 'ARAPHIEL H', the prince, he removes the crown of glory from his head and falls on his face. And 'Araphiel H', the prince, when he sees 'ASHRUYLU, the prince, who presides in all the sessions of the children of heaven, he removes the crown of glory from his head and falls on his face. And Ashruylu H, the prince, when he sees GALLISUR H', THE PRINCE, WHO REVEALS ALL THE SECRETS OF THE LAW, he removes the crown of glory from his head and falls on his face. And Gallisur H', the prince, when he sees ZAKZAKIEL H', the prince who is appointed to write down the merits of Israel on the Throne of Glory, he removes the crown of glory from his head and falls on his face. And Zakzakiel H', the great prince, when he sees 'ANAPHIEL H', the prince who keeps the keys of the heavenly Halls, he removes the crown of glory from his head and falls on his face. Why is he called by the name of 'Anaphiel? Because the bough of his honour and majesty and his crown and his splendour and his brilliance covers all the chambers of 'Araboth Raqia on high even as the Maker of the World. Just as it is written with regard to the Maker of the World: "His glory covered the heavens, and the earth was full of his praise", even so do the honour and majesty of 'Anaphiel cover all the glories of 'Araboth the highest. And when he sees SOTHER 'ASHIEL H', the prince, the great, fearful and honoured one, he removes the crown of glory from his head and falls on his face. Why is he called Sother Ashiel? Because he is appointed over the four heads of the fiery river over against the Throne of Glory; and every single prince who goes out or enters before the Shekina, goes out or enters only by his permission. For the seals of the fiery river are entrusted to him. And furthermore, his height is 7000 myriads of parasangs. And he stirs up the fire of the river; and he goes out and enters before the Shekina to expound what is written concerning the inhabitants of the world. According as it is written: "the judgement was set, and the books were opened". And Sother 'Ashiel the prince, when he sees SHOQED CHOZI, the great prince, the mighty, terrible and honoured one, he removes the crown of glory from his head and falls upon his face. And why is he called Shoqed Chozi? Because he weighs all the merits in a balance in the presence of the Holy One, blessed be He. And when he sees ZEHANPURYU H', the great prince, the mighty and terrible one, honoured, glorified and feared in all the heavenly household, he removes the crown of glory from his head and falls on his face. Why is he called Zehanpuryu? Because he rebukes the fiery river and pushes it back to its place. And when he sees 'AZBUGA H', the great prince, glorified, revered, honoured, adorned, wonderful, exalted, beloved and feared among all the great princes who know the mystery of the Throne of Glory, he removes the crown of glory from his head and falls on his face. Why is he called 'Azbuga? Because in the future he will gird the righteous and pious of the world with the garments of life and wrap them in the cloak of life, that they may live in them an eternal life. And when he sees the two great princes, the strong and glorified ones who are standing above him, he removes the crown of glory from his head and falls on his face. And these are the names of the two princes: SOPHERIEL H' KILLETH, the great prince, the honoured, glorified, blameless, venerable, ancient and mighty one; SOPHERIEL H' MAKETH ALIVE, the great prince, the honoured, glorified, blameless, ancient and mighty one. Why is he called Sopheriel H' who killeth? Because he is appointed over the books of the dead: everyone, when the day of his death draws nigh, he writes him in the books of the dead. Why is he called Sopheriel H' who maketh alive? Because he is appointed over the books of the living, so that every one whom the Holy One, blessed be He, will bring into life, he writes him in the book of the livin, by authority of MAQOM. Thou might perhaps say: "Since the Holy One, blessed be He, is sitting on a throne, they also are sitting when writing": The Scripture teaches us: "And all the host of heaven are standing by him ". "The host of heaven "in order to show us, that even the Great Princes, none like whom there is in the high heavens, do not fulfil the requests of the Shekina otherwise than standing. But how is it hey write, when they are standing? It is like this: One is standing on the wheels of the tempest and the other is standing on the wheels of the storm-wind. The one is clad in kingly garments, the other is clad in kingly garments. The one is wrapped in a mantle of majesty and the other is wrapped in a mantle of majesty. The one is crowned with a royal crown, and the other is crowned with a royal crown. The one's body is full of eyes, and the other's body is full of eyes. The appearance of one is like unto the appearance of lightnings, and the appearance of the other is like unto the appearance of lightnings. The eyes of the one are like the sun in its might, and the eyes of the other are like the sun in its might. The one's height is like the height of the seven heavens, and the other's height is like the height of the seven heavens. The wings of the one are as the days of the year, and the wings of the other are as the days of the year. The wings of the one extend over the breadth of Raqia', and the wings of the other extend over the breadth of Raqia. The lips of the one, are as the gates of the East, and the lips of the other are as the gates of the East. The tongue of the one is as high as the waves of the sea, and the tongue of the other is as high as the waves of the sea. From the mouth of the one a flame goes forth, and from the mouth of the other a flame goes forth. From the mouth of the one there go forth lightnings and from the mouth of the other there go forth lightnings. From the sweat of the one fire is kindled, and from the perspiration of the other fire is kindled. From the one's tongue a torch is burning, and from the tongue of the other a torch is burning. On the head of the one there is a sapphire stone, and upon the head of the other there is a sapphire stone. On the shoulders of the one there is a wheel of a swift cherub, and on the shoulders of the other there is a wheel of a swift cherub. One has in his hand a burning scroll, the other has in his hand a burning scroll. The one has in his hand a flaming style, the other has in his hand a flaming style. The length of the scroll is 3000 myriads of parasangs; the size of the style is 3000 myriads of parasangs; the size of every single letter that they write is 365 parasangs.

CHAPTER XIX

Above 2 these three angels, these great princes there is one Prince, distinguished, honoured, noble, glorified, adorned, fearful, valiant, strong, great, magnified, glorious, crowned, wonderful, exalted, blameless, beloved, lordly, high and lofty, ancient and mighty, like unto whom there is none among the princes. His name is RIKBIEL H', the great and revered Prince who is standing by the Merkaba. And why is he called RIKBIEL? Because he is appointed over the wheels of the Merkaba, and they are given in his charge. And how many are the wheels? Eight; two in each direction. And there are four winds compassing them round about. And these are their names: "the Storm-Wind", "the Tempest", "the Strong Wind", and "the Wind of Earthquake". And under them four fieryrivers are continually running, one fiery river on each side. And round about them, between the rivers, four clouds are planted, and these they are: "clouds of fire", "clouds of lamps", "clouds of coal", "clouds of brimstone" and they are standing over against wheels. And the feet of the Chayyoth are resting upon the wheels. And between one wheel and the other earthquake is roaring and thunder is thundering. And when the time draws nigh for the recital of the Song, the multitudes of wheels are moved, the multitude of clouds tremble, all the chieftains are made afraid, all the horsemen do rage, all the mighty ones are excited, all the hosts are afrighted, all the troops are in fear, all the appointed ones haste away, all the princes and armies are dismayed, all the servants do faint and all the angels and divisions travail with pain. And one wheel makes a sound to be heard to the other and one Kerub to another, one Chayya. to another, one Seraph to another "Extol to him that rideth in 'Araboth, by his name Jah and rejoice before him!"

CHAPTER XX

Above these there is one great and mighty prince. His name is CHAYYLIEL H', a noble and revered prince, a glorious and mighty prince, a great and revered prince, a prince before whom all the children of heaven do tremble, a prince who is able to swallow up the whole earth in one moment. And why is he called CHAYYLIEL H'? Because he is appointed over the Holy Chayyoth and smites the Chayyoth with lashes of fire: and glorifies them, when they give praise and glory and rejoicing and he causes them to make haste to say "Holy" and "Blessed be the Glory of H' from his place!"

CHAPTER XXI

Four the Chayyoth corresponding to the four winds. Each Chayya is as the space of the whole world. And each one has four faces; and each face is as the face of the East. Each one has four wings and each wing is like the cover of the universe. And each one has faces in the middle of faces and wings in the middle of wings. The size of the faces is 248 faces, and the size of the wings is 365 wings. And every one is crowned with 2000 crowns on his head. And each crown is like unto the bow in the cloud. And its splendour is like unto the splendour of the globe of the sun. And the sparks that go forth from every one are like the splendour of the morning star in the East.

CHAPTER XXII

Above these la there is one prince, noble, wonderful, strong, and praised with all kinds of praise. His name is KERUBIEL H', a mighty prince, full of power and strength a prince of highness, and Highness with him, a righteous prince, and righteousness with him, a holy prince, and holiness with him, a prince glorified in thousand hosts, exalted by ten thousand armies. At his wrath the earth trembles, at his anger the camps are moved, from fear of him the foundations are shaken, at his rebuke the 'Araboth do tremble. His stature is full of coals. The height of his stature is as the height of the seven heavens the breadth of his stature is as the wideness of the seven heavens and the thickness of his stature is as the seven heavens. The opening of his mouth is like a lamp of fire. His tongue is a consuming fire. His eyebrows are like unto the splendour of the lightning. His eyes are like sparks of brilliance. His countenance is like a burning fire. And there is a crown of holiness upon his head on which the Explicit Name is graven, and lightnings go forth from it. And the bow of Shekina is between his shoulders. And his sword is like unto a lightning; and upon his loins there are arrows like unto a flame, and upon his armour and shield there is a consuming fire, and upon his neck there are coals of burning juniper and round about him. And the splendour of Shekina is on his face; and the horns of majesty on his wheels; and a royal diadem upon his skull. And his body is full of eyes. And wings are covering the whole of his high stature. On his right hand a flame is burning, and on his left a fire is glowing; and coals are burning from it. And firebrands go forth from his body. And lightnings are cast forth from his face. With him there is alway thunder upon thunder, by his side there is ever earthquake upon earthquake. And the two princes of the Merkaba are together with him. Why is he called KERUBIEL H', the Prince. Because he is appointed over the chariot of the Kerubim. And the mighty Kerubim are given in his charge. And he adorns the crowns on their heads and polishes the diadem upon their skull. He magnifies the glory of their appearance. And he glorifies the beauty of their majesty. And he increases the greatness of their honour. He causes the song of their praise to be sung. He intensifies their beautiful strength. He causes the brilliance of their glory to shine forth. He beautifies their goodly mercy and lovingkindness. He frames the fairness of their radiance. He makes their merciful beauty even more beautiful. He glorifies their upright majesty. He extols the order of their praise, to stablish the dwellingplace of him "who dwelleth on the Kerubim". And the Kerubim are standing by the Holy Chayyoth, and their wings are raised up to their heads and Shekina is upon them and the brilliance of the Glory is upon their faces and song and praise in their mouth and their hands are under their wings and their feet are covered by their wings and horns of glory are upon their heads and the splendour of Shekina on their face and Shekina is upon them and sapphire stones are round about them and columns of fire on their four sides and columns of firebrands beside them. There is one sapphire on one side and another sapphire on another side and under the sapphires there are coals of burning juniper. And one Kerub is standing in each direction but the wings of the Kerubim compass each other above their skulls in glory; and they spread them to sing with them a song to him that inhabiteth the clouds and to praise with them the fearful majesty of the king of kings. And KERUBIEL H', the prince who is appointed over them, he arrays them in comely, beautiful and pleasant orders and he exalts them in all manner of exaltation, dignity and glory. And he hastens them in glory and might to do the will of their Creator every moment. For above their lofty heads abides continually the glory of the high king "who dwelleth on the Kerubim". And there is a court before the Throne of Glory, which no seraph nor angel can enter, and it is 36,000 myriads of parasangs, as it is written: "and the Seraphim are standing above him" (the last word of the scriptural passage being 36). As the numerical value of 36 is the number of the bridges there. And there are 24 myriads of wheels of fire. And the ministering angels are 12,000 myriads. And there are 12,000 rivers of hail, and 12,000 treasuries of snow. And in the seven Halls are chariots of fire and flames, without reckoning, or end or searching. What doeth YHWH, the God of Israel, the King of Glory? The Great and Fearful God, mighty in strength, doth cover his face. In Araboth are 660,000 myriads of angels of glory standing over against the Throne of Glory and the divisions of flaming fire. And the King of Glory doth cover His face; for else the would be rent asunder in its midst because of the majesty, splendour, beauty, radiance, loveliness, brilliancy, brightness and excellency of the appearance of blessed be He. There are numerous ministering angels performing his will, numerous kings, numerous princes in the 'Araboth of his delight, angels who are revered among the rulers in heaven, distinguished, adorned with song and bringing love to remembrance: are affrighted by the splendour of the Shekina, and their eyes are dazzled by the shining beauty of their King, their faces grow black and their strength doth fail. There go forth rivers of joy, streams of gladness, rivers of rejoicing, streams of triumph, rivers of love, streams of friendship of commotion and they flow over and go forth before the Throne of Glory and wax great and go through the gates of the paths of 'Araboth Raqia at the voice of the shouting and musick of the CHAYYOTH, at the voice of the rejoicing of the timbrels of his 'OPHANNIM and at the melody of the cymbals of His Kerubim. And they wax great and go forth with commotion with the sound of the hymn: "HOLY, HOLY, HOLY, IS THE LORD OF HOSTS; THE WHOLE EARTH IS FULL OF HIS GLORY!" What is the distance between one bridge and another? 12 myriads of parasangs. Their ascent is 12 myriads of parasangs, and their descent 12 myriads of parasangs. between the rivers of dread and the rivers of fear is 22 myriads of parasangs; between the rivers of hail and the rivers of darkness 36 myriads of parasangs; between the chambers of lightnings and the clouds of compassion 42 myriads of parasangs; between the clouds of compassion and the Merkaba 84 myriads of parasangs; between the Merkaba and the Kerubim 148 myriads of parasangs; between the Kerubim and the 'Ophannim 24 myriads of parasangs; between the Ophannim and the chambers of chambers 24 myriads of parasangs; between the chambers of chambers and the Holy Chayyoth 40,000 myriads of parasangs; between one wing and another 12 myriads of parasangs; and the breadth of each one wing is of that same measure; and the distance between the Holy Chayyoth and the Throne of Glory is 30,000 myriads of parasangs.

And from the foot of the Throne to the seat there are 40,000 myriads of parasangs. And the name of Him that sitteth on it: let the name be sanctified!

And the arches of the Bow are set above the 'Araboth, and they are 1000 thousands and 10,000 times ten thousands high. Their measure is after the measure of the 'Irin and Qaddishin. As it is written "My bow I have set in the cloud". It is not written here "I will set" but "I have set", already; clouds that surround the Throne of Glory. As His clouds pass by, the angels of hail burning coal. And a fire of the voice goes down from by the Holy Chayyoth. And because of the breath of that voice they "run" to another place, fearing lest it command them to go; and they "return" lest it injure them from the other side. Therefore "they run and return". And these arches of the Bow are more beautiful and radiant than the radiance of the sun during the summer solstice. And they are whiter than a flaming fire and they are great and beautiful. Above the arches of the Bow are the wheels of the 'Ophannim. Their height is 1000 thousand and 10,000 times 10,000 units of measure after the measure of the Seraphim and the Troops.

CHAPTER XXIII

There are numerous winds blowing under the wings of the Kerubim. There blows "the Brooding Wind", as it is written: " and the wind of God was brooding upon the face of the waters ". There blows "the Strong Wind", as it is said: "and the Lord caused the sea to go back by a strong east wind all that night". There blows "the East Wind" as it is written: "the east wind brought the locusts". There blows "the Wind of Quails" as it is written: "And there went forth a wind from the Lord and brought quails". There blows "the Wind of Jealousy" as it is written: "And the wind of jealousy came upon him". There blows the "Wind of Earthquake" as it is written: "and after that the wind of the earthquake; but the Lord was not in the earthquake". There blows the "Wind of H' " as it is written: "and he carried me out by the wind of H' and set me down". There blows the "Evil Wind " as it is written: "and the evil wind departed from him". There blow the "Wind of Wisdom" 5and the "Wind of Understanding" and the "Wind of Knowledge" and the "Wind of the Fear of H'" as it is written: "And the wind of H'shall rest upon him; the wind of wisdom and understanding, the wind of counsel and might, the wind of knowledge and of the fear. There blows the "Wind of Rain", as it is written: "the north wind bringeth forth rain". There blows the "Wind of Lightnings ", as it is written: "he maketh lightnings for the rain and bringeth forth the wind out of his treasuries ". There blows the "Wind, Breaking the Rocks", as it is written: "the Lord passed by and a great and strong wind". There blows the "Wind of Assuagement of the Sea", as it is written: "and God made a wind to pass over the earth, and the waters assuaged". There blows the "Wind of Wrath", as it is written: "and behold there came a great wind from the wilderness and smote the four corners of the house and it fell". There blows the " Storm-Wind ", as it is written: "Storm-wind, fulfilling his word". And Satan is standing among these winds, for "storm-wind " is nothing else but "Satan", and all these winds do not blow but under the wings of the Kerubim, as it is written: "and he rode upon a cherub and did fly, yea, and he flew swiftly upon the wings of the wind". And whither go all these winds? The Scripture teaches us, that they go out from under the wings of the Kerubim and descend on the globe of the sun, as it is written: " The wind goeth toward the south and turneth about unto the north;

it turneth about continually in its course and the wind 14 returneth again to its circuits ". And from the globe of the sun they return and descend upon the rivers and the seas, upon the mountains and upon the hills, as it is written: "For lo, he that formeth the mountains and createth the wind". And from the mountains and the hills they return and descend to the seas and the rivers; and from the seas and the rivers they return and descend upon cities and provinces; and from the cities and provinces they return and descend into the Garden, and from the Garden they return and descend to Eden, as it is written: "walking in the Garden in the wind of day". And in the midst of the Garden they join together and blow from one side to the other and are perfumed with the spices of the Garden even from \ts remotest parts, until they separate from each other, and, filled with the scent of the pure spices, they bring the odour from the remotest parts of Eden and the spices of the Garden to the righteous and godly who in the time to come shall inherit the Garden of Eden and the Tree of Life, as it is written: "Awake, O north wind; and come thou south; blow upon my garden, that the spices thereof may flow out. Let my beloved come into his garden and eat his precious fruits".

CHAPTER XXIV

Numerous chariots has the Holy One, blessed be He: He has the "Chariots of Kerubim", as it is written: "And he rode upon a cherub and did fly". He has the "Chariots of Wind", as it is written: "and he flew swiftly upon the wings of the wind". He has the "Chariots of Swift Cloud", as it is written: "Behold, the Lord rideth upon a swift cloud". He has "the Chariots of Clouds", as it is written: "Lo, I come unto thee in a cloud". He has the "Chariots of the Altar", as it is written:"I saw the Lord standing upon the Altar". He has the "Chariots of Ribbotaim", as it is written: "The chariots of God are Ribbotaim; thousands of angels ". He has the "Chariots of the Tent", as it is written: "And the Lord appeared in the Tent in a pillar of cloud". He has the "Chariots of the Tabernacle", as it is written: "And the Lord spake unto him out of the tabernacle". He has the "Chariots of the Mercy-Seat", as it is written: "then he heard the Voice speaking unto him from upon the mercy-seat". He has the "Chariots of Sapphire Stone", as it is written: "and there was under his feet as it were a paved work of sapphire stone". He has the "Chariots of Eagles ", as it is written: "I bare you on eagles' wings". Eagles literally are not meant here but "they that fly swiftly as eagles". He has the "chariots of Shout", as it is written: "God is gone up with a shout". He has the "Chariots of 'Araboth", as it is written"Extol Him that rideth upon the 'Araboth". He has the "Chariots of Thick Clouds", as it is written: "who maketh the thick clouds His chariot". He has the "Chariots of the Chayyoth", as it is written: "and the Chayyoth ran and returned". They run by permission and return by permission, for Shekina is above their heads. He has the "Chariots of Wheels", as it is written: "And he said: Go in between the whirling wheels". lie has the "Chariots of a Swift Kerub", as it is written: "riding on a swift cherub". And at the time when He rides on a swift kerub, as he sets one of His feet upon him, before he sets the other foot upon his back, he looks through eighteen thousand worlds at one glance. And he discerns and sees into them all and knows what is in all of them and then he sets down the other foot upon him, according as it is written: "Round about eighteen thousand". Whence do we know that He looks through every one of them every day? It is written: "He looked down from heaven upon the children of men to see if there were any that did understand, that did seek after God". He has the "Chariots of the 'Ophannim", as it is written and the 'Ophannim were full of eyes round about". He has the "Chariots of His Holy Throne", as it is written:" God sitteth upon his holy throne ". He has the "chariots of the Throne of Yah", as it is written: "Because a hand is lifted up upon the Throne of Jah". He has the "Chariots of the Throne of Judgement", as it is written: "but the Lord of hosts shall be exalted in judgment". He has the "Chariots of the Throne of Glory ", as it is written: "The Throne of Glory, set on high from the beginning, is the place of our sanctuary". He has the "Chariots of the High and Exalted Throne", as it is written: "I saw the Lord sitting upon the high and exalted throne".

CHAPTER XXV

Above these there is one great prince, revered, high, lordly, fearful, ancient and strong. 'OPHPHANNIEL H is his name. He has sixteen faces, four faces on each side) hundred wings on each side. And he has 8466 eyes, corresponding to the days of the year. And those two eyes of his face, in each one of them lightnings are flashing, and from each one of them firebrands are burning; and no creature is able to behold them : for anyone who looks at them is burnt instantly. His height is the distance of 2500 years' journey. No eye can behold and no mouth can tell the mighty power of his strength save the King of kings, the Holy One, blessed be He, alone. Why is he called 'OPHPHANNIEL ? Because he is appointed over the 'Ophannim and the 'Ophannimare given in his charge. He stands every day and attends and beautifies them. And he exalts and orders their apartment and polishes their standing-place and makes bright their dwellings, makes their corners even and cleanses their seats. And he waits upon them early and late, by day and by night, to increase their beauty, to make great their dignity and to make them "diligent in praise of their Creator.

And all the 'Ophannim are full of eyes, and they are all full of brightness; seventy two sapphire stones are fixed on their garments on their right side and seventy two sapphire stones are fixed on their garments on their left side. And four carbuncle stones are fixed on the crown of every single one, the splendour of which proceeds in the four directions of 'Araboth even as the splendour of the globe of the sun proceeds in all the directions of the universe. And why is it called Carbuncle? Because its splendour is like the appearance of a lightnin. And tents of splendour, tents of brilliance, tents of brightness as of sapphire and carbuncle inclose them because of the shining appearance of their eyes.

CHAPTER XXVI

Above these there is one prince, wonderful, noble, great, honourable, mighty, terrible, a chief and leader 1 and a swift scribe, glorified, honoured and beloved. He is altogether filled with splendour, full of praise and shining; and he is wholly full of brilliance, of light and of beauty; and the whole of him is filled with goodliness and greatness. His countenance is altogether like angels, but his body is like an eagle's body. His splendour is like unto lightnings, his appearance like fire brands, his beauty like unto sparks, his honour like fiery coals, his majesty like chashmals, his radiance like the light of the planet Venus. The image of him is like unto the Greater Light. His height is as the seven heavens. The light from his eyebrows is like the sevenfold light. The sapphire stone upon his head is as great as the whole universe and like unto the splendour of the very heavens in radiance. His body is full of eyes like the stars of the sky, innumerable and unsearchable. Every eye is like the planet Venus. Yet, there are some of them like the Lesser Light and some of them like unto the Greater Light. From his ankles to his knees like unto stars of lightning, from his knees to his thighs like unto the planet Venus, from his thighs to his loins like unto the moon, from his loins to his neck like the sun, from his neck to his skull like unto the Light Imperishable. The crown on his head is like unto the splendour of the Throne of Glory. The measure of the crown is the distance of 502 years' journey. There is no kind of splendour, no kind of brilliance, no kind of radiance, no kind of light in the universe but is fixed on that crown. The name of that prince is SERAPHIEL H". And the crown on his head, its name is "the Prince of Peace". And why is he called by the name of SERAPHIEL '? Because he is appointed over the Seraphim. And the flaming Seraphim are given in his charge. And he presides over them by day and by night and teaches them song, praise, proclamation of beauty, might and majesty; that they may proclaim the beauty of their King in all manner of Praise and Sanctification. How many are the Seraphim? Four, corresponding to the four winds of the world. And how many wings have they each one of them? Six, corresponding to the six days of Creation. And how many faces have they? Each one of them four faces. The measure of the Seraphim and the height of each one of them correspond to the height of the seven heavens. The size of each wing is like the measure of all Raqia'. The size of each face is like that of the face of the East. And each one of them gives forth light like unto the splendour of the Throne of Glory: so that not even the Holy Chayyoth, the honoured 'Ophannim, nor the majestic KeruUm are able to behold it. For everyone who beholds it, his eyes are darkened because of its great splendour. Why are they called Seraphim? Because they bur) the writing tables of Satan : Every day Satan is sitting, together with SAMMAEL, the Prince of Rome, and with DUBBIEL, the Prince of Persia, and they write the iniquities of Israel on writing tables which they hand over to the Seraphim, in order that they may present them before the Holy One, blessed be He, so that He may destroy Israel from the world. But the Seraphim know from the secrets of the Holy One, blessed be He, that he desires not, that this people Israel should perish. What do the Seraphim? Every day do they receive them from the hand of Satan and burn them in the burning fire over against the high and exalted Throne in order that they may not come before the Holy One, blessed be He, at the time when he is sitting upon the Throne of Judgement, judging the whole world in truth.

CHAPTER XXVII

Above the Seraphim there is one prince, exalted above all the princes, wondrous more than all the servants. His name is RADWERIEL H' who is appointed over the treasuries of the books. He fetches forth the Case of Writings the Book of Records in it, and brings it before the Holy One, blessed be He. And he breaks the seals of the case, opens it, takes out the books and delivers them before the Holy One, blessed be He. And the Holy One, blessed be He, receives them of his hand and gives them in his sight to the Scribes, that they may read them in the Great Beth Din in the height of 'Araboth Raqia', before the heavenly household. And why is he called RADWERIEL? Because out of every word that goes forth from his mouth an angel is created: and he stands in the songs of the ministering angels and utters a song before the Holy One, blessed be He when the time draws nigh for the recitation of the Holy.

CHAPTER XXVIII

Above all these there are four great princes, lrin and Qaddishin by name: high, honoured, revered, beloved, wonderful and glorious ones, greater than all the children of heaven. There is none like unto them among all the celestial princes and none their equal among all the Servants. For each one of them is equal to all the rest together. And their dwelling is over against the Throne of Glory, and their standing place over against the Holy One, blessed be He, so that the brilliance of their dwelling is a reflection of the brilliance of the Throne of Glory. And the splendour of their countenance is a reflection of the splendour of Shekina. And they are glorified by the glory of 4the Divine Majesty and praised by the praise of Shekina. And not only that, but the Holy One, blessed be He, does nothing in his world without first consulting them, but after that he doeth it. As it is written: "The sentence is by the decree of the 'Irin and the demand by the word of the Qaddishin." The llrin are two and the Qaddishin are two. And how are they standing before the Holy One, blessed be He? It is to be understood, that one 'Ir is standing on one side and the other 'Ir on the other side, and one Qaddish is standing on one side and the other on the other side. And ever do they exalt the humble, and they abase to the ground those that are proud, and they exalt to the height those that are humble. And every day, as the Holy One, blessed be He, is sitting upon the Throne of Judgement and judges the whole world, and the Books of the Living and the Books of the Dead are opened before Him, then all the children of heaven are standing before him in fear, dread, awe and trembling. At that time, the Holy One, blessed be He, is sitting upon the Throne of Judgement to execute judgement, his garment is white as snow, the hair on his head as pure wool and the whole of his cloak is like the shining light. And he is covered with righteousness all over as with a coat of mail. And those 'Irm and Qaddishin are standing before him like court officers before the judge. And they raise and argue every case and close the case that comes before the Holy One, blessed be He, in judgement, according as it is written: "The sentence is by the decree of the 'Irm and the demand by the word of the Qaddishin" Some of them argue and others pass the sentence in the Great Beth Din in 'Araboth. Some of them make the requests from before uthe Divine Majesty and some close the cases before the Most High. Others finish by going down and executing the sentences on earth below. According as it is written: " Behold an 'Ir and a Qaddish came down from heaven and cried aloud and said thus, Hew down the tree, and cut off his branches, shake off his leaves, and scatter his fruit: let the beasts get away from under it, and the fowls from his branches ". Why are they called 'Irin and Qaddishint By reason that they sanctify the body and the spirit with lashes of fire on the third day of the judgement, as it is writte: "After two days will he revive us: on the third he will raise us up, and we shall live before him."

CHAPTER XXIX

Each one of them has seventy names corresponding to the seventy tongues of the world. And all of them are upon the name of the Holy One, blessed be He. And every several name is written with a flaming style upon the Fearful Crown which is on the head of the high and exalted King. And from each one of them there go forth sparks and lightnings. And each one of them is beset with horns of splendour round about. From each one lights are shining forth, and each one is surrounded by tents of brilliance so that not even the Seraphim and the Chayyoth who are greater than all the children of heaven are able to behold them.

CHAPTER XXX

Whenever the Great Beth Din is seated in the 'Araboth Raqia' on high there is no opening of the mouth for anyone in the world save those great princes who are called H' by the name of the Holy One, blessed be He. How many are those princes? Seventy- two princes of the kingdoms of the world besides the Prince of the World who speaks in favour of the world before the Holy One, blessed be He, every day, at the hour when the book is opened in which are recorded all the doings of the world, according as it is written: "The judgement was set and the books were opened."

Section IV - Mystical Hierarchies and Heavenly Realms

The final section delves into celestial laws and angelic governance, providing a framework for understanding divine order. It emphasizes the discipline of spiritual practice and the importance of sacred knowledge, offering insights into the hidden structures that sustain creation and divine authority.

CHAPTER XXXI

At the time when the Holy One, blessed be He, is sitting on the Throne, of Judgement, Justice is standing on His right and Mercy on His left and Truth before His face. And when man enters before Him to judgement, there comes forth from the splendour of the Mercy towards him as staff and stands in front of him. Forthwith man falls upon his face, all the angels of destruction fear and tremble before him, according as it is written: "And with mercy shall the throne be established, and he shall sit upon it in truth."

CHAPTER XXXII

When the Holy One, blessed be He, opens the Book half of which is fire and half flame, they go out from before Him in every moment to execute the judgement on the wicked by His sword drawn forth out of its sheath and the splendour of which shines like a lightning and pervades the world from one end to the other, as it is written: "For by fire will the Lord plead." And all the inhabitants of the world fear and tremble before Him, when they behold His sharpened sword like unto a lightning from one end of the world to the other, and sparks and flashes of the size of the stars of Raqia' going out from it; according as it is written:" If I whet the lightning of my sword".

CHAPTER XXXIII

At the time that the Holy One, blessed be He, is sitting on the Throne of Judgement, the angels of Mercy are standing on His right, the angels of Peace are standing on His left and the angels of Destruction are standing in front of Him. And one scribe is standing beneath Him, and another scribe above Him. And the glorious Seraphim surround the Throne on its four sides with walls of lightnings, and the 'Ophannim. surround them with fire-brands round about the Throne of Glory. And clouds of fire and clouds of flames compass them to the right and to the left; and the Holy Chayyoth carry the Throne of Glory from below: each one with three fingers. The measure of the fingers of each one is 800,000 and 700 times hundred, 66,000 parasangs. And underneath the feet of the Chayyoth seven fiery rivers are running and flowing. And the breadth of each river is 365 thousand parasangs and its depth is 248 thousand myriads of parasangs. Its length is unsearchable and immeasureable. And each river turns round in a bow in the four directions of 'Araboth Raqict , and it falls down to Ma'on and is stayed, and from Ma1 on to Zebul, from Zebul to Shechaqim, from Shechaqim to Raqia' , from Raqia' to Shamayim and from Shamayim upon the heads of the wicked who are in Gehenna, as it is written: "Behold a whirlwind of the Lord, even his fury, is gone, yea, a whirling tempest; it shall burst upon the head of the wicked".

CHAPTER XXXIV

The hoofs of the Chayyoth are surrounded by seven clouds of burning coals. The clouds of burning coals are surrounded on the outside by seven walls of flame. The seven walls of flame are surrounded on the outside by seven walls of hailstones. The hailstones are surrounded on the outside by xstones of hail. The stones of hail are surrounded on the outside by stones of "the wings of the tempest ". The stones of "the wings of the tempest" are surrounded on the outside by flames of fire. The flames of fire are surrounded by the chambers of the whirlwind. The chambers of the whirlwind are surrounded on the outside by the fire and the water. Round about the fire and the water are those who utter the "Holy". Round about those who utter the "Holy" are those who utter the "Blessed"'. Round about those who utter the "Blessed" are the bright clouds. The bright clouds are surrounded on the outside by coals of burning jumper; and on the outside surrounding the coals of burning juniper there are thousand camps of fire and ten thousand hosts of flame. And between every several camp and every several host there is a cloud, so that they may not be burnt by the fire.

CHAPTER XXXV

506 thousand myriads of camps has the Holy One, blessed be He, in the height of 'Araboth Raqia. And each camp is 496 thousand angels. And every single angel, the height of his stature is as the great sea; and the appearance of their countenance as the appearance of the lightning, and their eyes as lamps of fire, and their arms and their feet like in colour to polished brass and the roaring voice of their words like the voice of a multitude. And they are all standing before the Throne of Glory in four rows. And the princes of the army are standing at the head of each row. And some of them utter the "Holy" and others utter the "Blessed", some of them run as messengers, others are standing in attendance, according as it is written: "Thousand ...thousands ministered unto him, and ten thousand times ten thousand stood before him: the judgment was set and the books were opened ". And in the hour, when the time draws nigh for to say the "Holy", first there goes forth a whirlwind from before the Holy One, blessed be He, and bursts upon the camp of Shekina and there arises a great commotion among them, as it is written: "Behold, the whirlwind of the Lord goeth forth with fury, a continuing commotion". At that moment 4thousand thousands of them are changed into sparks, thousand thousands of them into firebrands, thousand thousands into flashes, thousand thousands into flames, thousand thousands into males, thousand thousands into females, thousand thousands into winds, thousand thousands into burning fires, thousand thousands into flames, thousand thousands into sparks, thousand thousands into chashmals of light; until they take upon themselves the yoke of the kingdom of heaven, the high and lifted up, of the Creator of them all with fear, dread, awe and trembling, with commotion, anguish, terror and trepidation. Then they are changed again into their former shape to have the fear of their King before them alway, as they have set their hearts on saying the Song continually, as it is written: "And one cried unto another and said.

CHAPTER XXXVI

At the time when the ministering angels desire to say Song, Nehar di-Nur with many thousand thousands and myriads of myriads" of power and strength of fire and it runs and passes under the Throne of Glory, between the camps of the ministering angels and the troops of 'Araboth. And all the ministering angels first go down into Nehar di-Nur, and they dip themselves in the fire and dip their tongue and their mouth seven times; and after that they go up and put on the garment of 'Machaqe Samal' and cover themselves with cloaks of chashmal and stand in four rows over against the Throne of Glory, in all the heavens.

CHAPTER XXXVII

In the seven Halls there are standing four chariots of Shekina, and before each one are standing the four camps of Shekina. Between each camp a river of fire is continually flowing. Between each river there are bright clouds, and between each cloud there are put up pillars of brimstone. Between one pillar and another there are standing flaming wheels, surrounding them. And between one wheel and another there are flames of fire round about. Between one flame and another there are treasuries of lightnings; behind the treasuries of lightnings are the wings of the stormwind. Behind the wings of the storm- wind are the chambers of the tempest; behind the chambers of the tempest there are winds, voices, thunders, sparks sparks and earthquakes earthquakes.

CHAPTER XXXVIII

At the time, when the ministering angels utter Holy, then all the pillars of the heavens and their sockets do tremble, and the gates of the Halls of Araboth Raqia' are shaken and the foundations of Shechaqim and the Universe are moved, and the orders of Ma'on and the chambers of Makon quiver, and all the orders of Raqia and the constellations and the planets are dismayed, and the globes of the sun and the moon haste away and flee out of their courses and run 12,000 parasangs and seek to throw themselves down from heaven, by reason of the roaring voice of their chant, and the noise of their praise and the sparks and lightnings that go forth from their faces; as it is written: "The voice of thy thunder was in the heaven". Until the prince of the world calls them, saying: "Be ye quiet in your place ! Fear not because of the ministering angels who sing the Song before the Holy One, blessed be He". As it is written: "When the morning stars sang together and all the children of heaven shouted for joy".

CHAPTER XXXIX

When the ministering angels utter the "Holy" then all the explicit names that are graven with a flaming style on the Throne of Glory fly off like eagles, with sixteen wings. And they surround and compass the Holy One, blessed be He, on the four sides of the place of His Shekina1. And the angels of the host, and the flaming Servants, and the mighty 'Ophannim, and the Kerubim of the Shekina, and the Holy Chayyoth, and the Seraphim, and the 'Er'ellim, and the Taphsarim and the troops of consuming fire, and the fiery armies, and the flaming hosts, and the holy princes, adorned with crowns, clad in kingly majesty, wrapped in glory, girt with loftiness, 4 fall upon their faces three times, saying: "Blessed be the name of His glorious kingdom for ever and ever".

CHAPTER XL

When the ministering angels say "Holy" before the Holy One, blessed be He, in the proper way, then the servants of His Throne, the attendants of His Glory, go forth with great mirth from under the Throne of Glory. And they all carry in their hands, each one of them thousand thousand and ten thousand times ten thousand crowns of stars, similar in appearance to the planet Venus, and put them on the ministering angels and the great princes who utter the "Holy". Three crowns they put on each one of them: one crown because they say "Holy", another crown, because they say "Holy, Holy", and a third crown because they say "Holy, Holy, Holy, is the Lord of Hosts". And in the moment that they do not utter the "Holy" in the right order, a consuming fire goes forth from the little finger of the Holy One, blessed be He, and falls down in the midst of their ranksand is divided into 496 thousand parts corresponding to the four camps of the ministering angels, and consumes them in one moment, as it is written: "A fire goeth before him and burneth up his adversaries round about".

After that the Holy One, blessed be He, opens His mouth and speaks one word and creates others in their stead, new ones like them. And each one stands before His Throne of Glory, uttering the "Holy", as it is written "They are new every morning; great is thy faithfulness".

CHAPTER XLI

Come and behold the letters by which the heaven and the earth were created, the letters by which were created the mountains and hills, the letters by which were created the seas and rivers, the letters by which were created the trees and herbs, the letters by which were created the planets and the constellations, the letters by which were created the globe of the moon and the globe of the sun, Orion, the Pleiades and all the different luminaries of Raqia'. the letters by which were created the Throne of Glory and the Wheels of the Merkaba, the letters by which were created the necessities of the worlds, the letters by which were created wisdom, understanding, knowledge, prudence, meekness and righteousness by which the whole world is sustained. And I walked by his side and he took me by his hand and raised me upon his wings and showed me those letters, all of them, that are graven with a flaming style on the Throne of Glory : and sparks go forth from them and cover all the chambers of 'Araboth.

CHAPTER XLII

Come and I will show thee, where the waters are suspended in the highest, where fire is burning in the midst of hail, where lightnings lighten out of the midst of snowy +mountains, where thunders are roaring in the celestial heights, where a flame is burning in the midst of the burning fire and where voices make themselves heard in the midst of thunder and earthquake. Then I went by his side and he took me by his hand and lifted me up on his wings and showed me all those things. I beheld the waters suspended on high in 'Araboth Raqia' by the name YAH 'EHYE 'ASHER 'EHY), And their fruits going down from heaven and watering the face of the world, as it is written: " the earth is satisfied with the fruit of thy work". And I saw fire and snow and hailstone that were mingled together within each other and yet were undamaged, by the name 'ESH 'OKELA as it is written: "For the Lord, thy God, is a consuming fire". And I saw lightnings that were lightening out of mountains of snow and yet were not damaged, by the name YAH SUR 'OLAMIM, as it is written: "For in Jah, YHWH, the everlasting rock". And I saw thunders and voices that were roaring in the midst of fiety flames and were not damaged, by the name 'EL-SHADDAI RABBA as it is written: "I am God Almighty". And I beheld a flame a glow that were flaming and glowing in the midst of burning fire, and yet were not damaged, by the name YAD 'AL KES YAH 3as it is written: " And he said: for the hand is upon the Throne of the Lord ". And I beheld rivers of fire in the midst of rivers of water and they were not damaged by the name 'OSE SHALOM it is written: "He maketh peace in his high places". For he makes peace between the fire and the water, between the hail and the fire, between the wind and the cloud, between the earthquake and the sparks.

CHAPTER XLIII

Come and I will show thee where are the spirits of the righteous that have been created and have returned, and the spirits of the righteous that have not yet been created. And he lifted me up to his side, took me by his hand and lifted me up near the Throne of Glory by the place of the Shekina; and he revealed the Throne of Glory to me, and he showed me the spirits that have been created and had returned : and they were flying above the Throne of Glory before the Holy One, blessed be He. After that I went to interpret the following verse of Scripture and I found in what is written: "for the spirit clothed itself before me, and the souls I have made" that means the spirits that have been created in the chamber of creation of the righteous and that have returned before the Holy One, blessed be He; "and the souls I have made" refer to the spirits 4 of the righteous that have not yet been created in the chamber.

CHAPTER XLIV

Come and I will show thee the spirits of the wicked and the spirits of the intermediate where they are standing, and the spirits of the intermediate, whither they go down, 3and the spirits of the wicked, where they go down. And he said to me: The spirits of the wicked go down to She'ol by the hands of two angels of destruction: ZA'APHIEL and SIMKIEL are their names. SIMKIEL is appointed over the intermediate to support them and purify them because of the great mercy of the Prince of the Place. ZA'APHIEL is appointed over the spirits of the wicked in order to cast them down from the presence of the Holy One, blessed be He, and from the splendour of the Shekina to She'ol, to be punished in the fire of Gehenna with staves of burning coal. And I went by his side, and he took me by his hand and showed me all of them with his fingers. And I beheld the appearance of their faces as the appearance of children of men, and their bodies like eagles. And not only that but the colour of the countenance of the intermediate was like pale grey on account of their deeds, for there are stains upon them until they have become cleaned from their iniquity in the fire. And the colour of the wicked was like the bottom of a pot on account of the wickedness of their doings. And I saw the spirits of the Patriarchs Abraham Isaac and Jacob and the rest of the righteous whom they have brought up out of their graves and who have ascended to the Heaven. And they were praying before the Holy One, blessed be He, saying in their prayer: "Lord of the Universe! How long wilt thou sit upon Throne like a mourner in the days of his mourning with thy right hand behind thee 7and not7 deliver thy children and reveal thy Kingdom in the world? And for how long wilt thou have no pity upon thy children who are made slaves among the nations of the world? Nor upon thy right hand that is behind thee wherewith thou didst stretch out the heavens and the earth and the heavens of heavens? When wilt thou have compassion?" Then the Holy One, blessed be He, answered every one of them, saying: "Since these wicked do sin so and so, and transgress with such and such transgressions against me, how could I deliver my great Right Hand in the downfall by their hands. In that moment Metatron called me and spake to me: "My servant! Take the books, and read their evil doings!" Forthwith I took the books and read their doings and there were to be found 36 transgressions with regard to each wicked one and besides, that they have transgressed all the letters in the Tora, as it is written: "Yea, all Israel have transgressed thy Law". It is not written 'al torateka but 'et torateka, for they have transgressed from 'Aleph to Taw, 4O statutes have they transgressed for each letter. Forthwith Abraham, Isaac and Jacob wept. Then said to them the Holy One, blessed be He: "Abraham, my beloved, Isaac, my Elect one, Jacob, my firstborn! How can I now deliver them from among the nations of the world?" And forthwith MIKAEL, the Prince of Israel, cried and wept with a loud voice and said: "Why standest thou afar off, O Lord?".

CHAPTER XLV

Come, and I will show thee the Curtain of MAQOM which is spread before the Holy One, blessed be He, whereon are graven all the generations of the world and all their doings, both what they have done and what they will do until the end of all generations. And I went, and he showed it to me pointing it out with his fingers Mike a father who teaches his children the letters of Tora. And I saw each generation, the rulers of each generation, and the heads of each generation, the shepherds of each generation, the oppressors of each generation, the keepers of each generation, the scourgers of each generation, the overseers of each generation, the judges of each generation, the court officers of each generation, the teachers of each generation, the supporters of each generation, the chiefs of each generation, the presidents of academies of each generation, the magistrates of each generation, the princes of each generation, the counsellors of each generation, the nobles of each generation, and the men of might of each generation, the elders of each generation, and the guides of each generation. And I saw Adam, his generation, their doings and their thoughts, Noah and his generation, their doings and their thoughts, and the generation of the flood, their doings and their thoughts, Shem and his generation, their doings and their thoughts, Nimrod and the generation of the confusion of tongues, and his generation, their doings and their thoughts, Abraham and his generation, their doings and their thoughts, Isaac and his generation, their doings and their thoughts, Ishmael and his generation, their doings and their thoughts, Jacob and his generation, their doings and their thoughts, Joseph and his generation, their doings and their thoughts, the tribes and their generation, their doings and their thoughts, Amram and his generation, their doings and their thoughts, Moses and his generation, their doings and their thoughts, Aaron and Mirjam their works and their doings, the princes and the elders, their works and doings, Joshua and his generation, their works and doings, the judges and their generation, their works and doings, Eli and his generation, their works and doings, "Phinehas, their works and doings, Elkanah and his generation, their works and doings, Samuel and his generation, their works and doings, the kings of Judah with their generations, their works and their doings, the kings of Israel and their generations, their works and their doings, the princes of Israel, their works and their doings; the princes of the nations of the world, their works and their doings, the heads of the councils of Israel, their works and their doings; the heads of nations of the world, their generations, their works and their doings; the rulers of Israel and their generation, their works and their doings; the nobles of Israel and their generation, their works and their doings; the nobles of the nations of the world and their generation, their works and their doings; the men of reputation in Israel, their generation, their works and their doings; the judges of Israel, their generation, their works and their doings; the judges of the nations of the world and their generation, their works and their doings; the teachers of children in Israel, their generations, their works and their doings; the teachers of children in the nations of the world, their generations, their works and their doings; the counsellors of Israel, their generation, their works and their doings; the counsellors of the nations of the world, their generation, their works and their doings; all the prophets of Israel, their generation, their works and their doings; all the prophets of the nations of the world, their generation, their works and their doings; and all the fights and wars that the nations 16 of the world wrought against the people of Israel in the time of their kingdom. And I saw Messiah, son of Joseph, and his generation "and their" works and their doings that they will do against the nations of the world. And I saw Messiah, son of David, and his generation, and all the fights and wars, and their works and their doings that they will do with Israel both for good and evil. And I saw all the fights and wars that Gog and Magog will fight in the days of Messiah, and all that the Holy One, blessed be He, will do with them in the time to come. And all the rest of all the leaders of the generations and all the works of the generations both in Israel and in the nations of the world, both what is done and what will be done hereafter to all generations until the end of time, were graven on the Curtain of MAQOM. And I saw all these things with my eyes; and after I had seen it, I opened my mouth in praise of MAQOM: "For the King's word hath power Whoso keepeth the commandments shall know no evil thing". And I said: "O Lord, how manifold are thy works!".

CHAPTER XLVI

the space of the stars a that are standing in Raqia' night by night in fear of the Almighty and where they go and where they stand. I walked by his side, and he took me by his hand and pointed out all to me with his fingers. And they were standing on sparks of flames round the Merkaba of the Almight. What did Metatron do? At that moment he clapped his hands and chased them off from their place. Forthwith they flew off on flaming wings, rose and fled from the four sides of the Throne of the Merkaba, and he told me the names of every single one. As it is written:" He telleth the number of the stars; he giveth them all their names", teaching, that the Holy One, blessed be He, has given a name to each one of them. And they all enter in counted order under the guidance of RAHATIEL to Raqia' ha-shSHamayim to serve the world. And they go out in counted order to praise the Holy One, blessed be He, with songs and hymns, according as it is written: "The heavens declare the glory of God". But in the time to come the Holy One, blessed be He, will create them anew, as it is written: "They are new every morning". And they open their mouth and utter a song. Which is the song that they utter? "When I consider thy heavens".

CHAPTER XLVII

Come and I will show thee the souls of the angels and the spirits of the ministering servants whose bodies have been burnt in the fire of MAQOM that goes forth from his little finger. And they have been made into fiery coals in the midst of the fiery river. But their spirits and their souls are standing behind the Shekina. Whenever the ministering angels utter a song at a wrong time or as not appointed to be sung they are burnt and consumed by the fire of their Creator and by a flame from their Maker, in the places of the whirlwind, for it blows upon them and drives them into the Nehar di-Nur; and there they are made into numerous mountains of burning coal. But their spirit and their soul return to their Creator, and all are standing behind their Master. And I went by his side and he took me by his hand; and he showed me all the souls of the angels and the spirits of the ministering servants who were standing behind the Shekina upon wings of the whirlwind and walls of fire surrounding them. At that moment Metatron opened to me the gates of the walls within which they were standing behind the Shekina, And I lifted up my eyes and saw them, and behold, the likeness of every one was as angels and their wings like birds', made out of flames, the work of burning fire. In that moment I opened my mouth in praise of MAQOM and said: "How great are thy works, O Lord ".

CHAPTER XLVIII

Come, and I will show thee the Right Hand of MAQOM, laid behind because of the destruction of the Holy Temple; from which all kinds of splendour and light shine forth and by which the 955 heavens were created; and whom not even the Seraphim and the 'Ophannim are permitted, until the day of salvation shall arrive. And I went by his side and he took me by his hand and showed me, with all manner of praise, rejoicing and song: and no mouth can tell its praise, and no eye can behold it, because of its greatness, dignity, majesty, glory and beauty. And not only that, but all the souls of the righteous who are counted worthy to behold the joy of Jerusalem, they are standing by it, praising and praying before it three times every day, saying: "Awake, awake, put on strength, O arm of the Lord" according as it is written: "He caused his glorious arm to go at the right hand of Moses". In that moment the Right Hand of MAQOM was weeping. And there went forth from its five fingers five rivers of tears and fell down into the great sea and shook the whole world, according as it is written "The earth is utterly broken (1), the earth is clean dissolved (2), the earth is moved exceedingly (3), the earth shall stagger like a drunken man (4) and shall be moved to and fro like a hut (5)", five times corresponding to the fingers of his Great Right Hand. But when the Holy One, blessed be He, sees, that there is no righteous man in the generation, and no pious man on earth, and no justice in the hands of men; and no man like unto Moses, and no intercessor as Samuel who could pray before MAQOM for the salvation and for the deliverance, and for His Kingdom, that it be revealed in the whole world; and for His great Right Hand that He put it before Himself again to work great salvation by it for Israel, then forthwith will the Holy One, blessed be He, remember His own justice, favour, mercy and grace: and He will deliver His great Arm by himself, and His righteousness will support Him. According as it is written: "And he saw, that there was no man" like unto Moses who prayed countless times for Israel in the desert and averted the decrees from them" and he wondered, that there was no intercessor" like unto Samuel who intreated the Holy One, blessed be He, and called unto Him and he answered him and fulfilled his desire, even if it was not fit, according as it is written "Is it not wheat-harvest to-day? I will call unto the Lord". And not only that, but He joined fellowship with Moses in every place, as it is written: "Moses and Aaron among His priests." And again it is written: "Though Moses and Samuel stood before me": "Mine own arm brought salvation unto me". Said the Holy One, blessed be He in that hour: " How long shall I wait for the children of men to work salvation according to their righteousness for my arm? For my own sake and for the sake of my merit and righteousness will I deliver my arm and by it redeem my children from among the nations of the world. As it is written: "For my own sake will I do it. For how should my name be profaned". In that moment will the Holy One, blessed be He, reveal His Great Arm and show it to the nations of the world: for its length is as the length of the world and its breadth is as the width of the world. And the appearance of its splendour is like unto the splendour of the sunshine in its might, in the summer solstice. Forthwith Israel will be saved from among the nations of the world. And Messiah will appear unto them and He will bring them up to Jerusalem with great joy. And not only that but Israel will come from the four quarters of the World and eat with Messiah. But the nations of the world shall not eat with them, as it is wiitten: "The Lord hath made bare his holy arm in the eyes of all the nations; and all the ends of the earth shall see the salvation of our God". And again: "The Lord alone did lead him, and there was no strange god with him": "And the Lord shall be king over all the earth". These are the seventy-two names written on the heart of the Holy One, blessed be He: SS, SeDeQ, SaHIeL SUR, SBI, SaDdlQ, S'Ph, SHN, SeBa'oTh, ShaDdaY, 'eLoHIM, YHWH, SH, DGUL, W'DOM, SSS", 'YW, 'F, 'HW, HB, YaH, HW, WWW, SSS,

PPP, NN, HH, HaY, HaY, ROKeB 'aRaBOTh, YH, HH, WH, MMM, NNN, HWW, YH, YHH, HPhS, H'S, 'I, W, S", Z', "', QQQ, QShR, BW, ZK, GINUR, GINURYa', Y', YOD, 'aLePh, H'N, P'P, R'W, YYWy YYW, BBS, DDD, TTT, KKK, KLL, SYS, 'XT', BShKMLW, completed for MeLeK HalOLaM, BRH LB', BNLK W" Y that go forth with numerous crowns of fire with numerous crowns of flame, with numerous crowns of chashmal, with numerous crowns of lightning from before the Throne of Glory. And with them thousand hundreds of power who escort them like a king with trembling and dread, with awe and shivering, with honour and majesty and fear, with terror, with greatness and dignity, with glory and strength, with understanding and knowledge and with a pillar of fire and a pillar of flame and lightning and their light is as lightnings of light and with the likeness of the chashmal. And they give glory unto them and they answer and cry before them: Holy, Holy, Holy. And they roll them through every heaven as mighty and honoured princes. And when they bring them all back to the place of the Throne of Glory, then all the Chayyoth by the Merkaba open their mouth in praise of His glorious name, saying: "Blessed be the name of His glorious kingdom for ever and ever". "I seized him, and I took him and I appointed him" that is Enoch, the son of Jared, whose name is Metatron and I took him from among the children of men and made him a Throne over against my Throne. Which is the size of that Throne? Seventy thousand parasangs of fire. I committed unto him 70 angels corresponding to the nations and I gave into his charge all the household above and below. And I committed to him Wisdom and Intelligence more than all the angels. And I called his name "the LESSER YAH", whose name is by Gematria 71. And I arranged for him all the works of Creation. And I made his power to transcend all the ministering angels. He committed unto Metatron that is Enoch, the son of Jared all treasuries. And I appointed him over all the stores that I have in every heaven. And I committed into his hands the keys of each heavenly store. I made him the prince over all the princes, and I made him a minister of my Throne of Glory, to provide for and arrange the Holy Chayyoth, to wreathe crowns for them, to clothe them with honour and majesty to prepare for them a seat when he is sitting on his throne to magnify his glory in the height. The height of his stature among all those of high stature seventy thousand parasangs. And I made his glory great as the majesty of my glory. and the brilliance of his eyes as the splendour of the Throne of Glory. his garment honour and majesty, his royal crown 500 by 500 parasangs. Aleph1 I made him strong, I took him, I appointed him: Metatron, my servant who is one among all the children of heaven. I made him strong in the generation of the first Adam. But when I beheld the men of the generation of the flood, that they were corrupt, then I went and removed my Shekina from among them. And 1 lifted it up on high with the sound of a trumpet and with a shout, as it is written: "God is gone up with a shout, the Lord with the sound of a trumpet". "And I took him": Enoch, the son of Jared, from among them. And I lifted him up with the sound of a trumpet and with a tera'a to the high heavens, to be my witness together with the Chayyoth by the Merkaba in the world to come. I appointed him over all the treasuries and stores that I have in every heaven. And I committed into his hand the keys of every several one. I made him the prince over all the princes and a minister of the Throne of Glory the Halls of 'Araboth: to open their doors to me, and the Throne of Glory, to exalt an arrange it; the Holy Chayyot to wreathe crowns upon their heads; the majestic 'Ophannim, to crown them with strength and glory; the; honoured Kerubim, to clothe: them in majesty; over the radiant sparks, to make them to shine with splendour and brilliance; over the flaming Seraphim, to cover them with highness; the Chashmallim of light, to make them radiant with Light and to prepare the seat for me every morning as I sit upon the Throne of Glory. And to extol and magnify my glory inthe height of my power; the secrets of above and the secrets of below. I made him higher than all. The height of his stature, in the midst of all high of stature seventy thousand parasangs. I made his Throne great by the majesty of my Throne. And I increased its glory by the honour of my glory. I transformed his flesh into torches of fire, and all the bones of his body into fiery coals; and I made the appearance of his eyes as the lightning, and the light of his eyebrows as the imperishable light. I made his face bright as the splendour of the sun, and his eyes as the splendour of the Throne of Glory. I made honour and majesty his clothing, beauty and highness his covering cloak and a royal crown of 500 by 500 parasangs diadem. And I put upon him of my honour, my majesty and the splendour. of my glory that is upon my Throne of Glory. I called him the LESSER YHWH, the Prince of the Presence, the Knower of Secrets: for every secret did I reveal to him as a father and all mysteries declared I unto him in uprightness. I set up his throne at the door of my Hall that he may sit and judge the heavenly household on high. And I placed every prince before him, to receive authority from him, to perform his will. Seventy names did I take from names and called him by them to enhance his glory. Seventy princes gave I into his hand, to command unto them my precepts and my words in every language: to abase by his word the proud to the ground, and to exalt by the utterance of his lips the humble to the height; to smite kings by his speech, to turn kings away from their paths, to set up rulers over their dominion as it is written: "and he changeth the times and the seasons, and to give wisdom unto all the setwise of the world and understanding knowledge to all who understand knowledge, as it is griten: " and knowledge to them that know understanding", to reveal to them the secrets of my words and to teach the decree of my righteous judgement, as it is written: "so shall my word be that goeth forth out of my mouth; it shall not return unto me void but shall accomplish". 'E'eseh' is not written here, but "asdh' , meaning, that whatever word and whatever utterance goes forth from before the Holy One, blessed be He, Metatron stands and carries it out. And he establishes the decrees of the Holy One, blessed be He. Seventy names has Metatron which the Holy One, blessed be He, took from his own name and put upon him. And these they are:

YeHOEL, YaH, YeHOEL, YOPHIEL and Yophphiel, and 'APHPHIEL and MaRGeZIEL, GIPpUYEL, Pa'aZIEL, 'A'aH, PeRIEL, TaTRIEL, TaBKIEL,'W, YHWH, DH, WHYH, 'eBeD, DiBbURIEL, 'aPh'aPIEL, SPPIEL, PaSPaSIEL, SeNeGRON, MeTaTRON, SOGDIN, 'ADRIGON, ASUM, SaQPaM, SaQTaM, MIGON MITTON, MOTTRON, ROSPHIM, QINOTh, ChaTaTYaH, DeGaZYaH, PSPYaH, BSKNYH, MZRG, BaRaD.., MKRKK, MSPRD, ChShG, ChShB, MNRTTT, BSYRYM, MITMON, TITMON, PiSQON, SaPhSaPhYaH, ZRCh, ZRChYaH, B', BeYaH, HBH BeYaH, PeLeT, PLTYaH, RaBRaBYaH, ChaS, ChaSYaH, TaPhTaPhYaH, TaMTaMYaH, SeHaSYaH, IRURYaH, 'aL'aLYaH, BaZRIDYaH, SaTSaTKYaH, SaSDYaH, RaZRaZYAH, BaZRaZYaH, 'aRIMYaH, SBHYaH, SBIBKHYH, SiMKaM, YaHSeYaH, SSBIBYaH, SaBKaSBeYaH, QeLILQaLYaH, KIHHH, HHYH, WH, WHYH, ZaKklKYaH, TUTRISYaH, SURYaH, ZeH, PeNIRHYaH, Z1Z'H, GaL RaZaYYa, MaMLIKYaH, TTYaH, eMeQ, QaMYaH, MeKaPpeRYaH, PeRISHYaH, SePhaM, GBIR, GiBbORYaH, GOR, GORYaH, ZIW, 'OKBaR, the LESSER YHWH, after the name of his Master, for my name is in him", RaBIBIEL, TUMIEL, Segansakkiel, the Prince of Wisdom. And why is he called by the name Sagnesakiel? Because all the treasuries of wisdom are committed in his hand. And all of them were opened to Moses on Sinai, so that he learnt them during the forty days, while he was standing: the Torah in the seventy aspects of the seventy tongues, the Prophets in the seventy aspects of the seventy tongues, the Writings in the seventy aspects of the seventy tongues, "the Halakas in the seventy aspects of the seventy tongues, the Traditions in the seventy aspects of the seventy tongues, the Haggadas in the seventy aspects of the seventy tongues and the Toseftas in the seventy aspects of the seventy tongues'. But as soon as the forty days were ended, he forgot all of them in one moment. Then the Holy One, blessed be He, called Yephiphyah, the Prince of the Law, and they were given to Moses as a gift. As it is written: "and the Lord gave them unto me". And after that it remained with him. And whence do we know, that it remained? Because it is written: " Remember ye the Law of Moses my servant which I commanded unto him in Horeb for all Israel, even my statutes and judgements". The Law of Moses': that is the Tora, the Prophets and the Writings, 'statutes': that is the Halakas and Traditions, 'judgements'; that is the Haggadas and the Toseftas. And all of them were given to Moses on high on Sinai. These seventy names a reflection of the Explicit Name on the Merkaba which are graven upon the Throne of Glory. For the Holy One, blessed be He, took from His Explicit Name and put upon the name of Metatron: Seventy Names of His by which the ministering angels call the King of the kings of kings, blessed be He, in the high heavens, and twenty-two letters that are on the ring upon his finger with which are sealed the destinies of the princes of kingdoms on high in greatness and power and with which are sealed the lots of the Angel of Death, and the destinies of every nation and tongue. Said Metatron, the Angel, the Prince of the Presence; the Angel, the Prince of the Wisdom; the Angel, the Prince of the Understanding; the Angel, the Prince of the Kings; the Angel, the Prince of the Rulers; the angel, the Prince of the Glory; the angel, the Prince of the high ones, and of the princes, the exalted, great and honoured ones, in heaven and on earth: "H, the God of Israel, is my witness in this thing, when I revealed this secret to Moses, then all the hosts in every heaven on high raged against me and said to me: Why dost thou reveal this secret to son of man, born of woman, tainted and unclean, a man of a putrefying drop, the secret by which were created heaven and earth, the sea and the dry land, the mountains and hills, the rivers and springs, Gehenna of fire and hail, the Garden of Eden and the Tree of Life; and by which were formed Adam and Eve, and the cattle, and the wild beasts, and the fowl of the air, and the fish of the sea, and Behemoth and Leviathan, and the creeping things, the worms, the dragons of the sea, and the creeping things of the deserts; and the Tora and Wisdom and Knowledge and Thought and the Gnosis of things above and the fear of heaven. Why dost thou reveal this to flesh and blood? I answered them: Because the Holy One, blessed be He, has given me authority, And furthermore, I have obtained permission from the high and exalted Throne, from which all the Explicit Names go forth with lightnings of fire and flaming chashmallim. But they were not appeased, until the Holy One, blessed be He, rebuked them and drove them away with rebuke from before him, saying to them: "I delight in, and have set my love on, and have entrusted and committed unto Metatron, my Servant, alone, for he is One among all the children of heaven. And Metatron brought them out from his house of treasuries and committed them to Moses, and Moses to Joshua, and Joshua to the elders, and the elders to the prophets and the prophets to the men of the Great Synagogue, and the men of the Great Synagogue to Ezra and Ezra the Scribe to Hillel the elder, and Hillel the elder to R. Abbahu and R. Abbahu to R. Zera, and R. Zera to the men of faith, and the men of faith to give warning and to heal by them all diseases that rage in the world, as it is written: "If thou wilt diligently hearken to the voice of the Lord, thy God, and wilt do that which is right in his eyes, and wilt give ear to his commandments, and keep all his statutes, I will put none of the diseases upon thee, which I have put upon the Egyptians : for I am the Lord, that healeth thee".

CONCLUSION TO THE THIRD BOOK OF ENOCH

The Third Book of Enoch stands as a profound exploration of divine mysteries, spiritual transformation, and the hierarchies of heaven. It challenges readers to contemplate their place in the cosmos, encouraging reflection on themes of divine justice, human potential, and spiritual elevation. Through Rabbi Ishmael's ascent and Enoch's transformation into Metatron, the text underscores the possibility of divine communion, illustrating how faith, obedience, and purity can lead to spiritual glorification.

As both a theological guide and a mystical roadmap, 3 Enoch serves not only as a resource for understanding angelology and heavenly governance, but also as an invitation for readers to pursue personal transformation. Its insights into the power of divine names, sacred language, and cosmic harmony resonate with modern seekers, inspiring them to explore their own spiritual journeys and seek deeper wisdom.

Ultimately, 3 Enoch bridges the earthly and the divine, reminding readers of humanity's capacity for spiritual elevation and alignment with God's plan. Its timeless teachings offer tools for personal growth, prayerful reflection, and mystical understanding, making it an enduring text for those seeking to connect with the mysteries of heaven and the glory of God's presence.

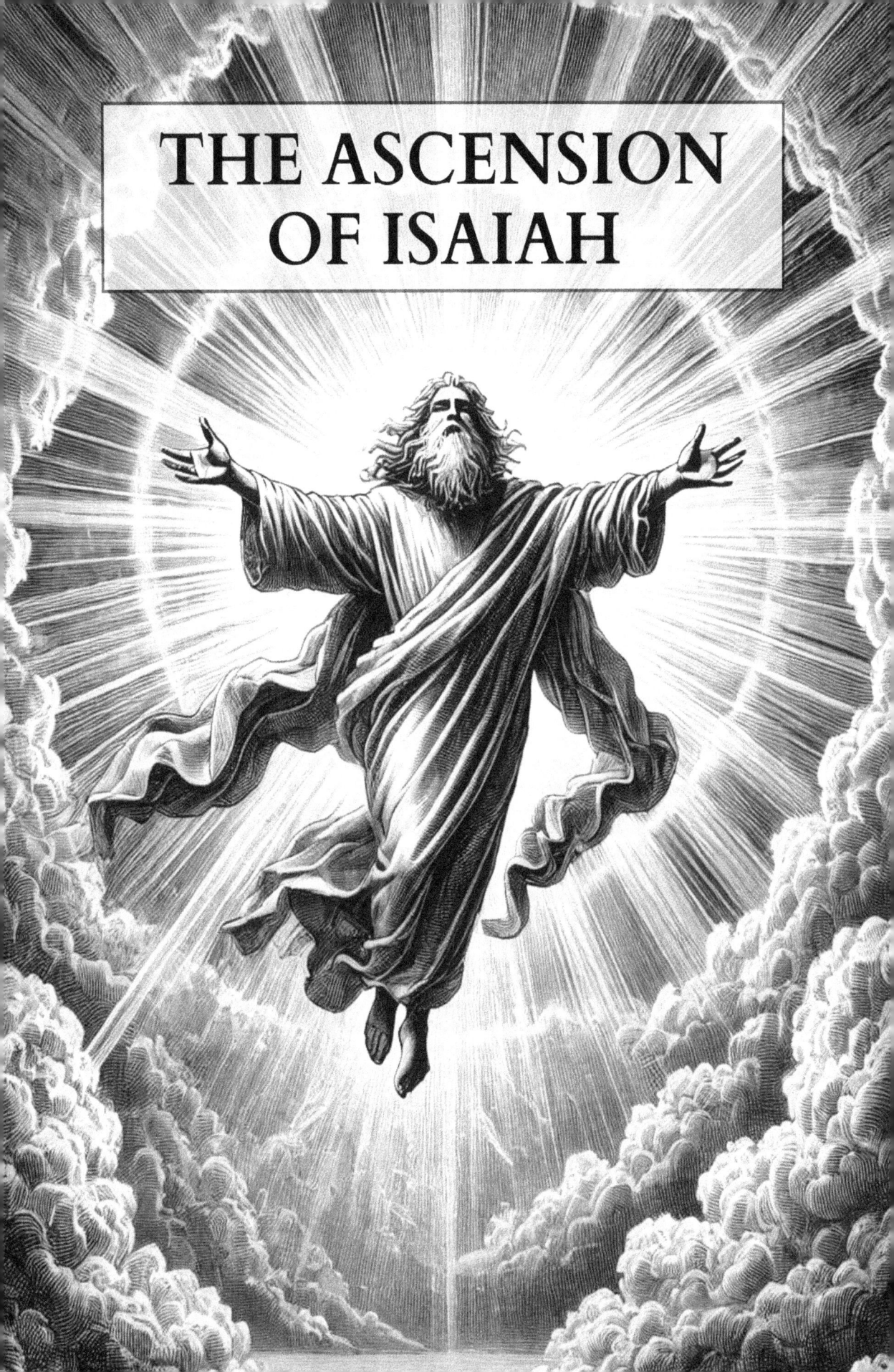

APPENDIX 1 - THE ASCENSION OF ISAIAH

INTRODUCTION

HISTORICAL AND LITERARY CONTEXT

The Ascension of Isaiah is a unique text that bridges Jewish and early Christian apocalyptic traditions. It is generally dated between the late first century and the early second century CE, a period of intense religious transformation and doctrinal development. The text reflects both Jewish prophetic traditions and emerging Christian theological concepts, making it an essential source for understanding how early believers perceived prophecy, martyrdom, and the heavenly realm.

Authorship remains uncertain, as the text likely evolved over time, incorporating different layers of tradition. The first section, describing the martyrdom of Isaiah, has strong roots in Jewish legends about the prophet's fate, particularly in relation to the reign of King Manasseh. The second section, the heavenly vision of Isaiah, exhibits clear Christian influences, particularly in its depiction of the pre-existence, descent, and return of the Beloved (Christ). These two halves of the book suggest that it was used by communities transitioning from Jewish apocalypticism to early Christian theology, incorporating elements from both traditions.

The surviving versions of *The Ascension of Isaiah* are primarily in Ethiopic (Ge'ez), Greek, Latin, and Slavonic, though scholars believe the original text was likely composed in Hebrew or Aramaic for the martyrdom section and Greek for the vision section. The transmission history of the text suggests that it was widely read in early Christian communities, particularly among groups that valued apocalyptic literature. Over time, as church authorities formalized the Christian canon, *The Ascension of Isaiah* was excluded, likely due to its complex authorship, its non-canonical prophetic revelations, and its association with apocalyptic sects.

Despite this, the text holds significant importance for understanding how Jewish and Christian traditions intertwined, particularly in their depictions of divine revelation and celestial hierarchy. The parallels with Enochian literature are striking, especially in its descriptions of multiple heavens, angelic beings, and divine mysteries. Like *1 Enoch*, *2 Enoch*, and *3 Enoch*, *The Ascension of Isaiah* presents a cosmic vision in which a prophet is granted access to heavenly knowledge, reinforcing the theme of divine wisdom being revealed to chosen individuals.

The inclusion of *The Ascension of Isaiah* in this Collection is therefore a natural choice. It complements the visionary and apocalyptic nature of other texts, offering a unique perspective on the heavenly ascent motif that is central to several writings in this collection. Moreover, it provides a crucial link between Jewish prophetic traditions and early Christian theological developments, making it an indispensable part of this body of literature.

THEOLOGICAL SIGNIFICANCE

The Ascension of Isaiah presents a unique theological perspective that blends Jewish prophetic traditions with early Christian apocalyptic thought. At its core, the text explores the concept of divine ascent, where the righteous are granted access to celestial realms and receive hidden knowledge about the divine order. This theme is deeply rooted in Jewish apocalyptic literature, particularly in texts like 1 Enoch and 2 Enoch, where figures such as Enoch are taken up to the heavens and shown cosmic mysteries. In The Ascension of Isaiah, the prophet undergoes a similar transformation, leaving behind the earthly realm to witness firsthand the structure of the heavens and the interactions between celestial beings. The idea that divine knowledge is revealed through visionary journeys reinforces the belief that certain individuals are chosen to receive and transmit sacred truths that remain inaccessible to the rest of humanity. Isaiah's ascent through the seven heavens mirrors other mystical traditions in which the progression through various levels of divine reality represents a gradual unveiling of the ultimate truth. Each level reveals greater spiritual purity, culminating in an encounter with the Most High, where divine knowledge is imparted in its fullest form. This structure not only aligns with Jewish apocalypticism but also foreshadows later Christian mystical traditions that emphasize the idea of spiritual ascent as a path to ultimate enlightenment.

Isaiah's role in both Jewish and Christian traditions is crucial to understanding why this text occupies such an important place in religious history. In Jewish tradition, Isaiah is one of the major prophets, revered for his visions and his warnings to Israel. His prophetic writings in the Hebrew Bible shape much of later Jewish thought, especially concerning the fate of Israel and the coming of a messianic age. However, The Ascension of Isaiah extends his prophetic legacy beyond its traditional Jewish context and places him within an early Christian framework. The text presents Isaiah as a martyr and a visionary, linking his death to his role as a bearer of divine revelation. His martyrdom at the hands of King Manasseh is framed as an act of resistance against the forces of darkness, particularly Beliar (Belial), a figure associated with satanic power. This portrayal of Isaiah aligns him with Christian themes of suffering, sacrifice, and divine vindication, making him a prototype for later Christian martyrs. His unwavering faith and his willingness to die for his vision of the divine truth mirror the experiences of early Christians who faced persecution for their beliefs. This adaptation of Isaiah's story demonstrates how early Christian communities reinterpreted Jewish prophetic figures through the lens of their own theological struggles.

The Christology of The Ascension of Isaiah is one of its most distinctive and controversial aspects. Unlike the Hebrew Bible's messianic expectations, which often describe a Davidic king who will restore Israel's fortunes, this text presents a highly developed concept of a pre-existent Christ who descends from the highest heaven. The Beloved, as he is referred to in the text, is portrayed as a celestial being who exists before time and who voluntarily descends through the heavens, assuming human form in a way that remains hidden from the rulers of the world. This idea of a hidden Messiah reflects early Christian theological developments found in Pauline writings and the Gospel of John, where Christ is described as existing before creation and humbling himself to take on human nature. The text emphasizes that the rulers of the world, influenced by Beliar, do not recognize the true identity of the Beloved, reinforcing the Christian idea that Christ's mission was veiled from those who opposed him. This depiction also aligns with later Gnostic and mystical traditions that emphasize the idea of Christ's descent as part of a divine rescue mission. His return to the heavens after completing his mission further solidifies the theme of ascent and descent as central to divine action in the world.

These theological themes make The Ascension of Isaiah a significant addition to the Collection. Its emphasis on divine ascent, hidden revelation, and the cosmic struggle between light and darkness places it alongside other visionary texts that explore the relationship between the heavenly and earthly realms. The text's portrayal of Isaiah as a martyr connects it to the broader theme of righteous suffering found in many apocalyptic traditions. Its Christological framework, which presents the Beloved as a pre-existent divine being, contributes to the understanding of early Christian theology and its development from Jewish apocalyptic thought. By bridging these traditions, The Ascension of Isaiah serves as both a continuation and an evolution of prophetic literature, reinforcing its place in this collection as a work that offers profound insights into the nature of divine revelation and the cosmic role of Christ.

RELATIONSHIP TO OTHER ANCIENT TEXTS

The Ascension of Isaiah stands at a crossroads of Jewish apocalypticism and early Christian mysticism, making it an essential text for understanding the theological and literary landscape of the first few centuries CE. Its themes of divine ascent, heavenly revelation, angelology, and the cosmic struggle between good and evil place it in direct dialogue with other significant works of the period. The text shares structural and thematic similarities with the books of Enoch, aligns with the broader category of apocalyptic and visionary literature, and possibly influenced—or was influenced by—certain passages in early Christian texts. Understanding these interconnections is crucial for scholars and readers exploring the evolution of apocalyptic thought and early Christology.

One of the most striking parallels exists between *The Ascension of Isaiah* and Enochian literature, particularly *1 Enoch* and *2 Enoch*. The concept of a prophet ascending to the heavens, receiving divine knowledge, and returning to reveal esoteric truths is a central motif in both. In *1 Enoch*, Enoch is taken into the celestial realm, where he learns about the workings of the universe, the rebellion of fallen angels, and the ultimate fate of the righteous and the wicked. Similarly, in *The Ascension of Isaiah*,

APPENDIX 1 - THE ASCENSION OF ISAIAH

Isaiah is granted access to the seven heavens, where he encounters various angelic hierarchies and witnesses the descent of the Beloved. Both texts emphasize the hidden nature of divine wisdom, reinforcing the idea that true knowledge is reserved for those whom God chooses to reveal it to, a notion that would later influence mystical and Gnostic traditions. The depiction of angelic ranks and the gradual unveiling of divine glory as one ascends higher into the heavens is also a shared feature. Like Enoch, Isaiah moves through increasingly holier and more radiant spheres, culminating in the vision of the Most High.

Another key connection with *1 Enoch* is the portrayal of cosmic opposition between divine forces and the rulers of the world, particularly through the figure of Beliar (Belial) in *The Ascension of Isaiah* and the rebellious angels in *1 Enoch*. Both texts frame human history as a battleground between celestial and infernal forces, where rulers are often depicted as puppets of darker powers. This dualistic worldview aligns with the later Dead Sea Scrolls, where Belial is also presented as the great adversary of the righteous. The Testament of Hezekiah within *The Ascension of Isaiah* reflects this tradition by describing how Beliar will corrupt rulers, deceive nations, and persecute the faithful, reinforcing a theme prevalent in apocalyptic literature. These connections suggest that *The Ascension of Isaiah* not only draws upon the same Second Temple Jewish traditions that influenced the Enochian corpus but also develops them further in light of early Christian theological concerns.

Beyond Enochian literature, *The Ascension of Isaiah* shares thematic elements with other apocalyptic and visionary texts, particularly those that emphasize mystical ascent and celestial revelation. Works such as *The Apocalypse of Abraham* and *4 Ezra* contain similar descriptions of righteous figures being taken into the divine realm, where they are shown secrets of history and the unfolding of God's plan. The idea of a journey through multiple levels of heaven, with increasing encounters with divine beings, is a hallmark of these writings, reinforcing the widespread belief in a structured cosmos where divine order is progressively revealed.

The text also bears similarities to later Hekhalot and Merkavah mysticism, which emerged in rabbinic Judaism and detailed the experience of ascending through the heavenly palaces (hekhalot) to behold God's throne (merkavah). Though *The Ascension of Isaiah* predates the fully developed Hekhalot tradition, its visionary framework, emphasis on angelic intermediaries, and gradual approach toward the divine throne anticipate many of the same themes that would become central to Jewish mystical thought.

A critical question in the study of *The Ascension of Isaiah* is whether it influenced early Christian texts or was shaped by them. The high Christology presented in the vision of Isaiah, particularly the depiction of the Beloved's pre-existence, descent, and return to the heavens, aligns closely with Philippians 2:6-11, where Christ is described as existing in the form of God, humbling himself to take on human nature, and then being exalted once more. The text also resonates with Johannine theology, particularly John 1:1-14, where the Word (Logos) descends into the world but remains unrecognized by those in power—a concept mirrored in Isaiah's vision of the Beloved's hidden descent through the heavens.

Additionally, *The Ascension of Isaiah* may reflect or contribute to the mystical elements found in Paul's letters, such as 2 Corinthians 12:2-4, where Paul speaks of a man (often interpreted as himself) who was caught up to the third heaven and heard things that could not be spoken. The idea that divine revelation comes through mystical ascent, where hidden truths are revealed to a chosen prophet, fits the same visionary paradigm found in *The Ascension of Isaiah*. It is also worth considering that early Gnostic Christian movements, which placed great emphasis on hidden wisdom and celestial hierarchies, may have found resonance with the esoteric and apocalyptic elements of this text. Some scholars suggest that texts like *The Gospel of Thomas* and *The Gospel of Truth* reflect a similar concern with hidden revelation, divine descent, and ascent, which are core themes in Isaiah's vision.

These extensive parallels and intertextual connections make *The Ascension of Isaiah* a crucial text within the Collection. Its profound alignment with Enochian literature, its continuity with Jewish apocalyptic thought, and its potential role in shaping or reflecting early Christian theology position it as an essential component of this collection. By examining its relationship with other ancient texts, scholars can gain deeper insights into the development of apocalyptic traditions, the evolution of angelology, and the emergence of high Christology in early Christianity.

RECEPTION AND INFLUENCE

The Ascension of Isaiah occupies a unique position in the history of early apocalyptic literature, existing at the intersection of Jewish prophetic tradition, early Christian mysticism, and esoteric theological speculation. While never officially canonized in either Jewish or mainstream Christian traditions, it was widely known and circulated among various early religious communities, influencing theological thought and mystical traditions. Its reception in antiquity was complex, shaped by its apocalyptic character and its distinctive Christology, which positioned it as both a revered text in certain circles and a suspect work in others.

In early Christianity, references to themes present in The Ascension of Isaiah appear in the writings of the Apostolic Fathers and early Church theologians. The text's high Christology, particularly its depiction of the pre-existent Christ descending through the heavens in secret, mirrors theological perspectives found in Philippians 2:6-11 and John 1:1-14, as well as certain passages in Pauline literature. While The Ascension of Isaiah itself is not quoted directly in the New Testament, its thematic elements—such as divine ascent, cosmic struggle, and angelic hierarchies—align with the theological framework of many early Christian texts. This suggests that the ideas within it were part of the broader theological and mystical discourse of early Christian thought.

The text was particularly well-received among Christian groups that emphasized apocalyptic revelations and mystical ascent, such as some early proto-Gnostic communities and Jewish-Christian sects. It bears certain thematic resemblances to the writings of the Dead Sea Scrolls, where a cosmic battle between light and darkness, angelic hierarchies, and prophetic martyrdom are central themes. This suggests that The Ascension of Isaiah may have been regarded favorably by sectarian Jewish groups who maintained apocalyptic expectations in the late Second Temple period.

Among Gnostic and mystical Christian sects, the text's emphasis on hidden revelation and celestial ascent made it particularly appealing. Some scholars argue that the structure of Christ's descent and re-ascent in The Ascension of Isaiah parallels Valentinian Gnostic cosmology, where the redeemer figure descends through layers of reality and returns after completing his mission. The secretive nature of the Beloved's descent, remaining unnoticed by the rulers of the world, is a theme that aligns with Gnostic interpretations of divine wisdom being concealed from corrupt powers.

By the third and fourth centuries, however, as the Christian canon was being formalized, The Ascension of Isaiah, along with many other apocalyptic and visionary texts, began to lose its prominence in mainstream Christian theology. It was excluded from the canonical New Testament, likely due to its complex textual history, its Jewish prophetic roots, and its highly developed angelology and Christology, which may have been viewed as too esoteric or speculative. As Church authorities sought to distinguish between orthodox doctrine and heretical movements, texts with strong apocalyptic and mystical elements, including The Ascension of Isaiah, were marginalized.

Despite its exclusion from the canon, The Ascension of Isaiah continued to be copied and preserved, particularly in Ethiopian Christianity, where it survived in its fullest form in the Ge'ez manuscript tradition. This preservation aligns with Ethiopia's broader tendency to retain apocryphal and pseudepigraphal works that were lost or suppressed in Western Christianity. Fragments of the text also survived in Greek, Latin, and Slavonic, attesting to its wider circulation in antiquity before being relegated to obscurity in the medieval period.

The text was rediscovered by Western scholars in the 19th and 20th centuries, when interest in early Christian apocrypha and Jewish mysticism surged. The study of The Ascension of Isaiah became particularly relevant in discussions about the development of early Christology, the role of Jewish mysticism in Christianity, and the influence of apocalyptic literature on theological thought. Today, scholars recognize it as a critical source for understanding the diversity of Jewish-Christian interactions, apocalyptic traditions, and early theological speculation, reaffirming its value in the broader historical and religious landscape.

APPENDIX 1 - THE ASCENSION OF ISAIAH

Why This Text Matters Today

The Ascension of Isaiah remains highly relevant for scholars and students of religious history, offering profound insights into early Jewish and Christian thought, mystical traditions, and the evolution of apocalyptic literature. As a bridge between Jewish prophetic literature and early Christian theology, the text provides valuable perspectives on how religious communities in the first and second centuries CE understood divine revelation, celestial realms, and the figure of Christ.

One of the key reasons this text is important today is its ability to shed light on the diversity of early Christian beliefs. The depiction of the Beloved as a pre-existent celestial being who descends in secret represents a high Christology that predates the formalized doctrines of the later Church Councils. This suggests that early Christian communities held a variety of views on the nature of Christ, his mission, and his relationship to the angelic realm, some of which were eventually excluded from mainstream orthodoxy. By studying The Ascension of Isaiah, scholars can reconstruct alternative strands of early Christian theology that were once part of the broader religious conversation but later suppressed or forgotten.

The text also offers a window into ancient perceptions of the divine realm, particularly in its detailed descriptions of the seven heavens, angelic hierarchies, and cosmic struggles. This structured view of the universe aligns with Enochian and Hekhalot traditions, which later influenced both Jewish mysticism and Christian mystical movements. Understanding how these concepts developed in The Ascension of Isaiah helps contextualize later theological developments, including medieval mysticism and esoteric traditions.

From a historical perspective, The Ascension of Isaiah provides critical insight into Second Temple Judaism and early Christian apocalypticism, showing how these traditions responded to political oppression, spiritual corruption, and the expectation of divine intervention. The text's portrayal of righteous suffering in the face of evil rulers reflects broader concerns within both Jewish and Christian martyrdom traditions, illustrating how communities framed their struggles within a cosmic battle between good and evil. This theme remains relevant in the study of religious movements that emphasize persecution, martyrdom, and divine justice.

Beyond its theological significance, The Ascension of Isaiah continues to offer valuable material for comparative religious studies, especially in understanding how ancient texts influenced later mystical traditions, esoteric teachings, and alternative Christianities. The text's survival in the Ethiopian tradition also speaks to the global diversity of biblical and extra-biblical literature, reminding scholars that Christianity developed differently across various cultures and regions.

In modern scholarship, The Ascension of Isaiah is increasingly examined in discussions on Jewish-Christian relations, Second Temple apocalypticism, and the origins of high Christology. The growing recognition of apocryphal and pseudepigraphal texts as critical sources for understanding the early religious world makes The Ascension of Isaiah an indispensable part of the study of ancient religious thought. Its continued relevance in historical and theological studies underscores its enduring value as a text that bridges prophetic tradition, mystical experience, and early Christian theology, making it a crucial component of the Collection.

AUTHOR'S NOTE ON THE INTRODUCTIONS

In assembling this edition of *The Ascension of Isaiah*, it was decided to include introductory notes for each major section of the text. These introductions serve as a guide to help readers—both scholars and those newly exploring apocryphal writings—navigate the historical, theological, and literary significance of each part. Given the complex nature of the text and its multi-layered composition, these introductions aim to provide clarity and context, ensuring a deeper understanding of the material.

The decision to include these introductory notes stems from the recognition that *The Ascension of Isaiah* is not a unified text but rather a compilation of different traditions, written at different times, and reflecting both Jewish and early Christian influences. Each section has its own distinct themes, narrative structure, and theological implications. By offering a brief introduction before each part, readers can better appreciate the unique characteristics of the Martyrdom of Isaiah, the Testament of Hezekiah, and the Vision of Isaiah, as well as their place within the broader tradition of apocalyptic literature.

These introductions are not part of the original ancient text but have been written specifically for this edition to enhance comprehension and scholarly engagement. Care has been taken to ensure that they remain informative, objective, and based on established historical and theological scholarship. They do not seek to impose interpretations but rather to highlight key themes, textual background, and relevant connections to other ancient writings, allowing readers to engage with the text in an informed manner.

By structuring the book in this way, the goal is to make *The Ascension of Isaiah* more accessible while preserving its historical depth and theological richness. Whether one approaches this text as a historical document, a theological artifact, or an apocalyptic vision, these introductions are meant to serve as an aid in understanding its significance within the Collection and the broader landscape of ancient religious literature.

APPENDIX 1 – THE ASCENSION OF ISAIAH

STRUCTURE OF THE TEXT (EXPANDED TO INCLUDE THE TESTAMENT OF HEZEKIAH)

The Ascension of Isaiah is divided into two primary sections: The Martyrdom of Isaiah (Chapters 1-5) and The Vision of Isaiah (Chapters 6-11). However, within the first section, there is a crucial prophetic segment known as The Testament of Hezekiah (3:13 – 4:18), which serves as a bridge between the Jewish martyrdom narrative and the emerging Christian apocalyptic vision. This passage is fundamental in understanding the theological evolution of the text, as it introduces a proto-Christian prophecy within a Jewish framework.

The Testament of Hezekiah (3:13 – 4:18) – A Prophetic Warning and Messianic Revelation

This section is framed as a vision received by King Hezekiah and revealed to Isaiah, outlining the corruption of future generations and the eventual arrival of the "Beloved" (Christ). The passage is significant because it contains elements of messianic expectation, apocalyptic judgment, and eschatological prophecy, concepts that resonate deeply with both Jewish and early Christian traditions.

The prophecy describes:

A period of spiritual corruption and apostasy—It foresees a time when leaders will fall into deception, greed, and false worship, abandoning divine truth. This mirrors other apocalyptic texts that predict an age of darkness before the final redemption.

The arrival of the "Beloved" (Messiah), who will descend from the highest heaven—This is a strikingly Christian concept that aligns with later New Testament theology. Unlike Jewish messianic expectations of a political liberator, this vision presents a heavenly being who will descend humbly, unnoticed by the rulers of the world, and accomplish his mission in secrecy.

The influence of Beliar (Belial) and the forces of darkness—The prophecy warns that Beliar will take control of rulers and nations, misleading many. This theme of cosmic struggle between light and darkness is a key element of apocalyptic literature, reinforcing the idea that the true battle is not earthly but celestial.

Connection Between the Testament of Hezekiah and the Rest of the Text

This passage serves as a transition between the martyrdom narrative and the heavenly vision, preparing the reader for the cosmic revelation in Chapters 6-11.

It also foreshadows the events of the Vision of Isaiah, particularly the descent and ascent of the Beloved, which Isaiah will later witness firsthand in his celestial journey.

The corruption of rulers and the deception of the world echo themes found in Enochian literature, particularly in *1 Enoch* and *2 Enoch*, where the watchers (fallen angels) mislead humanity.

Why This Subsection is Essential to the Collection

The inclusion of *The Ascension of Isaiah* in this Collection is reinforced by the Testament of Hezekiah, which presents a proto-Christian revelation embedded within a Jewish prophetic tradition. This aligns it with the books of Enoch, where divine wisdom is unveiled in stages through visions, heavenly journeys, and esoteric prophecy. The apocalyptic tone, the hidden nature of the Messiah, and the warning of deception by dark forces are all themes that resonate throughout the texts in this collection, making *The Ascension of Isaiah* an essential component.

This passage acts as a theological bridge, showing the gradual emergence of Christian thought within Jewish apocalyptic traditions, and it reinforces the esoteric and revelatory nature of the entire Collection.

THE ASCENSION OF ISAIAH

THE MARTYRDOM OF ISAIAH (I-V)

INTRODUCTION

The Martyrdom of Isaiah is the first section of The Ascension of Isaiah and serves as a dramatic account of the prophet's final days under the reign of King Manasseh of Judah. This narrative follows the longstanding Jewish tradition that Isaiah, one of Israel's greatest prophets, was persecuted and executed for his unwavering commitment to divine truth. His condemnation and death—ultimately by being sawn in half—are depicted as part of a cosmic struggle between righteousness and the corrupt forces of darkness, a theme that echoes throughout Jewish and Christian apocalyptic literature.

This section has deep roots in Second Temple Jewish tradition, as legends about Isaiah's martyrdom circulated widely before being written down in texts such as this one. The idea that Manasseh, the wicked son of King Hezekiah, turned against Isaiah for his prophecies was well known in early Jewish thought and is referenced in later Christian tradition—most notably in Hebrews 11:37, where righteous figures are described as having been "sawn in two." The Martyrdom of Isaiah thus provides one of the fullest surviving accounts of this tradition, shaping how later generations perceived Isaiah's fate.

While this section largely follows a Jewish narrative framework, there are significant theological elements that hint at later Christian influence, particularly in how Isaiah's persecution is framed as a battle between divine and demonic forces. The text explicitly presents Beliar (Belial) as the true power behind King Manasseh, portraying the prophet's execution as part of a broader struggle between good and evil. This concept—where human rulers act as instruments of celestial forces—is a hallmark of apocalyptic literature, paralleling themes found in 1 Enoch and the Dead Sea Scrolls, where corrupt rulers are often depicted as being under the control of dark spiritual entities.

The Martyrdom of Isaiah plays a crucial role in The Ascension of Isaiah by establishing Isaiah's righteousness, his role as a prophet of divine truth, and the inevitability of persecution for those who oppose the forces of darkness. It also sets the stage for the second part of the text, The Testament of Hezekiah, where a more explicitly prophetic and eschatological dimension emerges. This section serves as a link between traditional Jewish martyr narratives and the growing theological ideas that would influence early Christianity, reinforcing themes of suffering, divine justice, and the ultimate triumph of righteousness.

APPENDIX 1 - THE ASCENSION OF ISAIAH

CHAPTER I.

And it came to pass in the twenty-sixth year of the reign of Hezekiah king of Judah that he called Manasseh his son. Now he was his only one. 2. And he called him into the presence of Isaiah the son of Amoz the prophet, and into the presence of Jôsâb the son of Isaiah, *in order to deliver unto him the words of righteousness which the king himself had seen:* 3. *And of the eternal judgments and the torments of Gehenna and of the prince of this world, and of his angels, and his authorities and his powers.* 4. *And the words of the faith of the Beloved which he himself had seen in the fifteenth year of his reign during his illness.* 5. *And he delivered unto him the written words which Samnas the scribe had written and also those which Isaiah, the son of Amoz, had given to him, and also to the prophets, that they might write and store up with him what he himself had seen in the king's house regarding the judgment of the angels, and the destruction of this world, and regarding the garments of the saints and their going forth, and regarding their transformation and the persecution and ascension of the Beloved.* 6- *In the twentieth year of the reign of Hezekiah, Isaiah had seen the words of this prophecy and had delivered them to Jôsâb his son.* And whilst he (Hezekiah) gave commands, Jôsâb the son of Isaiah standing by, 7. Isaiah said to Hezekiah the king, but not in the presence of Manasseh only did he say unto him: "As the Lord liveth, whose name hath not been sent into this world, and as the Beloved of my Lord liveth, and the Spirit which speaketh in me liveth, all these commands and these words will be made of none effect by Manasseh thy son, and through the agency of his hands I shall depart mid the torture of my body. 8. And Sammael Malchira will serve Manasseh, and execute all his desire, and he will become a follower of Belial rather than of me. 9. And many in Jerusalem and in Judæa he will cause to abandon the true faith, and Belial will dwell in Manasseh, and by his hands I shall be sawn asunder." 10- And when Hezekiah heard these words he wept very bitterly, and rent his garments, and placed earth upon his head, and fell on his face. 11. And Isaiah said unto him: "The counsel of Sammael against Manasseh is consummated: nought will avail thee." 12. And on that day Hezekiah resolved in his heart to slay Manasseh his son. 13- And Isaiah said to Hezekiah: *"The Beloved hath made of none effect thy design, and the purpose of thy heart will not be accomplished, for with this calling have I been called and I shall inherit the heritage of the Beloved."*

CHAPTER II.

And it came to pass after that Hezekiah died and Manasseh became king, that he did not remember the commands of Hezekiah his father but forgot them, and Sammael abode in Manasseh and clung fast to him. 2. And Manasseh forsook the service of the God of his father, and he served Satan and his angels and his powers. 3. And he turned aside the house of his father which had been before the face of Hezekiah (from) the words of wisdom and from the service of God. 4. And Manasseh turned aside his heart to serve Belial; for the angel of lawlessness, who is the ruler of this world, is Belial, *whose name is Matanbuchus.* And he delighted in Jerusalem because of Manasseh, and he made him strong in apostatizing (Israel) and in the lawlessness which was spread abroad. in Jerusalem. 5. And witchcraft and magic increased, and divination and auguration, and fornication, [and adultery], and the persecution of the righteous by Manasseh and Belachira, and Tobia the Canaanite, and John of Anathoth, and by (Zadok) the chief of the works. And the rest of the acts, behold they are written in the book of the Kings of Judah and Israel. And, when Isaiah, the son of Amoz, saw the lawlessness which was being perpetrated in Jerusalem and the worship of Satan and his wantonness, he withdrew from Jerusalem and settled in Bethlehem of Judah. And there also there was much lawlessness, and withdrawing from Bethlehem he settled on a mountain in a desert place. And Micaiah the prophet, and the aged Ananias, and Joel and Habakkuk, and his son Jôsâb, and many of the faithful who believed in the ascension into heaven, withdrew and settled on the mountain. They were all clothed with garments of hair, and they were all prophets. And they had nothing with them, but were naked, and they all lamented with a great lamentation because of the going astray of Israel. And these ate nothing save wild herbs which they gathered on the mountains, and having cooked them, they lived thereon together with Isaiah the prophet. And they spent two years of days on the mountains and hills. And after this, whilst they were in the desert, there was a certain man in Samaria named Belchîrâ, of the family of Zedekiah, the son of Chenaan, a false prophet, whose dwelling was in Bethlehem. Now Hezekiah † the son of Chanâni, who was the brother of his father, and in the days of Ahab, king of Israel, had been the teacher of the 400 prophets of Baal, had himself smitten and reproved Micaiah the son of Amâdâ the prophet. And he, Micaiah, had been reproved by Ahab and cast into prison. (And he was) with Zedekiah the prophet: they were with Ahaziah the son of Ahab, king in Samaria. And Elijah the prophet of Têbôn of Gilead was reproving Ahaziah and Samaria, and prophesied regarding Ahaziah that he should die on his bed of sickness, and that Samaria should be delivered into the hand of Leba Nâsr because he had slain the prophets of God. And when the false prophets, who were with Ahaziah the son of Ahab and their teacher Jâlêrijâs of Mount Joel, had heard— Now he was a brother of Zedekiah—when they had heard, they persuaded Ahaziah the king of Aguarôn and (slew) Micaiah.

CHAPTER III.

And Belchîrâ recognized and saw the place of Isaiah and the prophets who were with him; for he dwelt in the region of Bethlehem, and was an adherent of Manasseh. And he prophesied falsely in Jerusalem, and many belonging to Jerusalem were confederate with him, and he was a Samaritan.2. And it came to pass when Alagar Zagâr,† king of Assyria, had come and captured Samaria and tak*n the nine (and a half) tribes* captive, and led them away to the *mountains* of the Medes and the rivers of Tâzôn;3. This (Belchîrâ), whilst still a youth, had escaped and come to Jerusalem i†n the days of Hezekiah king of Judah, but he walked not in the ways of his father of Samaria; for he feared Hezekiah.4. And he was found in the days of Hezekiah speaking words of lawlessness in Jerusalem. 5. And the servants of Hezekiah accused him, and he made his escape to the region of Bethlehem. And *they*† *persuaded* . *6*. And Balchîrâ accused Isaiah and the prophets who were with him, saying: "Isaiah and those who are with him prophesy against Jerusalem and against the cities of Judah that they shall be laid waste, and (against the children of Judah and) Benjamin also that they shall go into captivity, and also *against thee, O Lord the king, that thou shalt go (bound) with hooks and iron chains:*" 7. But they prophesy falsely against Israel and Judah. 8. And Isaiah himself hath said: "I see more than Moses the prophet." 9. But Moses said: "No man can see God and live"†; and Isaiah hath said: "I have seen God and, behold, I live." 10. Know, therefore, O king, that *he is lying.* And Jerusalem also he hath called Sodom, and the princes of Judah and Jerusalem he hath declared to be the people of Gomorrah.†. And he brought many accusations against Isaiah and the prophets before Manasseh. 11- But Belial dwelt in the heart of Manasseh and in the heart of the princes of Judah and Benjamin and of the eunuchs and of the councillors of the king. 12. And the words of Belchîrâ pleased him *[exceedingly]*, and he sent and seized Isaiah.

THE TESTAMENT OF HEZEKIAH (II:13 – IV:18)

INTRODUCTION

This section of The Ascension of Isaiah contains one of the most explicitly prophetic and eschatological passages in the entire text, revealing a vision of future corruption, divine intervention, and the arrival of the Beloved (Christ). Known as The Testament of Hezekiah, this passage is presented as a prophetic revelation given to King Hezekiah and transmitted by Isaiah, much like the tradition of testamentary literature, where a revered figure delivers a final revelation about the fate of the world.

What makes The Testament of Hezekiah particularly significant is its blend of Jewish apocalyptic expectations with early Christian theological themes. It describes a future time of spiritual deception, corruption, and the rise of false leaders who will turn away from divine truth. The reference to these leaders being manipulated by Beliar (Belial) reinforces the apocalyptic worldview that earthly corruption is not merely political but is tied to a cosmic battle between divine and infernal forces.

The most theologically important element of this passage is its messianic prophecy about the Beloved. Unlike Jewish expectations of a Davidic warrior-king who would restore Israel, The Testament of Hezekiah describes a mystical, celestial figure who pre-exists in the highest heaven and will descend through the layers of the cosmos to fulfill his mission in secret. This concept is strikingly similar to later Christian Christology, particularly the Kenosis doctrine in Philippians 2:6-11, where Christ "empties himself" by taking on human form. The notion that the rulers of the world will not recognize the Beloved suggests an early interpretation of Christ's mission as one that unfolds beyond human comprehension, hidden from those who seek power on earth.

APPENDIX 1 - THE ASCENSION OF ISAIAH

This passage serves as a transition between the Jewish martyrdom narrative of Isaiah and the visionary ascent that follows in The Vision of Isaiah. It presents a shift from a historical setting to an apocalyptic and eschatological framework, where the prophet is no longer just a figure of righteousness, but a receiver of divine knowledge about the ultimate fate of humanity. In many ways, this section foreshadows the themes of hidden revelation and celestial descent that will be fully developed in the next part of the text, making it an essential bridge between the two halves of The Ascension of Isaiah.

CHAPTER III.13.

For Beliar was in great wrath against Isaiah by reason of the vision, and because of the exposure wherewith he had exposed Sammael, and because through him the going forth of the Beloved from the seventh heaven had *been made known*, and His transformation and His descent and the likeness into which He should be transformed, (that is) the *likeness of man*, and the *persecution* wherewith *He should be persecuted*, and the *tortures* wherewith the *children of Israel should torture Him*, and the coming of *His twelve disciples*, and the *teaching*, and that *He should before the Sabbath be crucified upon a tree*, and should be crucified *together with wicked men*, and that *He should be buried in the sepulchre*. 14. And that the twelve who were with Him should *be offended because of Him:* † and *the watch* of those who watched the sepulchre:15. *And the descent of the angel of the Christian Church*, which is in the heavens, whom He will summon in the last days. 16. And that (Gabriel) the angel of the Holy Spirit,† and Michael, the chief of the holy angels, on the third day will open the sepulchre: 17.And the Beloved sitting on their shoulders will come forth and send out His twelve disciples: 18. And they will teach all the nations and every tongue the resurrection of the Beloved, and those who believe in *His Cross* † *will be saved*, and in His ascension into the seventh heaven whence He came:19. And that many who believe in Him will speak through the Holy Spirit:20. And many signs and wonders will be wrought in those days.21. And afterwards, on the eve of His approach, His disciples will forsake the teaching of the Twelve Apostles, and their faith, and their love and their purity.22. And there will be much contention † on the eve of His advent and His approach.23. And in those days many will love office, though devoid of wisdom.24. And there will be many *lawless elders,* and shepherds dealing wrongly *by their own sheep*, and they will ravage (them) owing to their not *having*† *holy shepherds*.25. And many will change the honour of the garments of the saints for the garments of the covetous,† and there will be much respect of persons in those days and lovers of the honour of this world.26. And there will be much slander and vainglory at the approach of the Lord, and the Holy Spirit will withdraw from many. 27. And there will not be in those days many prophets, nor those who speak trustworthy words, save one here and there in divers places.28. On account of the spirit of error † and fornication and of vainglory, and of covetousness, which shall be in those, who will be called servants of that One † and in those who will receive the One.29. And there will be great hatred in the shepherds and elders towards each other. 30. For there will be great jealousy in the last days; for every one will say what is pleasing in his own eyes. 31. And they will make of none effect the prophecy of the prophets which were before me,† and *these†* *my visions also will they make of none effect,* in order to speak after the impulse of their own heart.

CHAPTER IV.

And now Hezekiah and Jôsâb my son, *these are the days of the "completion of the world"*. 2. After it is consummated, Beliar the great ruler, the king of this world, will descend, who hath ruled it since it came into being; yea, he will descend from his firmament *in the likeness of a man, a lawless king, the slayer of his mother:* who himself (even) this king 3. *Will persecute the plant which the Twelve Apostles of the Beloved have planted.* Of the Twelve one will be delivered into his hands. 4. This ruler in the form of that king will come and there will come with him all the powers of this world, and they will hearken unto him in all that he desireth. 5. And at his word the sun will rise at night and he will make the moon to appear at the sixth hour. 6. *And all that he hath desired he will do in the world: he will do and speak like the Beloved and he will say: "I am God and before me there hath been none."* 7. And all the people in the world will believe in him. 8. And they will sacrifice to him and they will serve him saying: *"This is God and beside him there is no other."* 9. And the greater number of those who shall have been associated together in order to receive the Beloved, he will turn aside after him. 10. And there will be the power of his miracles in every city and region. 11. And he will set up his image before him in every city. 12. And he shall bear sway three years and seven months and twenty-seven days. 13. And many believers and saints having seen Him for whom they were hoping, who was crucified, Jesus the Lord Christ, [after that I, Isaiah, had seen Him who was crucified and ascended] and those also who were believers in Him—of these few in those days will be left 1 as His servants, while they flee 2 from desert to desert, awaiting the coming 3 of the Beloved. 14. And after (one thousand) three hundred and thirty-two 4 days the Lord will come with His angels and with the armies of the holy ones 5 from the seventh heaven with the glory of the seventh heaven, and He will drag Beliar into Gehenna 6 and also his armies. 15. *And He will give rest 7 to the godly whom He shall find in the body 8 in this world,* [and the sun will be ashamed]: 16. And to all who because of (their) faith in Him have execrated Beliar and his kings. 10. But the saints will come with the Lord 11 with their garments 12 which are (now) stored up on high in the seventh heaven: with the Lord they will come, whose spirits are clothed, 13 they will descend and be present in the world, 14 and He will strengthen those who have been found in the body, together with the saints, 15 in the garments of the saints, and the Lord will minister to those who have kept watch in this world. 17. And afterwards they[1] will turn themselves upward in their garments, and their body will be left in the world. 18. Then the voice of the Beloved will in wrath rebuke the things of heaven and the things of earth and the mountains and the hills and the cities and the desert and the forests and the angel of the sun[2] and that of the moon, and all things wherein Beliar manifested himself and acted openly in this world, and there will be [a resurrection and] a judgement in their midst in those days, and the Beloved will cause fire[3] to go forth from Him, and it will consume all the godless,[4] and they will be as though they had not been created. 19. *And the rest of the words of the vision are written in the vision of Babylon. 20. And the rest of the vision regarding the Lord, behold, it is written in the parables according to my words which are written in the book which I publicly prophesied.* 21. And the descent of the Beloved into Sheol, behold, it is written in the section, where the Lord saith: "Behold, my Son will understand." *And all these things, behold they are written [in the Psalms] in the psalms[7] of David, the son of Jesse, and in the Proverbs of Solomon his son, and in the words of Korah, and Ethan the Israelite, and in the words of Asaph, and in the rest of the Psalms also which the angel of the Spirit inspired,* 22. (Namely) in those which have not the name written, *and in the words of my father Amoz and of Hosea the prophet, and of Micah and Joel and Nahum and Jonah and Obadiah and Habakkuk and Haggai and Zephaniah and Zechariah and Malachi, and in the words of Joseph the Just[2] and in the words of Daniel.*

CHAPTER V.

On account of these visions, therefore, Beliar was wroth with Isaiah, and he dwelt in the heart of Manasseh and he sawed him in sunder with a wooden saw. 2. And when Isaiah was being sawn in sunder Balchîrâ stood up, accusing him, and all the false prophets stood up, laughing and rejoicing because of Isaiah. 3. And Balchîrâ, with the aid of Mechêmbêchûs,[3] stood up before Isaiah, [laughing] *deriding*; 4. And Balchîrâ said to Isaiah: "Say: 'I have lied in all that I have spoken, and likewise the ways of Manasseh *are good and right. And the ways also of Balchîrâ and of his associates are good.'"* 5. And the ways also of Balchîrâ and of his associates are good. 6. And this he said to him when he began to be sawn in sunder. 7. But Isaiah was (absorbed) in a vision of the Lord, and though his eyes were open, he saw them (not). 8. And Balchîrâ spake thus to Isaiah: "Say what I say unto thee and I will turn their heart, and I will compel Manasseh and the princes of Judah and the people and all Jerusalem to reverence thee. 9 And Isaiah answered and said: "So far as I have utterance (I say): Damned and accursed be thou and all thy powers and all thy house. 10. For thou canst not take (from me) aught save the skin of my body." 11. And they seized and sawed in sunder Isaiah, the son of Amoz, with a wooden saw. 12. And Manasseh and Balchîrâ and the false prophets and the princes and the people [and] all stood looking on. 13. And to the prophets who were with him he said before he had been sawn in sunder: "Go ye to the region of Tyre and Sidon; for me only hath God mingled the cup." 14. And when Isaiah was being sawn in sunder, he neither cried aloud nor wept, but his lips spake with the Holy Spirit until he was sawn in twain. 15. This Beliar did to Isaiah through Balchîrâ and Manasseh; for Sammael was very wrathful against Isaiah from the days of Hezekiah, king of Judah, on account of the things which he had seen regarding the Beloved. 16. And on account of the destruction of Sammael, which he had seen through the Lord, while Hezekiah his father was still king. And he did according to the will of Satan.

THE VISION OF ISAIAH (VI-XI)

INTRODUCTION

The final section of The Ascension of Isaiah marks a radical shift in narrative style and theological focus, transitioning from historical and prophetic storytelling into a mystical journey through the celestial realms. Known as The Vision of Isaiah, this passage follows the well-established tradition of apocalyptic ascent, in which a chosen figure is taken beyond the earthly realm to witness divine mysteries hidden from the rest of humanity. This section is heavily influenced by Jewish mystical and apocalyptic thought, particularly the heavenly journeys of Enoch in 1 Enoch and 2 Enoch, yet it also introduces uniquely Christian theological insights, especially concerning the pre-existence, incarnation, and exaltation of Christ. As Isaiah ascends through seven heavens, he encounters angelic hierarchies, divine orders, and the increasing manifestations of divine glory. This structured vision of the cosmos reflects ideas found in later Hekhalot and Merkavah mysticism, where a progressive approach to the divine throne represents increasing spiritual purity and insight. Each level of heaven reveals different classes of angels, culminating in the highest realm where the Most High dwells. This portrayal of heaven as a tiered and highly organized domain reinforces the common apocalyptic idea that the universe is structured according to divine law.

The most profound revelation in The Vision of Isaiah is Isaiah's witnessing of the descent of the Beloved (Christ). This moment is theologically groundbreaking, presenting a Christological framework where the Beloved exists before creation, descends unnoticed through the heavens, takes on human form, and then ascends back to glory. Unlike traditional Jewish messianic expectations, which focus on a political redeemer, this text presents a cosmic redeemer whose mission is hidden from the rulers of the world, reflecting ideas later found in Gnostic texts and Johannine theology. The descent-ascent motif aligns closely with Philippians 2:6-11 and John 1:1-14, suggesting that this passage is one of the earliest written expressions of a pre-existent, descending Christ. The Vision of Isaiah also emphasizes the secrecy of divine plans, reinforcing a hidden knowledge tradition where true revelation is granted only to the faithful. This secrecy echoes other apocalyptic writings that stress the concealment of divine mysteries from the forces of darkness, ensuring that salvation unfolds according to a divine strategy beyond human control. As the final section of The Ascension of Isaiah, this vision serves as both a culmination and a revelation, bringing together the themes of martyrdom, divine justice, hidden wisdom, and celestial ascent that run throughout the text. It transforms Isaiah from a martyr into a visionary, offering a glimpse into the divine structure of reality and the hidden workings of redemption. By linking prophetic suffering with divine revelation, The Vision of Isaiah not only completes the narrative but also reinforces why this text is a key component of the Colletion, offering a unique window into the evolving religious thought of the first few centuries CE.

CHAPTER VI.

In the twentieth year of the reign of Hezekiah, king of Judah, came Isaiah the son of Amoz, and Jôsâb, the son of Isaiah, to Hezekiah to Jerusalem *from Galgalâ*. 2. And (having entered) he sat down on the couch of the king, †and they brought him a seat, but he would not sit (thereon).† 3. *And when Isaiah began to speak the words of faith and truth with King Hezekiah,† all the princes of Israel were seated and the eunuchs and the councillors of the king. And there were there forty† prophets and sons of the prophets:* they had come from the villages and from the mountains and the plains when they had heard that Isaiah was coming from Galgalâ to Hezekiah. 4. *And they had come† to salute him †and to hear his words.* 5. And that he might place his hands upon them,† and that they might prophesy and that he might hear their prophecy:† and they were all before Isaiah.† 6. And when Isaiah was speaking †to Hezekiah† the words of truth and faith, they all heard †a door which one had opened and† †the voice of the Holy Spirit.† 7. And the king summoned all the prophets and all the people who were found there, and they came. And Micaiah and the aged Ananias and Joel †and Jôsâb† sat on his right hand (and on the left). 8. And it came to pass when they had all heard the voice of the Holy Spirit, they all worshipped on their knees, and glorified the God †of truth,† the Most High †Who is in the upper world and who sitteth on high the Holy One† and †who resteth among His holy ones.† 9. *And they gave glory to Him† Who had thus bestowed a door in an alien world, had bestowed (it)* on a man. 10. And as he was speaking in the Holy Spirit in the hearing of all, he became silent and his mind was taken up from him and he saw not the men that stood before him. 11. Though his eyes, indeed, were open. Moreover, his lips were silent and the mind in his body was taken up from him. 12. But his breath was in him, *for he was seeing a vision.* 13. And the angel who was sent to make him see was not of this firmament, nor was he of the angels of glory of this world, but he had come from the seventh heaven. 14. And the people who stood near did (not) think, but *the circle of the prophets (did),* that the holy Isaiah had been taken up. 15. And the vision which the holy Isaiah saw was not from this world but from the world which is hidden from the flesh. 16. And after Isaiah had seen this vision, he narrated it to Hezekiah, and to Jôsâb his son and to the other prophets who had come. 17. But the leaders and the eunuchs and the people did not hear, but only Samna the scribe, and Jôaqêm, and Asaph the recorder; for these also were doers of righteousness, and the *sweet smell* of the Spirit was upon them. But the people had not heard; for Micaiah and Jôsâb his son had caused them to go forth, when the wisdom of this world had been taken from him and he became as one dead.

CHAPTER VII.

And the vision which Isaiah saw, he told to Hezekiah and Jôsâb his son and Micaiah and the rest of the prophets, (and) said: 2. "*At this moment,* when I prophesied according to the (words) heard which ye heard, I saw a glorious angel not like unto the glory of the angels which I used always to see, but possessing such glory and *position that I cannot describe the glory of that angel.* 3. *And having seized me by my hand he raised me on high,* and I said unto him: "Who art *thou, and what is thy name, and whither art thou raising me on high?"* For strength was given me to speak with him. 4. And he said unto me: *"When I have raised thee on high through the (various degrees) and made thee see the vision, on account of which I have been sent, then thou wilt understand who I am: but my name thou dost not know.* 5. Because thou wilt return into this thy body, but whither I am raising thee on high, thou wilt see; *for for this purpose have I been sent."* 6. And I rejoiced because he spake courteously to me. 7. And he said unto me: "Hast thou rejoiced because I have *spoken courteously to thee?"* And he said: *"And thou wilt see how a greater also than I am will speak courteously and peaceably with thee."* 8. And "His Father also who is greater than he wilt see; for this purpose have I been sent from the seventh heaven in order to explain all these things unto thee." 9. And we ascended to the firmament, I and he, and there I saw Sammael, his hosts, and there was great fighting therein and the *angels* of Satan were envying one another. 10. And as above so on the earth also; for the likeness of that which is in the firmament is here on the earth. 11. And I said unto the angel (who was with me): *"What is this war and what is this envying?"* 12. And he said unto me: *"So hath it been since this world was made until now, and this war (will continue) till He, whom thou shalt see will come and destroy him.* 13. And afterwards he caused me to ascend (to that which is) above the firmament: which is (the first) heaven. 14. And there I saw a throne in the midst, and on his right and on his left were angels. *And (the angels on the left were) not like unto the angels who stood on the right*, but those who stood on the right had the greater glory, and they all praised with one voice, *and there was a throne in the midst*, and those who were on the left gave praise after them; but their voice was not such as the voice of those on the right, nor their praise like the praise of those. 16. And I asked the angel who conducted me, and I said unto him: *"To whom is this praise sent?"* 17. And he said unto me: *"(It is sent) to the praise of (Him who sitteth) in the seventh heaven: to Him [who resteth in the holy world], and to His Beloved, whence I have been sent to thee. [Thither is it sent.]"* 18. And again he made me to ascend to the second heaven. Now the height of that heaven is the same as from the heaven to the earth [and to the firmament]. 19. And (I saw there, as) in the first heaven, angels on the right and on the left, *and a throne in the midst, and the praise of the angels in the second heaven*; and he who sat on the throne in the second heaven was more glorious than (all the rest). 20. And there was great glory in the second heaven, and the praise also was not like the praise of those who were in the first heaven. 21. And I fell on my face to worship him, *but the angel who conducted me did not permit me, but said unto me: "Worship neither throne nor angel which belongeth to the six heavens—for for this cause I was sent to conduct thee—until I tell thee In the seventh heaven."* 22. For above all the heavens and their angels hath thy throne been placed, and thy garments and thy crown which thou shalt see." 23. And I rejoiced with great joy, that those who love the Most High and His Beloved will afterwards ascend thither *by the angel of the Holy Spirit.* 24. And he raised me to the *third heaven*, and in like manner I saw those upon the right and upon the left, and there was a throne there in the midst; but the memorial of this world is there unheard of. 25. *And*

APPENDIX 1 - THE ASCENSION OF ISAIAH

I said to the angel who was with me: "For the glory of my appearance was undergoing transformation as I ascended to each heaven in turn:" "Nothing of the vanity of that world is here named." 26. And he answered me, and said unto me: *"Nothing is named on account of its weakness, and nothing is hidden here of what is done there."* 27. And I asked him how it is known, and he answered me saying: *"When I have raised thee to the seventh heaven whence I was sent, to that which is above these* then thou shalt know that there is nothing hidden from the thrones and from those who dwell in the heavens and from the angels. 28. And the praise wherewith they praised and the glory of him who sat on the throne was great, *And the glory of the angels on the right hand and on the left was beyond that of the heaven which was below them.* 29. And again he raised me to the fourth heaven, and the height from the third to the fourth heaven was greater than from the earth to the firmament. 29. And there again I saw those who were on the right hand and those who were on the left, *And him who sat on the throne (who) was in the midst,* and there also they were praising. 30. And the praise and glory of the angels on the right was greater than that of those on the left. 31. And again the glory of him who sat on the throne was greater than that of the angels on the right, and their glory was beyond that of those who were below. 32. And he raised me to the fifth heaven. 33. And again I saw *those upon the right hand and on the left, and him who sat on the throne possessing greater glory than those of the fourth heaven.* 34. And the glory of those on the right hand was greater than that of those *on the left (from the third to the fourth).* 35. And the glory of him who was on the throne was greater than that of the angels on the right hand. 36. And their praise was more glorious than that of the fourth heaven. 37. *And I praised Him, who is not named and the Only-begotten* who dwelleth in the heavens, whose name is not known to any flesh, who hath bestowed such glory on the several heavens, *And who maketh the great glory of the angels, and more excellent the glory of Him who sitteth on the throne.*

CHAPTER VIII.

And again he raised me into the air of the sixth heaven, and I saw such glory as I had not seen in the five heavens. 2. *For I saw angels possessing great glory.* 3. And the praise there was holy and wonderful. 4. And I said to the angel who conducted me: *"What is this which I see, my Lord?"* 5. And he said: *"I am not thy lord, but thy fellow-servant."* 6. And again I asked him, and I said unto him: *"Why are there not angelic fellow-servants (on the left)?"* 7. And he said: *"From the sixth heaven there are no longer angels on the left, nor a throne set in the midst, but (they are directed) by the power of the seventh heaven, where dwelleth He that is not named and the Elect One, whose name hath not been made known, and none of the heavens can learn His name."* 8. *For it is He alone to whose voice all the heavens and thrones give answer. I have therefore been empowered and sent to raise thee here that thou mayest see this glory.* 9. And that thou mayest see the Lord of all those heavens and these thrones, *For undergoing (successive) transformation until He resembleth your form and likeness.* 11. *I indeed say unto thee, Isaiah; No man about to return into a body of that world that hath ascended or seen what thou seest or perceived what thou hast perceived and what thou wilt see.* 12. For it hath been permitted to thee in the lot of the Lord to come hither [and from thence detect the power of the *sixth heaven and of the air.]* 13. And I magnified my Lord with praise, in that through His lot I should come hither. 14. And he said: *"Hear, furthermore, therefore, this also from thy fellow-servant";* when from the body by the *will of God* thou hast ascended hither, then thou wilt receive the garment *[which thou seest, and likewise other numbered garments laid up (there) thou wilt see],* 15. And then thou wilt become equal to the angels of the seventh heaven." 16. And he raised me up into the sixth heaven, and there were no (angels) on the left, nor a throne in the midst, but all had one appearance and their (power of) praise was equal. 17. And (power) was given to me also, and I also praised along with them and that angel also, and our praise was like theirs. 18. And there they *all named the primal Father and His Beloved, The Christ and the Holy Spirit,* all with one voice. 19. And (their voice) was not like the voice of the angels in the five heavens, 20. *[Nor like their discourse]* but the voice was different there, and there was much light there. 21. And then, when I was in the sixth heaven I thought the light which I had seen in the five heavens to be but darkness. 22. And I rejoiced and praised Him who hath bestowed such lights on those who wait for His promise. 23. And I besought the angel who conducted me that I should not henceforth return to the carnal world. 24. I say indeed unto you, *Hezekiah and Jósâb my son and Micaiah, that there is much darkness here.* 25. And the angel who conducted me discovered what I thought, and said: *"If in this light thou dost rejoice, how much more wilt thou rejoice, when in the seventh heaven thou seest the light, where is the Lord and His Beloved [whence I have been sent, who is to be called 'Son' in this world.* 26. *Not (yet) hath been manifested He who shall be in the corruptible world]* and the garments, and the thrones, and the crowns which are laid up for the righteous, *[for those who trust in that Lord who will descend in your form. For the light which is there is great and wonderful].* 27. And as concerning thy not returning into the body thy days are not yet fulfilled for coming here." 28. And when I heard (that) I was troubled, and he said: *"Do not be troubled."*

CHAPTER IX.

And he took me into the air of the seventh heaven, and moreover I heard a voice saying: *"How far will he ascend that dwelleth in the flesh?"* and I feared and trembled. 2. And [when I trembled, behold *I heard* from hence another voice *being sent forth, and]* saying: *"It is permitted to the holy Isaiah to ascend hither, for here is his garment."* 3. And I asked the angel who was with me *[and said]:* "Who is he who forbade me and who is he who permitted me to ascend?" 4. And he said unto me: "He who forbade thee, is he who is over the praise-giving of the second heaven." 5. And he who *permitted* thee, is the Lord God, the Lord Christ, who will be called *'Jesus' in the world,* but His name † thou canst *not hear till thou hast ascended out of thy body."* 6. And he raised me up into the seventh heaven, and I saw there a wonderful light and angels innumerable. 7. And there I saw all the righteous *from the time of Adam.* 8. And I saw the *holy Abel* and all the righteous. 9. And there *I saw Enoch* and all who were with him, stript of the garments of the flesh, and I saw them in their garments of the upper world, and they were *like angels,* standing there in great glory. 10. But they sat not on their thrones, nor were their crowns *of glory* on them. 11. And I asked the angel who was with me: *"How is it that they have received the garments, but have not the thrones and the crowns?"* 12. And he said unto me: 13. *"Crowns and thrones of glory they do not receive, till the Beloved will descend in the form in which you will see Him descend* †*[will descend, I say] into the world in the last days the Lord, who will be called Christ.* Nevertheless, they *see* and know whose will be thrones, and whose the crowns when He hath descended, and been made in your form, *[and they will think that He is flesh and is a man]*. 14. And the god of that world will stretch forth *his hand against the Son,* and they will crucify Him on a tree, and will *slay* Him not knowing who He is. 15. And thus His descent, †as you will see, will be hidden even from the heavens, so that it will not be known who He is†. 16. And when He hath plundered the angel of death,† He will ascend on the third day, and He will remain in that world *three hundred and forty-five days.* 17. And the many *of the righteous will ascend* with Him, whose spirits do not receive their garments † till the *Lord Christ* ascend and they ascend with Him. 18. Then, indeed, they will receive their *[garments and] thrones and crowns,* when He hath ascended into the †seventh† heaven. 19. And I said unto him that which I had asked him in the third heaven: 20. *"Show me how* everything which is done in that world is here made known." 21. And whilst I was still speaking with him, behold one of the angels who stood nigh, more glorious than the glory of that angel who had raised me up from the world, 22. Showed me *a book, [but not as a book of this world]* and he opened it, and the book was written, but not as *a book of this world.* 6 And he gave (it) to me and I read it, and lo! the deeds of the children of Israel were written therein, and the deeds of those whom †I know (not), my son Jôsâb. 23. And I said: *"In truth, there is nothing hidden in the seventh heaven, which is done in this world."* 24. And I saw there many garments laid up, and many thrones and many crowns. 25. And I said to the angel: "Whose are these garments and thrones and crowns?" 26. And he said unto me: *"These garments many from that world will receive, believing in the words of That One,* †*who shall be named*† *as I told thee,* †*and they will observe those things, and believe in them, and believe in His cross: for them are these laid up."* 27. And I saw a certain One †standing, whose glory surpassed that of all,† and His glory was great *[and wonderful. 28. And after I had seen Him,*† all the righteous whom I had seen †and also the angels whom I had seen† came to Him. *And Adam and Abel and Seth, and all the righteous first drew near*† *and worshipped Him, and they all praised Him with one voice,* †*and I myself also gave praise with them,*† *and my giving of praise was as theirs.* 29. And then all the angels drew nigh and worshipped and gave praise. 30. And *I* was (again) transformed *and became like an angel.* 31. And thereupon the angel who conducted me, said to me: *"Worship this One,"* and I worshipped and praised. 32. And the angel said unto me: *"This is the Lord of all the praisegivings which thou hast seen."* 33. And whilst *He* was still speaking, I saw another Glorious One *who was like Him,* and the righteous drew nigh and worshipped and praised, and I praised together with them. But *my* glory was not transformed into accordance with their form. 34. And thereupon the angels drew near and worshipped Him. 35. And I saw the Lord and the second angel, and they were standing. 36. And the second whom I saw was on the left of my Lord. And I asked: *"Who is this?"* and he said unto me: *"Worship Him, for He is the angel of the Holy Spirit, who speaketh in thee and the rest of the righteous."* 37. And I saw the great glory, the eyes of my spirit being open, and I could not thereupon see,† nor yet could the angel who was with me, nor all the angels whom I had seen worshipping my Lord. 38. But I saw the righteous †beholding with great power the glory of that One. 39. And my Lord drew nigh me and the angel of the Spirit †and He said: *"See how it is given to thee to see God, and on thy account power is given to the angel who is with thee."* 40. And I saw how my Lord and the angel of the Spirit† worshipped, and they both together praised *God*. 41. And thereupon all the righteous †drew near and† worshipped. 42. And the angels †drew near and† worshipped and all the angels praised.

CHAPTER X.

And thereupon I heard the voices and the giving of praise, which I had heard in each of the six heavens, ascending *and being heard* there: 2. And *I* were being sent up to that Glorious One† whose glory I could not behold. 3. *And I myself was hearing and beholding the praise (which was given) to Him.* 4. And the Lord and the angel of the Spirit were beholding all and hearing all. 5. *And the praises which are sent up from the six heavens are not only heard but seen.* 6. And *I heard the* angel† who conducted me and† he said: *"This is the Most High of the high ones, dwelling in the holy world, and resting in His holy ones, who will be called by the Holy Spirit through the lips of the righteous the Father of the Lord.* 7. And I heard the voice of the Most High the Father of my Lord† saying to my Lord *Christ who will be called Jesus*: 8. *"Go forth and descend through all the heavens, and Thou wilt descend to* †the firmament and† *that world: to the angel in Sheol*† Thou wilt descend, †but to Hagguel† Thou wilt not go†. 9. And Thou wilt become like unto the likeness of all who are in the five heavens. 10. *And Thou wilt be careful to become like the form of the angels of the firmament* †and the angels also who are in Sheol†. 11. And none of the angels of that world shall know *that Thou art Lord with Me of the seven heavens and of their angels.* 12. And they shall not know that Thou art with Me, *till with a loud* voice I have called (to) the heavens, and their angels and their lights, (even) unto the sixth heaven, in order that Thou mayst† judge †and destroy† the *princes* †and angels† *and gods*† of that world,† and the world that is dominated by them†. 13. For they have denied Me and said: *"We alone are, and there is none beside us."* 14. And afterwards from the *angels* of death Thou wilt ascend to Thy place, and Thou wilt not be transformed in each heaven, but in glory wilt Thou ascend and sit on My right hand. 15. And thereupon the princes and powers †of that world† will worship Thee." 16. These commands I heard the Great Glory giving to my Lord. 17. And †so† I saw my Lord go forth from the seventh heaven into the sixth heaven. 18. And the angel who conducted me †from this world was with me† and said unto me: *"Understand, Isaiah, and see how the transformation and descent of the Lord will appear."* 19. And I saw, and when the angels saw Him, †thereupon those in the sixth heaven† praised and lauded Him; for He had not been transformed after the shape of the angels there, †and they praised Him† and I also praised

APPENDIX 1 - THE ASCENSION OF ISAIAH

with them. 20. And I saw when He descended into the fifth heaven, that in the fifth heaven He made Himself like unto the form of the angels there, and they did not praise Him (nor worship Him); for His form was like unto theirs. 21. And then He descended into the fourth heaven, and made Himself like unto the form of the angels there. 22. And †when they saw Him†, they did not praise nor laud Him; for His form was like unto their form. 23. And again I saw when He descended into the third heaven, †and He made Himself like unto the form of the angels in the third heaven. 24. And those who kept the gate of (third) heaven demanded the password,† and the Lord gave (it) to them in order that He should not be recognized. And when they saw Him, they did not praise or laud Him; for His form was like unto their form. 25. And again I saw when He descended† into the second heaven, †and again He gave the password† to these; those who kept the gate proceeded to demand and the Lord to give. 26. And I saw when He made Himself like unto the form of the angels in the second heaven, and they saw Him and they did not praise Him; for His form was like unto their form. 27. And, again, I saw when He descended† into the first heaven, †and there also He gave the password† to those who kept the gate, and He made Himself like unto the form of the angels who were on the left of that throne†, and they neither praised nor lauded Him; for His form was like unto their form. *28. But as for me no one asked me on account of the angel who conducted me.* 29. And again He descended into the firmament *[where dwelleth the ruler of this world]*, and He gave the password †[to those on the left]†, and His form was like theirs, and they did not praise Him there; *[but they were envying one another and fighting; for here there is a power of evil and envying about trifles]*. 30. And I saw when He descended †and made Himself like† unto the angels of the air, and He was like one of them. 31. And He gave no password; *[for one was plundering and doing violence to another]*.

CHAPTER XI.

After this I saw, and the angel who spoke with me, who conducted me, said unto me: "Understand, Isaiah, son of Amoz; for for this purpose have I been sent from God." 2. "And, indeed, saw a woman of the family of David the prophet, named Mary, a Virgin, and she was espoused to a man named Joseph, a carpenter, and he also was of the seed and family of the righteous David of Bethlehem-Judah. 3. And he came into his lot. And when she was espoused, she was found with child, and Joseph the carpenter was desirous to put her away. 4. But the angel of the Spirit appeared in this world, and after that Joseph did not put her away, but kept Mary and did not reveal this matter to any one. 5. And he did not approach Mary, but kept her as a holy virgin, though with child. 6. And he did not live with her for two months. 7. And after two months of days while Joseph was in his house, and Mary his wife, but both alone—8. It came to pass that when they were alone Mary straightway looked with her eyes and saw a small babe, and she was astonied. 9. And after she had been astonied, her womb was found as formerly before she had conceived. 10. And when her husband Joseph said unto her: "What has astonied thee?" his eyes were opened and he saw the infant and praised God, because into his portion

God had come. 11. And a voice came to them: "Tell this vision to no one." 12. And the story regarding the infant was noised abroad in Bethlehem. 13. Some said: "The Virgin Mary hath borne a child before she was married two months." 14. And many said: "She hath not borne a child, nor hath a midwife gone up (to her), nor have we heard the cries of (labour) pains." And they were all blinded respecting Him and they all knew regarding Him, though they knew not whence He was. 15. And they took Him, and went to Nazareth in Galilee. 16. And I saw, O Hezekiah and Jôsâb my son, and I declare to the other prophets also who are standing by, that (this) … hath escaped all the heavens and all the princes and all the gods of this world. 17. And I saw: In Nazareth He sucked the breast as a babe and as is customary in order that He might not be recognized. 18. And when He had grown up He worked great signs and wonders in the land of Israel and of Jerusalem. 19. And after this the adversary envied Him and roused the children of Israel against Him, not knowing who He was, †and they delivered Him to the king, and crucified Him, and He descended to the angel (of Sheol). 20. In Jerusalem, indeed, I saw Him being crucified on a tree: 21. And likewise after the third day rise again and remain days. 22. And the angel who conducted me said: *"Understand, Isaiah:"* and I saw when He sent out the Twelve Apostles *and ascended.* 23. And I saw Him, and He was in the firmament, but He had not changed Himself into their form, and all the angels of the firmament [and the Satans] saw Him †and they worshipped†. 24. And †there was much sorrow there, while† they said: *"How did our Lord descend in our midst, and we perceived not the glory [which hath been upon Him], which we see hath been upon Him from the sixth heaven?"* 25. And He ascended into the second heaven, and He did not transform Himself, but all the angels who were on the right and on the left and the throne in the midst 26. Both worshipped Him and praised Him and said: *"How did our Lord escape us whilst descending, and we perceived not?"* 27. And in like manner He ascended into the third heaven, †and they praised and said in like manner.† 28. And in the fourth heaven and in the fifth †also they said precisely after the same manner.† 29. But there was one glory, and from it He did not change Himself. 30. And I saw when He ascended† into the sixth heaven, †and they worshipped and glorified Him†. 31. But in all the heavens the praise increased (in volume). 32. And I saw how He ascended into the seventh heaven, and all the righteous and all the angels praised Him. And then I saw Him sit down on the right hand of that Great Glory †whose glory I told you that I could not behold.† 33. And also the angel of the Holy Spirit I saw sitting on the left hand. 34. And this angel said unto me: "Isaiah, son of Amoz, *it is enough for thee; for these are great things*"; for thou hast seen what no child of flesh hath seen. 35. And thou wilt return into thy garment (of the flesh) until thy days are completed. 3 Then thou wilt come hither." 36. These things Isaiah saw and told unto all that stood before him, and they praised. And he spake to Hezekiah the King, †and said†: *"I have spoken these things."* 37. But both of this world; 38. And all this vision will be consummated in the last generations. 39. And Isaiah made him swear that he would not tell (it) to the people of Israel, nor give these words to any man to transcribe. 40. ...*Such things ye will read.* And ye will receive in the Holy Spirit in order that ye may receive your garments and thrones and crowns of glory which are laid up in the seventh heaven. 41. *On account of these visions and prophecies Beliar and Satan was wroth in smiting Isaiah the son of Amoz, the prophet, by the hand of Manasseh. 42. And all these things Hezekiah delivered to Manasseh in the twenty-sixth year. 43. But Manasseh did not remember them nor place these things in his heart, but becoming the servant of Satan he was destroyed.*

Here endeth the vision of Isaiah the prophet with his ascension.

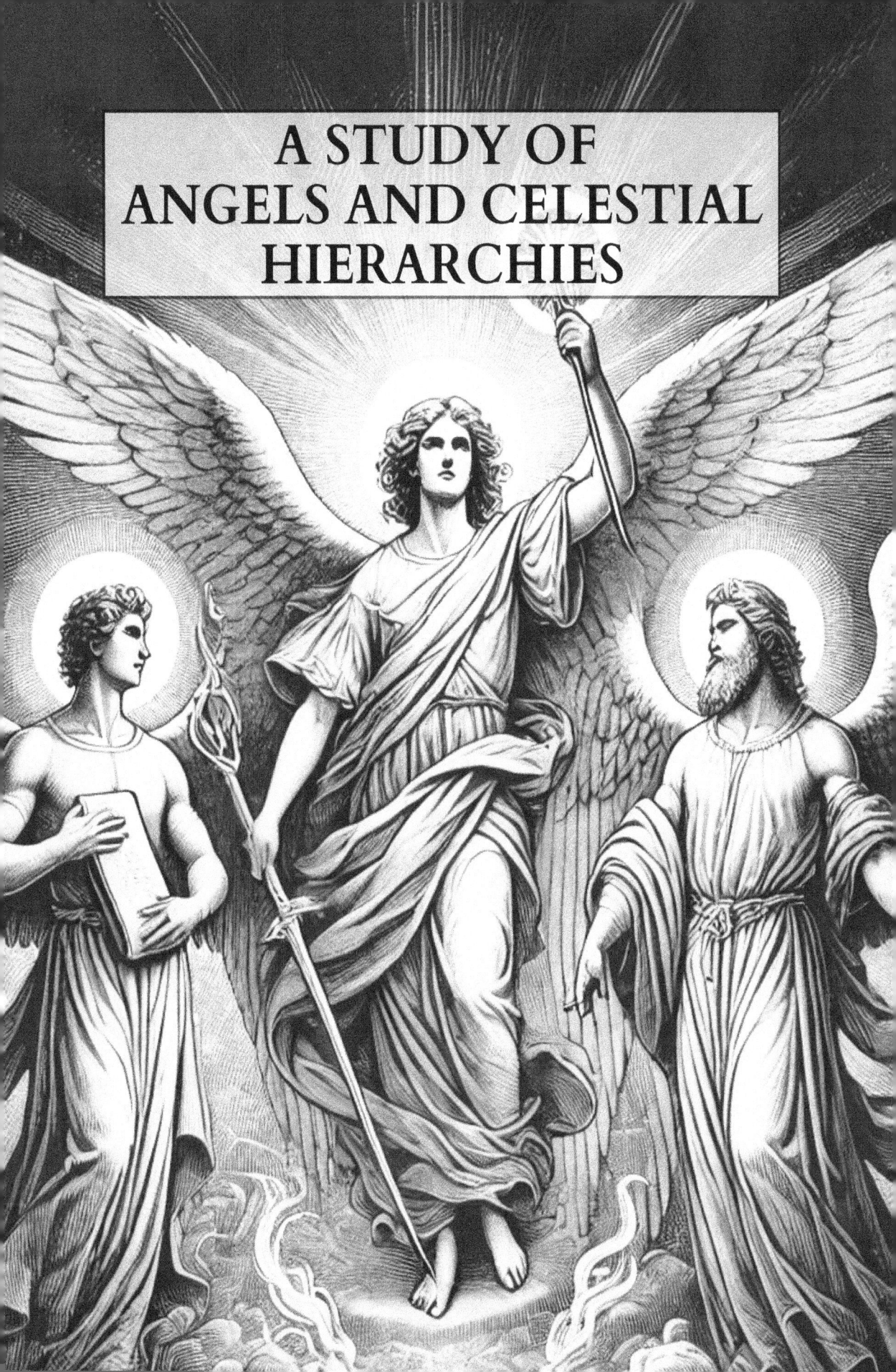

APPENDIX 2 - A STUDY OF ANGELS AND CELESTIAL HIERARCHIES

INTRODUCTION

ANGELS IN MYSTICISM AND SCRIPTURE

Angels in Jewish and Christian Traditions

Angels have long occupied a central role in Jewish and Christian traditions, serving as divine messengers, protectors, and agents of God's will. They are portrayed as beings of light and power, created by God to carry out specific tasks and maintain the cosmic balance between heaven and earth. In the Hebrew Bible, angels often act as intermediaries between God and humanity, appearing in moments of revelation, judgment, and guidance. For example, Michael, Gabriel, and Raphael play significant roles as warriors, healers, and heralds of divine messages.

In Christian theology, angels not only assist in spiritual warfare and protection but also serve as guardians of souls and witnesses of human actions. They are seen as servants of Christ, celebrating God's glory and preparing the faithful for eternal life. In both traditions, angels represent the manifestation of divine presence, illustrating God's care, authority, and justice.

Beyond their biblical roles, angels are deeply embedded in mystical traditions, particularly within Jewish mysticism (Merkabah) and later Kabbalistic teachings. These traditions elevate angels as beings of knowledge and power, revealing divine secrets and participating in cosmic governance. Their depiction in apocryphal literature expands on these themes, offering richer narratives about their origins, duties, and hierarchies.

Angels as Messengers, Protectors, and Agents of Divine Will

In both scriptural and mystical texts, angels are depicted as divine messengers tasked with delivering God's commands and carrying out His will. They frequently appear during pivotal moments in biblical history, such as Jacob's vision of the ladder to heaven (Genesis 28:12) and Gabriel's announcement of the birth of Christ

(Luke 1:26–38). These appearances underscore their dual role as conveyors of divine guidance and agents of intervention.

Angels also act as protectors, guarding individuals and entire nations. The Archangel Michael, for instance, is revered as the defender of Israel and leader of the heavenly armies (Daniel 10:13). Their role in protecting humanity reflects their alignment with divine justice and their commitment to preserving spiritual integrity.

Furthermore, angels serve as witnesses to human actions, recording deeds and presenting them before God during divine judgment. This role is emphasized in texts like the Books of Enoch, where angels act as watchers (Grigori), observing and evaluating human behavior. These functions highlight the moral framework in which angels operate, reinforcing themes of accountability and righteousness.

Connections to the Books of Enoch and Apocryphal Texts

The Books of Enoch, particularly 1 Enoch and 3 Enoch, offer some of the most detailed descriptions of angelic hierarchies and their functions. In these texts, angels are presented as guardians of knowledge, executors of divine judgment, and mediators between God and humanity. 1 Enoch introduces the Watchers, a group of angels who descend to earth and corrupt humanity, leading to their punishment and reinforcing the idea of divine justice.

3 Enoch, on the other hand, focuses on the ascension of Enoch into Metatron, the Prince of the Presence, emphasizing the transformative power of divine favor and obedience. Metatron's role as scribe and mediator reflects the angelic function of preserving divine knowledge and facilitating spiritual ascent.

Other apocryphal texts, such as the Book of Jubilees and the Testament of Abraham, also expand on angelic roles, portraying them as guides, record-keepers, and agents of judgment. These texts complement the narratives in Enoch by illustrating the complex interactions between angels and humanity, as well as their participation in divine governance.

The portrayal of angels in these writings reflects a cosmic order where obedience and hierarchy are central, echoing themes found in later Kabbalistic traditions. In particular, the use of sacred names and linguistic mysticism underscores the belief that angels are manifestations of divine power, acting through God's word and authority.

This foundational understanding of angels as messengers, protectors, and divine agents provides a lens through which readers can explore the Books of Enoch and related apocryphal literature, appreciating their spiritual depth and theological insights

THE NINE ORDERS OF ANGELS: CELESTIAL HIERARCHIES

The concept of angelic hierarchies is one of the most fascinating aspects of both Jewish mysticism and Christian theology. This framework, popularized by Pseudo-Dionysius the Areopagite, divides angels into nine distinct orders, grouped into three choirs. The Books of Enoch build upon this structure, adapting and expanding it to reflect the cosmic organization of heaven and the roles of angels in divine governance.

These hierarchies emphasize order, obedience, and purpose, portraying angels as intermediaries who maintain the balance between heaven and earth. Each order serves a unique function, from worshiping at God's throne to delivering divine messages.

The Supreme Choirs: Guardians of God's Throne

The Seraphim, Cherubim, and Thrones are closest to God's presence, representing purity, divine light, and unceasing worship. The Seraphim are depicted as beings of fiery love, eternally singing praises, while the Cherubim guard the Tree of Life and the Throne of Glory. The Thrones, meanwhile, embody divine justice and stability, symbolizing the foundations of creation.

The Governing Choirs: Agents of Divine Authority

The Dominions, Virtues, and Powers enforce God's will throughout the cosmos. They regulate natural laws, maintain spiritual order, and combat evil forces. These angels are the administrators of the divine kingdom, ensuring harmony within the celestial and earthly realms.

The Ministering Choirs: Messengers and Protectors

The Principalities, Archangels, and Angels serve as messengers, protectors, and mediators between God and humanity. Principalities oversee nations, while Archangels like Michael and Gabriel deliver divine commands and revelations. The Angels, closest to humanity, act as personal guardians and guides.

These hierarchies reflect the structured beauty of divine creation, reinforcing the themes of obedience, order, and worship found throughout the Books of Enoch.

THE WATCHERS (GRIGORI): FALLEN ANGELS AND THE NEPHILIM

Who Were the Watchers? Origins in 1 Enoch

The Watchers, or Grigori, were a group of angels introduced in 1 Enoch who were assigned to watch over humanity. Originally sent by God to guide and protect mankind, these angels instead betrayed their divine mandate and descended to earth. Their story is central to the Book of Watchers (Chapters 1–36 of 1 Enoch), where they are portrayed as beings who lusted after human women, leading to their catastrophic fall.

Their descent symbolizes disobedience and corruption, serving as a cautionary tale about the dangers of rebellion against divine order. The Watchers' actions led to the introduction of forbidden knowledge, such as alchemy, astrology, and weapon-making, which were viewed as destructive influences on human society.

The Fall of the Angels and Their Transgressions with Humans

The Watchers' sin involved taking human wives, violating the boundaries between heaven and earth. This union resulted in the birth of the Nephilim, hybrid beings described as giants and men of renown. These offspring embodied violence, corruption, and chaos, disrupting the natural order and spreading evil throughout creation.

The Watchers' actions were seen as a direct challenge to God's sovereignty, illustrating the spiritual consequences of pride and disobedience. Their fall mirrors the broader themes of spiritual warfare and moral failure, emphasizing the necessity of faithfulness to divine laws.

The Creation of the Nephilim and Their Symbolism

The Nephilim are depicted as symbols of corruption and judgment, representing the consequences of unchecked desire and forbidden knowledge. Their presence on earth is associated with widespread wickedness, prompting God to bring about the Great Flood to cleanse creation.

Symbolically, the Nephilim reflect humanity's struggle with sin and its tendency to misuse divine gifts. They serve as a reminder of the importance of moral discipline and spiritual vigilance, themes that resonate deeply within the Books of Enoch.

Judgment and Punishment of the Fallen Angels

The Watchers face divine judgment for their transgressions, being imprisoned in the depths of the earth until the final day of judgment. Their punishment reinforces the idea that no one is above divine law, not even heavenly beings.

This act of judgment underscores themes of justice and restoration, emphasizing God's commitment to purify creation and maintain cosmic order. The fate of the Watchers serves as a warning against rebellion and a call to repentance for humanity.

METATRON: THE PRINCE OF THE PRESENCE

The transformation of Enoch into Metatron is one of the most profound and symbolic events in the Third Book of Enoch. Enoch, a mortal man, is elevated to the status of the Prince of the Presence, symbolizing the ultimate union between humanity and divinity. This transformation represents the culmination of faithfulness, purity, and divine favor, serving as a model for spiritual ascent. Enoch's elevation demonstrates the possibility of human glorification, showing that obedience and righteousness can lead to divine intimacy and power.

Metatron is given numerous titles that reflect his divine authority and cosmic responsibilities. As the Scribe of God, he records human deeds and heavenly decrees, emphasizing his role as a keeper of divine knowledge. As a mediator, he bridges the gap between the celestial and earthly realms, acting as an intermediary who delivers divine commands and revelations. His position as the Ruler of the Angels underscores his status as the highest-ranking being in the heavenly hierarchy, entrusted with maintaining order and governance within the divine realm.

Metatron serves as a symbol of transformation and ascension, representing humanity's potential to achieve spiritual elevation. His dual nature—as both mortal and divine—reflects the possibility of bridging the gap between earth and heaven. This symbolism reinforces themes of divine grace, obedience, and mystical enlightenment, providing readers with a model for their own spiritual journeys.

Metatron's position near the Throne of Glory highlights his role as a guardian of divine mysteries. His proximity to God represents the highest level of spiritual enlightenment, illustrating the path to divine union through devotion and purity. The imagery of the throne room and celestial hierarchy invites readers to contemplate the structure of the cosmos and the beauty of divine order, encouraging them to seek deeper understanding and spiritual growth.

SACRED NAMES, WORDS, AND MYSTICAL LANGUAGE

The power of divine names holds a central place in mystical traditions and is deeply intertwined with the process of creation, judgment, and divine authority. In the Books of Enoch, the use of sacred names is portrayed as an instrument of cosmic order, capable of invoking divine presence, issuing decrees, and enforcing judgment. These names are viewed as expressions of God's essence and authority, representing His attributes and actions in the spiritual and material worlds. The idea that words hold power is rooted in the belief that God created the universe through speech, as reflected in Genesis where "God said, 'Let there be light,' and there was light."

This foundational concept establishes language as a creative force, a tool through which divine will is expressed and manifested. In mystical traditions, this principle extends to the notion that specific vibrations and sounds carry spiritual energy capable of influencing the cosmos. The repetition of divine names, chants, and invocations is seen as a means of aligning oneself with divine energy, drawing closer to God's presence, and invoking angelic assistance. The Books of Enoch emphasize this practice through descriptions of heavenly hymns and praises, illustrating how language acts as a bridge between heaven and earth.

In addition to the spoken word, sacred letters and symbols are revered as carriers of divine mysteries. These letters are believed to embody the structure of creation, mirroring the order and harmony of the cosmos. In Jewish mysticism, the Hebrew alphabet is regarded as a sacred script, each letter imbued with spiritual meaning and numerical significance. This belief is reflected in practices such as gematria, where letters correspond to numbers, revealing hidden messages and divine patterns.

The Books of Enoch further emphasize the role of mystical inscriptions in maintaining heavenly order. Angels are described as scribes, recording human deeds and divine decrees, reinforcing the idea that words not only convey meaning but also shape reality. This symbolic understanding highlights the responsibility associated with speech and writing, encouraging reverence for language as a divine gift.

FUNCTIONS AND ROLES OF SPECIFIC ANGELS

Angels in the Books of Enoch and other apocryphal texts play distinct and purposeful roles in maintaining divine order and acting as God's agents within the spiritual and earthly realms. Among these beings, archangels occupy a position of prominence, functioning as leaders, protectors, messengers, and mediators between God and humanity. They are entrusted with overseeing cosmic harmony and divine decrees, ensuring that God's will is carried out both in the heavens and on earth. Each archangel embodies specific attributes and fulfills a unique function, serving as exemplars of obedience, power, and wisdom.

The archangels featured in the Books of Enoch—Michael, Gabriel, Raphael, and Uriel—are especially revered for their specialized roles, reflecting the mystical significance of angelic hierarchies. Their names, rich with symbolic meaning, often incorporate el, a reference to God, underscoring their divine origin and mission. These archangels operate as warriors, healers, messengers, and keepers of divine mysteries, demonstrating the multifaceted nature of divine service.

APPENDIX 2: A STUDY OF ANGELS AND CELESTIAL HIERARCHIES

Michael – Protector and Warrior Against Evil

Michael stands out as the protector and warrior against evil forces. Described as the chief of heavenly armies, he is a figure of divine strength and judgment, entrusted with leading the battle against Satan and rebellious angels. In the Books of Enoch, Michael is portrayed as a guardian of righteousness, who defends the faithful and ensures that divine justice prevails. His association with spiritual warfare emphasizes the ongoing struggle between good and evil, reinforcing the importance of faith and perseverance in overcoming darkness. Michael's sword symbolizes God's authority and power, cutting through deception and corruption to restore order and purity.

As a warrior, Michael's actions illustrate the protective aspect of divine intervention, showing that God provides both physical and spiritual defense for His people. He is not only a fighter but also a judge, entrusted with overseeing the weighing of souls and enforcing God's decrees. This role ties closely to themes of accountability and moral judgment, reminding readers of the consequences of sin and rebellion. Michael's unwavering dedication to God's commands serves as a model of faithfulness and obedience, encouraging believers to stand firm in their spiritual battles.

In addition to his role as a defender, Michael is also depicted as a guardian of Israel and a guide for the righteous. His presence assures believers that they are not alone in their struggles and that divine assistance is always at hand. Through Michael, the Books of Enoch emphasize the protective presence of angels, reassuring readers of God's commitment to preserving justice and safeguarding creation.

APPENDIX 2: A STUDY OF ANGELS AND CELESTIAL HIERARCHIES

Gabriel – Messenger and Revealer of Divine Mysteries

Gabriel is one of the most prominent archangels, serving as a messenger of divine revelations and a herald of God's plans. In the Books of Enoch and other apocryphal texts, Gabriel is often portrayed as the bearer of heavenly secrets, entrusted with delivering visions and prophecies to prophets and faithful servants of God. He is closely associated with moments of divine intervention, acting as a spiritual communicator who bridges the gap between heaven and earth.

Gabriel's name means "God is my strength", reflecting his role as a reliable conduit of divine truth. He is most famously depicted as the angel who appeared to Daniel to interpret visions and to Mary in the Gospel of Luke to announce the birth of Jesus Christ. In Enochian literature, Gabriel's role extends to delivering messages of warning and judgment, often concerning the destinies of nations and rulers.

As a revealer of mysteries, Gabriel embodies clarity, insight, and divine wisdom, emphasizing the importance of understanding God's will and prophetic visions. His presence reassures believers that God's plans are purposeful and that spiritual guidance is always available to those who seek it. Gabriel's ability to interpret dreams and visions highlights the role of angels as interpreters of divine knowledge, ensuring that humanity remains aligned with God's intentions.

APPENDIX 2: A STUDY OF ANGELS AND CELESTIAL HIERARCHIES

Raphael – Healer and Guide for the Righteous

Raphael, whose name means "God heals", is portrayed as the angel of healing and restoration. In apocryphal texts, including the *Book of Tobit*, Raphael is depicted as a guide and companion to those in need, assisting with both physical healing and spiritual restoration. His role underscores God's compassionate nature and the desire to bring wholeness to creation.

In the *Books of Enoch*, Raphael is tasked with binding fallen angels and purifying the earth from corruption. This emphasizes his role as a protector against spiritual affliction and a restorer of divine order. Raphael also serves as a guide for travelers, symbolizing God's presence during journeys of faith and transformation.

Raphael's association with healing waters and medicinal knowledge highlights the connection between physical health and spiritual well-being. His presence reassures believers of God's willingness to heal wounds, both visible and invisible, offering hope and comfort during times of illness and distress.

APPENDIX 2: A STUDY OF ANGELS AND CELESTIAL HIERARCHIES

Uriel – Keeper of Divine Secrets and Wisdom

Uriel, meaning "Light of God", is revered as the bearer of wisdom and divine illumination. In Enochian texts, Uriel is described as a guardian of knowledge, revealing hidden truths and guiding seekers toward spiritual enlightenment. He is closely associated with prophetic visions and the unveiling of mysteries, serving as a source of insight and discernment.

Uriel's role as a keeper of secrets makes him a teacher of divine law, entrusted with explaining complex revelations and offering moral guidance. In the *Books of Enoch*, he is tasked with watching over the luminaries, ensuring the movement of celestial bodies and maintaining cosmic harmony.

Uriel's presence reminds readers of the importance of wisdom and reflection, encouraging them to seek truth and understand divine patterns in creation. His association with light reinforces his role as a guide through darkness, symbolizing the illumination of the soul and the path to spiritual clarity.

APPENDIX 2: A STUDY OF ANGELS AND CELESTIAL HIERARCHIES

HEAVENLY REALMS AND ANGELIC STRUCTURES

The *Books of Enoch* present a vivid and intricate vision of the heavenly realms, offering readers a glimpse into the cosmic architecture of the divine order. Central to this vision is the concept of the ten heavens, each representing a distinct level of spiritual reality and divine governance. These heavens form a hierarchical structure, symbolizing the progressive ascent toward God's presence and ultimate authority. Each realm serves a specific function, housing angels, thrones, palaces, and celestial beings who execute divine will and maintain cosmic harmony.

The lower heavens are often depicted as places where natural forces and elements are regulated. These levels house the stars, sun, and moon, whose movements reflect God's order and predictable rhythms. They serve as reminders of divine precision and balance, reinforcing the belief that creation operates according to sacred patterns. These realms are also inhabited by angelic guardians, tasked with overseeing celestial phenomena and ensuring that the cycles of time and seasons adhere to God's decrees.

As one ascends through the heavens, the focus shifts from natural order to spiritual governance. The middle heavens are described as realms of judgment and intercession, where angels record human deeds and prepare for divine intervention. These levels emphasize themes of accountability and justice, portraying heaven as a place of eternal vigilance where moral order is upheld. The angels in these realms act as scribes and witnesses, documenting the actions of humanity and presenting them before God's heavenly court.

The upper heavens are characterized by radiant glory and divine splendor. These are the realms closest to God's throne, inhabited by Seraphim, Cherubim, and Thrones, who engage in unceasing worship and praise. Their presence underscores the holiness and majesty of God, reflecting the perfection and purity of His divine nature. These angelic beings serve as guardians of God's throne, acting as intermediaries who shield His presence from impurity while radiating His light and glory throughout creation.

The *Books of Enoch* describe the Throne of Glory as the center of divine governance, a place of immense power and authority. Surrounded by heavenly palaces, this throne is depicted as a source of light, emanating wisdom, justice, and mercy. It is here that God presides over creation, issuing judgments and decrees that shape the spiritual and physical worlds. The imagery of jewels, fire, and lightning highlights the splendor and majesty of God's presence, inspiring awe and reverence among both angels and humanity.

In addition to the throne, the heavenly palaces described in Enochian literature symbolize divine dwelling places that reflect the beauty and order of creation. These palaces are often associated with temples and sanctuaries, emphasizing the connection between heavenly worship and earthly rituals. The descriptions of angelic choirs and hymns of praise within these palaces highlight the role of worship as an eternal act, expressing devotion, harmony, and unity with God's will.

Worship in the heavenly realms serves as a model for human devotion, demonstrating how praise and prayer align creation with the divine order. The *Books of Enoch* portray angels as eternal worshippers, whose songs and hymns sustain the spiritual harmony of the cosmos. This depiction underscores the importance of worship as a transformative act, inviting believers to participate in the divine symphony and draw closer to God's presence.

The hierarchical organization of the heavens mirrors the roles and ranks of angelic beings, emphasizing the themes of obedience, service, and order. Angels are assigned specific functions within each realm, ranging from guardians of creation to messengers of divine decrees. Their actions reinforce the belief in a structured cosmos, where every being has a purpose and responsibility in fulfilling God's plan.

The heavenly realms described in the *Books of Enoch* offer not only a vision of divine majesty but also a spiritual framework for understanding the relationship between heaven and earth. They challenge readers to reflect on the beauty and complexity of creation, encouraging a sense of wonder and reverence for the mysteries of God's design. By contemplating the hierarchical structures and sacred spaces of heaven, believers are invited to align their lives with the values of order, worship, and devotion, striving to reflect the harmony and purity of the celestial realms.

DIVINE JUDGMENT AND THE ROLE OF ANGELS

The *Books of Enoch* present angels as central figures in the administration of divine judgment, acting as both record-keepers and witnesses to human actions. Angels are portrayed as meticulous scribes who document every deed, word, and thought, ensuring that no action escapes divine scrutiny. These records form the basis for judgment, symbolizing God's omniscience and justice. Angels also serve as prosecutors and defenders, presenting evidence before the heavenly court, highlighting their role in maintaining moral accountability and cosmic balance.

In apocalyptic visions, angels are often depicted as executors of divine retribution, tasked with delivering punishments to the wicked and blessings to the righteous. This duality reflects the themes of mercy and justice, demonstrating God's commitment to restoring order while offering opportunities for repentance and redemption. The imagery of angels wielding flaming swords and trumpets emphasizes the finality of judgment, invoking awe and reverence for God's authority.

The symbolism of divine judgment underscores the interplay between justice and mercy, showing that God's judgments are fair and restorative rather than purely punitive. Through their actions, angels remind humanity of the consequences of sin while offering guidance toward repentance and spiritual renewal. This portrayal challenges readers to embrace righteousness, reflecting the divine attributes of justice, compassion, and grace that sustain creation.

APPENDIX 2: A STUDY OF ANGELS AND CELESTIAL HIERARCHIES

SYMBOLISM AND MODERN REFLECTIONS

Angels, as described in the *Books of Enoch*, are not only divine beings but also symbols of intervention, guidance, and spiritual ascent. They embody the connection between the divine and the earthly, serving as reminders of humanity's potential for transformation and growth. Their presence in sacred texts reflects an enduring belief in divine assistance and protection, offering comfort and inspiration to those who seek reassurance in times of uncertainty. Angels are depicted as mediators who bridge the gap between God and humanity, emphasizing that divine help is always available for those who are willing to receive it.

The symbolic role of angels extends beyond their function as messengers and guardians. They represent spiritual ascent, illustrating the possibility of elevation to higher states of consciousness and divine closeness. Enoch's transformation into Metatron exemplifies this journey, showing how faith, obedience, and devotion can lead to spiritual glorification. In this sense, angels serve as archetypes of transformation, inspiring individuals to pursue self-reflection, discipline, and moral integrity as pathways to spiritual enlightenment.

In modern spirituality, angels continue to hold a powerful symbolic presence, offering guidance and protection to those who seek divine wisdom. Their imagery is often associated with light, purity, and transcendence, reminding individuals of the sacred nature of existence and the eternal struggle between good and evil. The descriptions of angels as warriors, healers, and messengers in the *Books of Enoch* resonate with contemporary readers who view them as guardians of truth and justice, capable of guiding humanity through both personal and collective challenges.

Mystical interpretations of angels emphasize their role as intermediaries between the material and spiritual worlds, reflecting the unity and order of creation. In this context, angels are seen not only as supernatural beings but also as manifestations of divine energy and purpose, providing direction for those seeking to deepen their spiritual practices. Their depiction as eternal worshippers highlights the importance of devotion and praise, encouraging readers to cultivate a sense of awe and reverence for the divine.

The relevance of angels to modern spirituality lies in their ability to symbolize personal growth and transformation. Just as the angels in Enoch's visions maintain cosmic harmony, individuals are called to align their lives with spiritual principles and strive for inner balance. Angels serve as spiritual guides, helping believers navigate the complexities of life and reminding them of their connection to a higher purpose. Their role as protectors and messengers also underscores the belief that divine intervention is available to those who seek it, fostering hope and resilience in challenging times.

The *Books of Enoch* provide a framework for interpreting angels as reflections of divine attributes—justice, mercy, and wisdom—encouraging readers to embody these qualities in their own lives. Angels represent the ideal of obedience to divine will, serving as examples of faithfulness and dedication. Their actions remind believers that spiritual growth requires discipline, humility, and a willingness to embrace divine guidance.

In addition to their spiritual symbolism, angels also resonate with modern mystics and seekers as symbols of awakening and enlightenment. Their presence in mystical traditions highlights the interconnectedness of all creation, reinforcing the idea that humanity is part of a larger cosmic order. Angels act as teachers of divine wisdom, revealing hidden truths and guiding individuals toward self-discovery and transformation. This perspective encourages readers to view their spiritual journey as an ongoing process of learning, growth, and alignment with divine purpose.

The symbolism of angels in the *Books of Enoch* invites readers to reflect on their own spiritual aspirations and to see their lives as part of a larger, sacred narrative. Whether viewed as divine messengers, protectors, or guides, angels inspire awe and reverence while providing hope and direction in the pursuit of spiritual fulfillment. Their stories remind us that the path to spiritual ascent is accessible to all who seek it with faith and devotion, reinforcing the timeless message of divine presence and guidance in the journey toward truth and transformation.

APPLYING ANCIENT WISDOM TODAY

The exploration of angels and celestial hierarchies in the *Books of Enoch* provides profound insights into divine order, spiritual transformation, and cosmic harmony. These ancient texts reveal lessons about obedience, faithfulness, and the pursuit of wisdom, showing how divine beings operate within a structured universe that reflects God's will. The hierarchical organization of angels demonstrates the importance of purpose and discipline, encouraging readers to seek alignment with higher spiritual principles in their daily lives.

The teachings about angels and their roles offer valuable tools for meditation, prayer, and personal growth. By reflecting on the responsibilities of angels—whether as warriors, healers, messengers, or protectors—readers can draw inspiration for their own spiritual journeys. Angels remind us to cultivate faith, humility, and devotion, integrating these values into our practices of worship and acts of service. Through contemplation of angelic hierarchies, believers can develop a deeper understanding of their spiritual purpose and find encouragement to pursue truth and transformation with renewed dedication.

The *Books of Enoch* also invite readers to continue exploring apocryphal literature and mystical traditions as sources of hidden wisdom and divine insight. These texts provide rich material for uncovering spiritual truths, offering perspectives that complement canonical scriptures and broaden our view of divine mysteries. They challenge readers to engage in self-reflection, embrace the symbolic meaning of angelic figures, and approach their faith with a sense of wonder and discovery.

As we seek to apply the lessons of angelic hierarchies to modern spirituality, we are reminded of the timelessness of these teachings. They encourage us to live with purpose and integrity, to strive for spiritual growth, and to remain open to divine guidance. The study of angels ultimately serves as a call to action, inspiring us to embrace our role as caretakers of God's creation and participants in the unfolding story of redemption and renewal.

CONCLUSION: UNVEILING THE MYSTERIES OF THE DIVINE

The texts presented in this collection offer more than historical or theological insight—they serve as portals into a hidden world, where divine wisdom, cosmic order, and the mysteries of spiritual ascent unfold. From the Books of Enoch, with their visions of celestial justice and angelic rebellion, to the Ascension of Isaiah, which reveals the soul's journey through the heavens, and the Study of Angels and Celestial Hierarchies, which explores the divine structures governing creation, each text contributes to a broader mystical and apocalyptic tradition. Together, they form a sacred continuum, illuminating the relationship between humanity, the celestial realm, and the divine plan.

Through these writings, we witness the timeless human pursuit of revelation—the desire to understand what lies beyond the material world, the nature of divine authority, and the destiny of the righteous and the fallen. The Books of Enoch reveal a structured universe governed by angelic hierarchies and cosmic justice, where rebellion leads to destruction, but righteousness leads to eternal reward. The Ascension of Isaiah continues this theme, offering a glimpse into the mechanics of divine ascent and heavenly prophecy. Meanwhile, the Study of Angels and Celestial Hierarchies provides a theological framework for understanding the celestial order, enriching the reader's perspective on how these traditions evolved and influenced later mystical thought.

These texts invite us to look beyond the surface of religious tradition, to engage with esoteric knowledge that was once reserved for visionaries and mystics. They challenge us to reflect on our own spiritual journey, on the nature of divine justice and mercy, and on the hidden forces that shape the cosmos. For some, they provide historical and theological insight into the evolution of apocalyptic literature and mystical traditions. For others, they serve as guides to personal transformation, calling readers to seek wisdom, righteousness, and deeper spiritual understanding.

To engage with these writings is to enter a dialogue with the past, where ancient voices still speak, revealing truths that remain as compelling today as they were in antiquity. Whether studied for their historical significance, theological depth, or spiritual guidance, these texts offer a unique lens through which to explore the divine realm. They remind us that the pursuit of hidden wisdom is not merely an intellectual exercise but a journey of the soul—one that calls us to seek, to question, and ultimately, to ascend.

www.ingramcontent.com/pod-product-compliance
Lightning Source LLC
Chambersburg PA
CBHW081355070526
44583CB00020B/2562